A History of Religious Educators

A History of Religious Educators

ELMER L. TOWNS
EDITOR

BAKER BOOK HOUSE
Grand Rapids, Michigan

"Augustine" is a revision of "St. Augustine on Teaching," *Religious Education* 54:171-76, by permission of the Religious Education Association.

"Erasmus" is reprinted by permission from *A History of Religious Education* (New York: New York University Press, 1968), pp. 100-104 and *History of Educational Thought* (New York: American Book Company, 1945), pp. 130-48.

"Martin Luther" is reprinted by permission from *Luther and Culture*, vol. 4 (Decorah, Iowa: Luther College Press, 1960), pp. 94-118.

"Nikolaus Ludwig Zinzendorf" is reprinted by permission from *Pioneers of Religious Education* (New York: Oxford University Press, 1939; reprinted — Freeport, N.Y.: Books for Libraries Press, 1969), pp. 76-88.

"John Wesley" is reprinted from "John Wesley and Religious Education," *Religious Education* 65:318-28, by permission of the Religious Education Association.

"Robert Raikes" is reprinted by permission from "Robert Raikes: A Comparison with Earlier Claims to Sunday School Origins," *The Evangelical Quarterly* 43:68-81.

Contents

Contributors 9
Preface 11

Part One A.D. 1-500 13

1 **Jesus** / Donald Guthrie 15
2 **Paul** / Richard N. Longenecker 39
3 **Augustine** / Howard Grimes 54

Part Two A.D. 500-1500 61

4 **Columba** / John Woodbridge 63
5 **Thomas Aquinas** / Joan Ellen Duval 71
6 **Geert Groote** / Julia S. Henkel 82

Part Three A.D. 1500-1750 89

7 **Erasmus** / Robert Ulich 92
8 **Martin Luther** / Harold J. Grimm 103
9 **Huldreich Zwingli** / H. Wayne Pipkin 124
10 **Ignatius of Loyola** / George E. Ganss 136

11   **Philip Melanchthon** / Carl S. Meyer   **144**
12   **John Knox** / Marshall Coleman Dendy   **161**
13   **John Calvin** / Elmer L. Towns   **167**
14   **John Amos Comenius** / William Warren Filkin, Jr.   **176**
15   **August Hermann Francke** / Kenneth O. Gangel   **190**
16   **Nikolaus Ludwig Zinzendorf** / T. F. Kinloch   **200**

Part Four A.D. 1750-1900   **209**

17   **John Wesley** / Elmer L. Towns   **212**
18   **Robert Raikes** / Elmer L. Towns   **226**
19   **Johann H. Pestalozzi** / Gerald Lee Gutek   **236**
20   **Johann Friedrich Herbart** / Abraham Friesen   **249**
21   **Thomas Arnold** / William R. Feyerharm   **264**
22   **John Henry Newman** / Bernard Ramm   **271**
23   **Horace Bushnell** / Elmer L. Towns   **278**
24   **Abraham Kuyper** / John H. Kromminga   **288**
25   **William James** / James Merritt   **297**
26   **John Dewey** / David H. Roper   **310**

Index of Persons   **327**

Contributors

Marshall Coleman Dendy (M.A., University of Tennessee), Retired Executive Secretary of the Board of Christian Education of the Presbyterian Church, U.S.

Joan Allen Duval (Ph.D., Catholic University of America), Chief, Early Childhood Branch, Division of School Programs, Bureau of Educational Personnel Development, United States Office of Education, Department of Health, Education, and Welfare

William R. Feyerharm (Ph.D., University of Wisconsin), Assistant Dean, College of Liberal Arts and Sciences, University of Illinois

William Warren Filkin, Jr. (Ph.D., Southern Baptist Theological Seminary), Professor Emeritus of Christian Education, Trinity Evangelical Divinity School.

Abraham Friesen (Ph.D., Stanford University), Assistant Professor of Renaissance and Reformation History, University of California (Santa Barbara)

Kenneth O. Gangel (Ph.D., University of Missouri), President, Miami Christian College

George E. Ganss, S.J. (Ph.D., St. Louis University), Professor Emeritus of Spirituality, School of Divinity, St. Louis University

9

Lewis Howard Grimes (Ph.D., Columbia University) Professor of Christian Education, Perkins School of Theology, Southern Methodist University

Harold J. Grimm (Ph.D., Ohio State University), Professor Emeritus of History, Ohio State University

Gerald Lee Gutek (Ph.D., University of Illinois), Professor of History and of Foundations of Education, Loyola University (Chicago)

Donald Guthrie (Ph.D., University of London), Registrar for Advanced Studies and Senior Lecturer ·in New Testament, London Bible College

Julia S. Henkel (Ph.D., University of Pittsburgh), Professor of Christian Education, Grand Rapids Baptist Seminary

T. F. Kinloch (M.A.), died 1953.

John H. Kromminga (Th.D., Princeton Theological Seminary), President and Professor of Historical Theology, Calvin Theological Seminary

Richard N. Longenecker (Ph.D., Edinburgh University), Professor of New Testament, Wycliffe College, University of Toronto

James Merritt (Ed.D., Harvard University), Professor of Education, Northern Illinois University

Carl S. Meyer (Ph.D., University of Chicago), died 1972. Formerly Graduate Professor of Church History, Concordia Theological Seminary (St. Louis)

H. Wayne Pipkin (Ph.D., Hartford Seminary Foundation), Assistant Professor of Religion, Baylor University

Bernard L. Ramm (Ph.D., University of Southern California), Professor of Theology, Eastern Baptist Theological Seminary

David H. Roper (Th.M., Dallas Theological Seminary), Director, Discovery Center, Peninsula Bible Church, Palo Alto, California

Elmer L. Towns (Th.M., Dallas Theological Seminary), Director, Sunday School Research Institute; and Executive Vice President, Baptist University of America

Robert Ulich (Dr.Phil., University of Leipzig), James Bryant Conant Professor of Education, Emeritus, Graduate School of Education, Harvard University

John D. Woodbridge (D.T.C., University of Toulouse), Associate Professor of Church History, Trinity Evangelical Divinity School

Preface

Historiography too often places more emphasis on events, dates, and places than on people. But people make history live. They dreamed of a better world, fought wars for their convictions, taught students, sacrificed, and died untimely deaths. Without them there is no history, nor is there a future.

This volume places the primary emphasis on people, on those men who have significantly influenced the history of Christian education. It is intended to be not a history of Christian education but historical studies of the giants in that field. Those chosen for inclusion in this work either represented the educational trends of their era or initiated reforms or movements which eventually, if not immediately, affected religious education.

Not all of the educators chosen were recognized widely during their lifetimes; John Amos Comenius, for example, received some recognition from his contemporaries but was almost forgotten for two centuries after his death. Now he is hailed by some as "the first modern educator." Nor were all of the educators included in this volume primarily educators; Martin Luther was first a reformer and preacher, but he did have a significant impact on the world of education. No educators more recent than John Dewey are in-

11

cluded, in part because primary and secondary sources are readily available, and in part because their influence on religious education has yet to be determined. The editor was helped greatly in making the choices by John Warwick Montgomery, as well as by the various contributing authors.

Each of the latter, incidentally, is a recognized authority on the figure about whom he writes. Most of the authors have written a dissertation or published scholarly articles or even books on their subjects. Several of the articles in this volume have already appeared in print.

Each article examines the subject's educational philosophy and the ways in which he implemented it, and each orients the reader to the original sources. Quotations from the writings of the subject of each article are, as much as possible, set off from the text through indentation. No quotations from secondary sources, on the other hand, are indented.

This is a reference work for all serious students of education, theology, and Christian education. It is valuable collateral reading for undergraduate and graduate courses in church history and the history of Christian education.

Two graduate assistants deserve recognition for their help: Glen Miller for his bibliographical research which served as the basis for assigning and selecting articles; and John Fischer for his help in checking the many details that naturally arise in a historical study. My thanks, too, to Mrs. Marie Chapman for reading and helping to edit the manuscript.

Part One

A.D. 1-500

Education is integral to the life of the Christian church, just as it has been to the Hebrew nation. Every Israelite is to be instructed in the law of God, given to the nation at Mt. Sinai: "And these words, which I command thee this day, shall be in thine heart: and thou shalt talk of them when thou sittest in thine house, and when thou walkest by the way, and when thou liest down, and when thou risest up. And thou shalt bind them for a sign upon thine hand, and they shall be as frontlets between thine eyes. And thou shalt write them upon the posts of thy house, and on thy gates." (Deut. 6:6-9) Since the Christian church was born and nurtured in the Hebrew milieu, it is natural that the church strongly emphasize the ministry of teaching.

It was the Jewish culture into which **Jesus** stepped and which He dominated. Concerning Him we read: ". . . seeing the multitudes, he went up into a mountain: and when he was set, his disciples came unto him: and he opened his mouth, and taught them" (Matt. 5:1, 2). When He finished, "the people were astonished at his doctrine: for he taught them as one having authority, and not as the scribes" (Matt. 7:28, 29). Christ was an outstanding educator, by virtue of both His methods and His message.

. The apostle **Paul,** who claimed to have seen Jesus in the flesh (II Cor. 5:16), was first an evangelist who carried the Christian message throughout Asia Minor and finally to Rome, but he was also an educator concerned about second- and third-generation Christians. "The things that thou hast heard of me among many witnesses, the same commit thou to faithful men, who shall be able to teach others also" (II Tim. 2:2).

Early in the third century a catechumenal system of instruction was instituted by which converts were prepared for Christian baptism in a three-year course. These schools evolved into centers for the defense of the gospel and the training of young men for the ministry. **Augustine** (354-430), the bishop of Hippo who greatly influenced the doctrinal development of the Western church, was also a master of catechizing, an art which he demonstrated in his book *The First Catechetical Instructor* and which declined after his death.

Christianity began as a seemingly obscure movement, one among many in the Roman world. Its object of reverence, Jesus Christ, had been put to death by the Roman government. That same government tried first to contain Christianity and then to destroy it through severe persecution. But the faith was spread by the early Christians, who fervently evangelized and then educated the heathen. Not only did Christianity survive, but in the first half of the fourth century, it was adopted as the official religion of the Roman Empire.

While Christianity came to be overly identified with the empire and its civilization, it survived both. In 410 the city of Rome was burned and sacked, and in 476 the last of the Roman emperors was overthrown. In 496 Clovis, King of the Franks, was baptized. Thus began the era in which the Germans were the champions of the faith in the West.

1

Donald Guthrie

Jesus

Christianity has historically stressed religious teaching since Jesus Himself was the supreme exponent of the art. His influence on education in the church cannot be overstressed, yet caution is needed in one respect: Jesus was more than an educator. Although He may be regarded as an Illuminator of the mind,[1] His mission was more basic. He came to bring redemption, and that redemption was the key to His teaching. Even if He had not come as Redeemer, His teaching, in both its content and its method, would be unique. His real claim to preeminence, however, rests in the fact that the practicability and relevance of His teaching depend on His work of atonement. In the following discussion of the teaching of Jesus, this must never be overlooked.

There has been a tendency in some quarters to reduce Jesus to the status of a social worker or a political revolutionary.[2] Although some aspects of His teaching may support such views, these concepts entirely miss the essential basis of His mission. Because of

---

1. The early Greek patristic authors, particularly Origen, laid stress on this.
2. S. G. F. Brandon recently attempted to establish some connection between Jesus and the revolutionary Zealot movement. *Jesus and the Zealots* (New York: Scribner, 1968).

His concern for men, He came to redeem them; and because of His redemptive purpose, His social concern was inescapable. His teaching was revolutionary because He expected men to do what was impossible in their own strength. A teacher who exhorts men to love their enemies (Matt. 5:44) cannot expect to escape clashes with those who regard such teaching as not only alien but contradictory. Nor can He evade the responsibility of giving men power to perform His impossible demands. In approaching Jesus as a religious teacher, we are considering more than a dynamic personality and more than a religious genius. We are examining the teaching methods of One who claimed to be the Son of God. This places our quest on a different basis from other approaches to religious education. In spite of His uniqueness, Jesus presents a pattern from which others have learned and are still learning. A study of His methods is entirely relevant precisely because in His ministry He was confronted with problems of communication similar to those confronted by men in all ages when seeking to impart religious truths. No philosophy of religious education can afford to ignore the basic principles of the approach of Jesus.

His Teaching Methods

In any assessment of Jesus as teacher, various basic questions must be asked. Since teaching methods can only be adequately understood against a knowledge of the background of the teacher, our first task is to establish the milieu in which Jesus taught. In this way, elements in His method which were determined exclusively by His environment may be distinguished from those which have universal validity. Following this, attention may be given to the various types of teaching which Jesus employed and His different methods of communicating the content of His message.

His background. Jesus taught in Palestine when that country was under the domination of imperial Rome. The Romans had recognized that the Jewish people represented a special category within the framework of the empire. Unlike most other subject peoples, their religious procedures could not be merged into the general religious syncretism which the Pantheon represented. They were not idol-worshipers and therefore had no image of Jehovah which the Romans could place alongside local deities collected from their various vassals. This meant that foreign domination had very little impact on the religious methods and approaches of the Jews. In spite of the fact that Palestine was a small pocket of Jewish culture in the midst of widespread Greek culture, the isolationism of the Jews, supported by strong religious convictions, was responsible for preserving them from the general tendency towards syncretism.

Jewish methods of teaching may give some help in understanding the methods of Jesus. There is some evidence that Jewish teachers followed well-defined pedagogical principles in instructing their pupils.[3] The first stage was always memorizing the text to be studied, without attempting to understand its meaning, a distinct second stage. Great emphasis was laid on the accurate transmission of texts, and many devices were used as aids to the memory. Much of the evidence for this is admittedly later than the time of Jesus, and it is therefore difficult to determine to what extent He was affected by such methods.[4] It must, of course, be recognized that Jesus was not a traditional rabbi. His unconventional purpose must have affected His methods, yet He could not have been unmindful of the need for both memorization and interpretation. This basic need may, in fact, provide a key to the purpose of the parables. The prime consideration was to store the mind with material which would spring to life when its true meaning was grasped. For example, much of the teaching of Jesus took on new meaning in the light of events subsequent to the passion. Prior to this it was impossible for men to understand teaching which depended for relevance on a new relationship with the risen Christ.

Some of the teaching methods of Jesus must be seen as preparatory rather than exemplary. As a teacher He was in a unique position since His doctrine revolved around His own person and work to such extent that it cannot be divorced from His mission. His methods were perfectly adapted to this special mission. In this they differ in marked degree from Jewish methods, which emphasized the importance of transmitting the teachings of established teachers. Their emphasis on precise traditions demanded techniques adequate to insure unperverted transmission. But Jesus promised

---

3. B. Gerhardsson, *Memory and Manuscript;* and *Tradition and Transmission,* trans. E. J. Sharpe (Lund: Gleerup, 1964).

4. For criticism of Gerhardsson, see A. N. Wilder, "Form-history and the Oldest Tradition," in *Neotestamentica et Patristica,* ed. W. C. van Unnik (Leiden: Brill, 1962), pp. 3-13; W. D. Davies, "The Gospel Tradition," in *Neotestamentica et Patristica,* pp. 14-34; and Davies, *The Setting of the Sermon on the Mount,* appendix 15.

better aid to memory than mnemonic devices when He assured His disciples that the Holy Spirit would bring to their minds all that He had taught them (John 14:26). This must be regarded as a special provision for the transmission of the teaching of Jesus.

His types of teaching. When comparisons are made between rabbinic methods and those of Jesus, it must be remembered that Jesus had an itinerant ministry. The rabbis could gather their pupils around them to give sustained instruction. Constant repetition of the same subject matter guaranteed that the pupil would be able to reproduce much of what was said. But Jesus could not and did not use such a method. His purpose was to adapt His teaching to make the most efficient use of the passing opportunity. The mechanical character of most traditional Jewish methods was wholly unsuited to such a purpose.

Although at times Jesus taught via sustained discourse—for example, in the Sermon on the Mount (Matt. 5-7) and the eschatological discourse (Matt. 24, 25)—His general method was to impart His teaching more concisely. It would be a mistake to suppose that all of Jesus' sustained discourses are recorded in the Gospels, for there are indications that at other times during His ministry He gathered audiences around Him and taught for sustained periods, as on the occasion of the feeding of the multitudes. It clearly requires greater skill to impress knowledge on fleeting occasions, and there is no doubt that Jesus possessed this skill to a superlative degree. Of all His teaching methods the use of parables (discussed later) illustrates how perfectly He chose the form of His teaching to make the most of each opportunity.

It would seem that Jesus aimed to implant in the memory of His hearers unforgettable illustrations which, reflected upon, would convey spiritual truth. His teaching abounds in metaphors so memorable that many of them have passed into common speech (e.g., "whited sepulchers"). The form in which Jesus expressed His teaching varied considerably. Sometimes an event gave rise to an epigram which summarized His comment on an important theme, as His remark about the tribute money, in which He urged men to render Caesar's things to Caesar and God's things to God (Matt. 22:21). Sometimes the teaching followed naturally from the event, as when a healing illustrated the necessity for faith or the superiority of spiritual healing over physical healing.

Although some analysis of the "forms" of Jesus' teaching is possible, it is noticeable that there is nothing approaching stereotyped patterns. Whatever rhetorical devices were employed, they were used as instruments and were never allowed to dominate the teaching. On occasions Jesus used Jewish methods of argument, but only to serve a specific purpose. He saw no virtue in conformity for its own sake. The variety of His methods brought unparalleled freshness to His teaching. He forced men to listen by perfectly adapting each saying to the needs of specific hearers, rather than using conventional forms. For instance, He addressed the Pharisees, who were abusing their privileges, with a sharper challenge than He addressed to the common people (as Matt. 23:13).

Another feature of His teaching was His relatively sparse use of abstract forms. This again illustrates an essentially Jewish method of thinking, for Semitic teachers' methods were more concrete than abstract.[5] Even when Jesus chose to speak of Truth or Light, He chose homespun illustrations to enable men to see its relevance to common life: for example, the lamps not designed to be placed under bushels (Matt. 5:15).

There is a living quality about the teaching of Jesus. He was never dull, as amply demonstrated by the variety of the forms He used for communicating truth. His aim was always to capture attention in order to implant ideas to stimulate further progressive thought.[6] Such virile teaching was mandatory in view of the fact that much of it could not be fully understood until after the passion. The early Christians would need to recall His essential teaching in order to interpret it in the light of His redemptive work and His resurrection power (John 7:38).

His methods of reasoning. All teaching must be aimed at the understanding. The teaching of Jesus furnishes many examples of His use of thought-forms which were perfectly adapted to the minds of the hearers. He employed the following methods of logical argument.

Frequently He used *analogy* to make spiritual truths more intelligible. Because men readily comprehend an earthly father's

---

5. The nearest approach to abstract forms in Jewish literature is found in the Qumran literature, but this is generally attributed to Hellenistic influence. On the use of *light*, cf. A. R. C. Leaney, *The Rule of Qumran and Its Meaning* (Philadelphia: Westminster, 1966).

6. For an example of virility of thought, cf. 12:24. Note also the poetic quality of much of the teaching of Jesus; cf. C. F. Burney, *The Poetry of Our Lord* (Oxford: Clarendon, 1925).

concern for His children's welfare, Jesus thus illustrated the much greater concern which God as Father has for His spiritual children (Matt. 7:10). A basic assumption underlying much of Jesus' teaching is that the physical world provides patterns for understanding the spiritual. The shepherding of sheep serves as a vivid and valid picture of the care of the Good Shepherd for His people (John 10:11).

Another common method was that of *argumentum ad absurdum.* When Jesus was accused of casting out demons by the prince of demons, He used this method to reduce His accusers to silence and to impress on His hearers a profound spiritual truth. "How can Satan cast out Satan?" He challenged (Mark 3:23; Matt. 12:55ff.; Luke 11:15ff.). His accusers had failed to grasp the logical outcome of the charge they had leveled against Him. They could not deny the absurdity of their position. Similarly, using the illustration of patches on garments and wine in leather bottles (Mark 2:21, 22), He showed the absurdity of attempting to confine His new teaching to the outdated forms of the old.[7] By these methods Jesus repeatedly pointed out the shallowness of men's thinking. He showed the inconsistency of His contemporaries who rejected John the Baptist for his asceticism and Jesus for His conviviality (Mark 11:17-19). Under these circumstances they were as fickle as children playing in the market place, who wanted neither to dance nor to mourn (Matt. 11:16; Luke 7:32).

Another method was *argumentum ad hominem,* which proceeds from the premises held by an opponent. Perhaps the most notable example of this is found in John's Gospel; Jesus answered a Jewish charge of blasphemy with an appeal to the Scripture containing the words "You are gods," implying that if earthly judges could be called "gods," there should be no objection to His claim to be the Son of God (John 10:34-36). The method of argument may seem strange, but Jewish hearers would have found it familiar—it was the kind of argument frequently employed in rabbinic discussions.

Similarly Jesus questioned His hearers or put counter-questions to His questioners. One example is His question concerning the origin of the authority of John the Baptist. His counter-question was addressed to those who asked on whose authority He Himself acted and taught. His counter-question posed a dilemma for His

---

7. Cf. Matt. 9:16ff.; Mark 2:21, 22; Luke 5:36, 37. According to A. Plummer, the piece torn from the new garment was "fasting." *The Gospel According to St. Luke* (Edinburgh: Clark, 1896).

critics (Matt. 21:23-27). By the same skillful manner, on more than one occasion, He silenced those who sought to catch Him. When the scribes and Pharisees quibbled about His disciples' plucking ears of corn on the sabbath, He asked whether they had read the account of what David did in a similar situation (Mark 2:23-27). There were many other occasions when Jesus showed the scribes' ignorance of their own Scriptures: for example, He referred to Moses' teaching about divorce (Matt. 19:3-6).

On occasion Jesus used the method known as *argumentum a fortiori*—arguing from the lesser to the greater. Here, Jesus established God's great willingness to give gifts to men by appealing to a human father's delight in giving gifts to his own children (Matt. 7:11). It requires no great leap of thought to catch the force of the argument, for it is self-evident that God must be superior to man. Again Jesus pointed out God's care for so common an item as grass to prove that He would have much greater care for man (Matt. 6:30). The same method is seen in reverse when, having washed His disciples' feet, Jesus challenged them to emulate His example on the grounds that a disciple is not superior to his master (John 13:14, 15).

In addition to counter-questions, Jesus frequently taught by the question-and-answer method. Often rhetorical questions occur in the course of a saying such as, "If you love those who love you, what reward have you?" (Matt. 16:26). Such penetrating questions cannot fail to stir the hearer to search for an adequate answer. Usually Jesus did not wait for the answer but assumed it, developing His line of thought on the basis of it. The important principle illustrated here is that Jesus clearly expected some mental participation on the part of His hearers. This fact has bearing on any assessment of His philosophy of religious education, which is discussed in the third section of this chapter.

His use of illustration. Among the most important teaching methods used by Jesus are verbal and visual illustration. The use of metaphor is especially striking. For instance, on many occasions figures of speech drawn from the body were used to convey spiritual truth. Physical blindness illustrated the far more serious blindness of the soul (John 9:39-41). Political bondage pointed up the bondage of the soul (John 8:31-36). Jesus keenly observed common things and aptly used them to illuminate His teaching. The ubiquitous sparrow could claim the heavenly Father's love (Matt. 10:29).

Splinters in eyes illustrate obstructions to spiritual discernment (Matt. 7:15); grass demonstrates the transiency of life (Matt. 6:50); and trees, the secret of true growth (Matt. 7:17, 18). Such illustrations impressed themselves on the mind more vividly than abstractions can. They draw attention to a fundamental facet of pedagogy. Teaching without illustration is like a house without windows: it may contain many treasures, but they may never be seen.

When describing His own mission, Jesus often resorted to metaphorical language. He claimed to be the Good Shepherd because everyone knew that true shepherds care for their flocks (John 10:11). He claimed to be the Light of the world to draw attention to His indisputable function of banishing moral darkness (John 8:12). One disciple later used the same comparison, commenting that the world did not comprehend the Light (John 1:5). Moreover, Jesus did not hesitate to use unexpected metaphors, as when He called Himself a door.[8]

The same is true of other facets of His teaching, as when He described the worthlessness of lives lived without God with such metaphors as tares (Matt. 13:18ff.), dung (Luke 14:35), and rotten fish (Matt. 13:47). This use of illustrations from common life—even distasteful ones—to shock people into serious thought was strongly characteristic of Jesus' ministry. As a religious teacher He is unequaled in regard to illustrations; not only did their vividness captivate His contemporaries, but many have become absorbed into modern life. For instance, such a proverb as "Do not cast your pearls before swine" (Matt. 7:6) generally illustrates the folly of expecting response from a totally unsuitable source. The incongruity of linking pearls with swine is so striking that hearers cannot easily forget.

The wide range of a teacher's illustrations reveals much about the teacher. In the case of Jesus it points to a mind keenly aware of its environment, a readiness to note insignificant things to illuminate profound truths. Jesus evidently loved the countryside since He so often drew his verbal pictures from it.[9] He could mean-

---

8. Both C. C. Torrey and M. Black suggested that the word *door* is a wrong translation from the Aramaic. *Our Translated Gospels* (New York: Harper, 1936), pp. 108, 111-13; *An Aramaic Approach to the Gospels and Acts,* 3rd ed. (Oxford: University Press, 1946), p. 193 (n. 1).

9. J. M. C. Crum considered the so-called document Q to have revealed much of Jesus' love of the countryside. *The Original Jerusalem Gospel* (New York: Macmillan, 1927), p. 62.

ingfully use the figure of a yoke because He may have fashioned yokes in the carpenter's shop (Matt. 11:29, 30). He watched merchants plying their trade and used them to illuminate His teaching (Matt. 13:45, 46). Similarly, He referred to fishermen and thieves. No educator can afford to ignore this method by which Jesus communicated to His contemporaries, for it is more vital than ever in an age when religion and the masses are drifting further apart.

His use of parables. The parables of Jesus deserve special comment for their distinctive contribution to His teaching method. Of the many examples preserved in the Gospels, a few are so important that they occur in all the Synoptics, but the majority are related by only one evangelist, suggesting that many others were not written. Each author chose those best suited to his purpose. As a medium for teaching, the parable possesses particular adaptability. It is especially geared to minds in the habit of thinking in pictures, since it aims to present basic truth by means of a simple story. The parables of Jesus, moreover, are particularly notable for their conciseness. For instance, it would be difficult to parallel a story with so much action in so few words as the parable of the good Samaritan (Luke 10:29ff.). It is the element of conciseness in the parables which makes them memorable.[10]

Much discussion has ranged around their interpretation, especially in view of Jesus' enigmatic response to a question by His disciples regarding their purpose. "This is why I speak to them in parables, because seeing they do not see, and hearing they do not hear, nor do they understand." The idea that Jesus chose a method of teaching with the express purpose of preventing hearers from knowing His meaning is unthinkable. Yet He was a realist, fully alive to the difficulties of communication. The parables offered a means of capturing the imagination even when the hearers' understanding is unenlightened. Once rooted in the memory, the parable might later lead to a fuller grasp of the basic truth. Yet the parabolic form has no significance to those whose minds are already closed to the truth.

Sometimes the focus of attention fell on the main characteristics

---

10. Cf. Matt. 13:3. R. V. G. Tasker commented that, unlike the parables of other teachers, those of Jesus are inseparable from Jesus Himself. "To fail to understand him is to fail to understand his parables." "Parable," in *New Bible Dictionary,* ed. J. D. Douglas (Grand Rapids: Eerdmans, 1962), p. 934.

of the central figure, as in the parable of the unjust judge,[11] but generally the characteristics of the subjects of the parables are left to be inferred from their actions or words. The essence of a parabolic method of teaching demands an uncomplicated plot. Characters appear on the scene without overlapping each other, as in the parable of the prodigal son, where the father, the younger son, and the elder son all come into focus at various points in the parable.[12] Scenic details are reduced to a minimum and are unessential to the interpretation. Many of these features are not unique to the parables of Jesus but conform to the conventional pattern.[13] Yet what distinguishes Jesus from all others who have taught in parables is the profundity of the truth which these stories convey. As the master educator, He chose the simplest medium to drive home ideas which have provided food for thought for the most profound minds.

In only two parables did Jesus supply His own interpretation (Matt. 3:18-23; 13:36-43). It is highly probable that his closest disciples sought some guidance regarding their meaning, and it may be supposed that Jesus was giving a general pattern for interpretation. In both the parable of the sower and the parable of the tares (Matt. 13:1ff., 24ff., 36ff.), the progress of the kingdom is in mind, and both show the importance of more than one detail of the parable. The basic principle of interpretation seems to be the analogy between the physical and the spiritual worlds. There is nothing of the fanciful allegorizing which has characterized some schools of interpretation.[14] Nevertheless there is still dispute over the key lesson of the parables. Some find it in eschatology, some in the kingdom theme, some in social and ethical teaching.[15] It is perhaps invalid to expect all the parables to address the same theme. It is reasonable to suppose that Jesus chose them in each case

11. Cf. Luke 18:1ff. The character of the judge has been a stumbling block to many exegetes. See recent discussions in J. Jeremias, *The Parables of Jesus,* p. 153; and E. Linnemann, *Parables of Jesus,* pp. 119ff.

12. For a modern exposition of the parable of the prodigal son (Luke 15), cf. Linnemann, *Parables of Jesus,* pp. 73ff.

13. Cf. R. Bultmann's discussion of the parable as a literary form in *History of the Synoptic Tradition,* trans. J. Marsh (Oxford: Blackwell, 1963), pp. 166ff. On the Jewish use of parables, cf. H. L. Strack, et al., *Kommentar zum Neue Testament aus Talmud und Midrasch,* vol. 1 (Munich: Beck, 1922), p. 654.

14. Among those patristic authors using allegorical methods, the most notable was Origen. Cf. also the Epistle of Barnabas.

15. For a discussion of various ideas regarding the key to the parables, cf. Tasker, "Parable"; Jeremias, *The Parables of Jesus;* and Linnemann, *Parables of Jesus.*

to express His immediate intentions, which varied with the occasion and the hearers.

The importance of His personality. Some educators rely on the excellency of their method and pay little regard to the impact of their personalties on their hearers. Other teachers use their personalities in the belief that once good relations are established, the hearers will learn more easily. In the case of Jesus, there was a perfect combination of establishing rapport and communicating the lesson. When He spoke, He spoke with authority. There was no question in His mind as to the validity and importance of His words. He spoke with such certainty that even His opponents were impressed. This authoritative approach contrasts vividly with much secular teaching, which is subjectively oriented. Jesus claimed a greater authority than the time-honored Jewish law. "Moses said, . . . but I say" was a formula frequently on his lips (Matt. 5:21, 27, 33, 43).[16]

Jesus' uniqueness is intimately bound up with His teaching. If any other person had conveyed the same teaching, the words would have lacked authority. Moreover, He is the only teacher who, having set up a high ethical ideal, has perfectly fulfilled it. He could rightly claim to be a pattern for others.[17] Even when He urged the seemingly impossible injunction that men should love their enemies (Matt. 5:44), He showed the way by seeking pardon for those who were crucifying Him.

It must not be forgotten that much of the warm humanity of Jesus shines through His sayings. There was nothing cold or abstract about any of His teaching. Even the profoundest sections were relevant to life. Some of His sayings were spiced with humor, as when He spoke of a camel passing through the eye of a needle or of a beam in a person's eye (Matt. 19:24; 23:24). Such examples suggest that He saw humor as a legitimate instrument for communicating his teaching.

As the content of the teaching is considered next, the supremely relevant quality of what Jesus said will be everywhere apparent. He had a message which met the needs not only of His own con-

---

16. On the implication of the introductory formula, "But I say to you . . ." Tasker commented, "In Judaism the Law occupied the supreme position. In Christianity that place is occupied by Christ Himself." "Gospel of Matthew," in *New Bible Dictionary,* p. 797.

17. Cf. John 13:15, where Jesus called His washing the disciples' feet an example *(hupodeigma).*

temporaries, but also of all men in every age who have been disposed to listen to His wisdom.

His Message

The greatness of Jesus in the field of religious education lies not so much in His effective methods as in what He taught. The methods were but instruments for the dissemination of ideas, which were more profound than any that men had heard previously or have heard since. It is possible to give only a brief summary of the most characteristic features of that teaching. It may be summarized as "good news," to use a modern rendering of the word *gospel*, which came in use to describe the Christian message (I Cor. 15:1-3).[18]

Good news about God. The major religious quest is for God, and many different ideas have been proposed. It is therefore necessary to inquire why Jesus' message about God was not only unique but superior to all others. Basically the reason lies in the idea of God as Father.[19] Such an idea was not altogether new to Jewish hearers, who regarded God as the Father of the Jewish nation in the sense of His having special care for His people.[20] But this notion of fatherhood was essentially corporate. It lacked the warm, personal note found in the message of Jesus. Nevertheless, it prepared the way for His more intimate approach.

The main trouble with the Jewish view of God in Jesus' time was its notion that God is too exalted to have personal contact with men, who then need some intermediary to negotiate approach to God. Jesus was no less convinced than His Jewish contemporaries that God was so holy that man cannot easily draw near to Him, but the purpose of Jesus' entire mission was to enable man to do so. In considering His special revelation of God as Father, it must be remembered that it was made on the basis that Jesus' mission made it possible for man to approach God.

18. For a full discussion of the word *gospel*, see G. Griedrich, *"Euangelion,"* in *Theological Dictionary of the New Testament*, ed. R. Kittel, vol. 2 (Grand Rapids: Eerdmans, 1954), pp. 718-35.

19. For a clear exposition of fatherhood in the teaching of Jesus, see H. E. W. Turner, *Jesus, Master and Lord*, 2nd ed. (Naperville, Ill.: Allenson, 1954), pp. 213ff.

20. In the Apocrypha the fatherhood of God is not prominent. The nearest approach to a personal, individual conception is found in Ecclus. 23:1,4.

In the pattern prayer (Matt. 6:9-13) which Jesus gave His disciples, He taught them to use the salutation "Father" because His purpose was to enable those responding to His gospel to be called the sons of God.[21] This was a tremendous leap forward from the idea of Israel as God's son. It brought God into intimate relationship with man. Its analogy was universally intelligible, although the figure of a human father but palely reflects the greater glory of the divine fatherhood.

When approached from the point of view that God is Father, the parallel truth that He is also Creator becomes less awesome.[22] Jesus assumed, rather than specified, the creative activity of God. For Him the world is presided over by the Father. Not even a common sparrow can fall without His knowledge. In this light His providential concern for men must be evident. To His disciples Jesus brought the news that their heavenly Father knows their needs (Matt. 6:8). It is impossible therefore to divorce the creatorship of God from His fatherhood. There was no room in the mind of Jesus for the idea that God is so remote that He has no concern for His creatures. Reaching those with this remote view of God demanded a radically different approach. Their minds must be conditioned for a basically new view of God. Jesus could not wait until men recognized their need for such a revelation; He took the initiative.

Good news about Himself. Many teachers have advanced claims about themselves, but none could make such profound claims as Jesus and, at the same time, substantiate them. Those claims are best illustrated by the titles Jesus used to describe Himself or that others used in referring to Him. On many occasions He used the title *Son of Man* (Matt. 16:27; Mark 8:31). No one else is recorded in the Gospels as using it. Differences of opinion exist regarding its interpretation.[23] Some deny that Jesus referred to Himself;

---

21. For studies on the pattern prayer, cf. E. Lohmeyer, *The Lord's Prayer,* trans. J. Bowden (London: Collins, 1965); and W. Lüthi, *The Lord's Prayer,* trans. K. Schoenenberger (Richmond: Knox, 1962).

22. W. N. Clarke pointed out that the Christian doctrine of God as Creator is based on the doctrine concerning God and men under the influence of the teaching of Jesus. "There is higher revelation in his dwelling with the humble than in his filling space." *The Christian Doctrine of God* (New York: Scribner, 1909), pp. 135ff.

23. Cf. G. S. Duncan, *Jesus, Son of Man* (New York: Macmillan, 1949); S. Mowinckel, *He That Cometh,* trans. G. W. Anderson (Oxford: Blackwell, 1956), pp. 346ff.; O. Cullmann, *Christology of the New Testament,* 2nd ed.

others suppose that only some instances of its use are authentic to Jesus; and still others regard the term as a deliberate choice on the part of Jesus to avoid using publicly the term *Messiah* because of contemporary ideas concerning it. The last of these is the most likely. Jesus may have had in mind certain Old Testament antecedents, such as in Ezekiel and Daniel. Jesus deemed it an appropriate term to express His perfect humanity and at the same time to stress His particular mission. Even if it cannot be supposed that His contemporaries fully understood it, there can be no doubt that for Jesus Himself it possessed Messianic significance. Different terms were used by others to describe Him, such as *Messiah* (John 4:25-29) and *Son of David* (Luke 18:38), although He did not use them of Himself. Much of His teaching nevertheless presupposed His acceptance of their truth. Many times, for instance, He referred to Himself as *Son* when calling God His Father, in such a way as to imply a special relationship (John 10:29-33).[24]

His awareness of Himself as Son of the heavenly Father is of utmost importance. Whatever He did was related to the Father's will. He was sent from God (John 5:37) and had come to glorify God (John 17:4). He was conscious of His uniqueness as the sole way to God (John 14:6). He affirmed that He was the *Light of the world* (John 8:12) and the *Life of men* (John 14:6). In the series of statements beginning with "I am," He reached a climax of remarkable assertions when He maintained, "Before Abraham was, I am" (John 8:58).[25] An informed Jewish hearer would detect a claim to deity since "I am" is akin to the name for God — *Yahweh* (Jehovah—Exod. 3:14, 15).

A fair summary of the claims of Jesus regarding Himself would be that He viewed Himself as perfectly human, capable of experiencing common human reactions such as thirst and tiredness, yet at the same time He claimed to be more than man. We are faced with the mystery of the incarnation. It is no wonder that as a religious teacher He was unique. It is not surprising that His listeners were also deeply interested in His actions: the actions of the Son of God in human form were bound to be insignificant.

(Philadelphia: Westminster, 1964), pp. 137-92; and E. Schweizer, "The Son of Man," *Journal of Biblical Literature* 79 (1960): 119-29.

24. On the title "Son of God" in general, cf. Turner, *Jesus, Master and Lord*, pp. 213ff. On Mark's use, cf. V. Taylor, *The Gospel According to St. Mark* (London: Macmillan, 1953), p. 120.

25. On the "I am" sayings, cf. J. H. Bernard, *The Gospel According to St. John* (New York: Scribner, 1929), pp. cxvi ff.

The activity of Jesus best illustrates His teaching.[26] The Gospels bear testimony to the early church's deep interest in the kind of person Jesus was and the things He did.

Good news about His mission. It is not possible in brief compass to explain completely what Jesus conceived to be the purpose of His life and death. But since this formed the core of what He taught, some summary of His mission is essential. First, His teaching about the *kingdom of God* is noted.

When Jesus spoke of the inauguration of the kingdom, He did not imply a domain as much as a reign.[27] The distinction is important because it draws attention to an activity rather than a state. What Jesus taught was a new relationship between the spiritual King and His people. There were two aspects to His teaching: one present, the other future. The most important evidence of the first is Luke 17:20, 21, where Jesus is recorded as saying, "The kingdom of God is in the midst of you."[28] This clearly relates to a present realization which has come through His mission. Similarly, when He cast out demons by the Spirit of God, He claimed that the kingdom had come (Matt. 12:28; Luke 11:20). This shows that power over evil agencies demonstrates the kingdom. It is a reminder that Jesus and His followers engaged in spiritual warfare. Moreover, even tax collectors and harlots were said to press into the kingdom ahead of the religious leaders (Matt. 21:31).[29]

The future aspect of the kingdom was frequently stressed by Jesus, especially in the parables. There was coming a time when the King would judge those who rejected Him. Such a mission is referred to in the so-called "eschatological discourse" (Mark 13; Matt. 24; Luke 21). But the primary mission of Jesus was not judgment. He came for the *salvation* of His people, and this saving work must next be outlined.

26. Cf. D. Guthrie, *New Testament Introduction*, rev. ed. (Downers Grove, Ill.: Inter-Varsity, 1971), pp. 55, 56. Many scholars deny that Jesus ever claimed this role of Son of God. His Lordship is, however, attested by the Gospel records. Cf. C. K. Barrett, *Jesus and the Gospel Tradition* (Philadelphia: Fortress, 1968).

27. Cf. G. E. Ladd, *Jesus and the Kingdom* (New York: Harper, 1964), pp. 118ff.

28. E. E. Ellis, commenting on Luke 17:20, 21, pointed out that the meaning "within" is unlikely since unbelieving Pharisees appear to be addressed. *The Gospel of Luke* (New York: Nelson, 1966).

29. These two classes were considered by the religious authorities to be the least eligible for entry into the kingdom. Cf. A. H. M'Neile's comment on Matt. 21:31 in *The Gospel According to Matthew* (London: Macmillan, 1915).

A glance at the Gospels shows a disproportionate amount of space devoted to the passion narratives, the only explanation for which is the importance Jesus attached to His death as a saving act. The passion was an essential part of His mission. It was predicted in Scripture (Matt. 26:24). There was a divine compulsion about it (Mark 9:12).

Several sayings of Jesus show that He taught that His death would have sacrificial significance. The central ordinance of Christian worship, the Lord's Supper, He instituted to commemorate His death. To achieve this purpose He chose the common elements of bread and wine, investing them with spiritual significance. Broken bread spoke of His own broken body and the wine of His shed blood, but the most significant feature is the reminder that His sacrificial act was on behalf of others, for the remission of their sins (Matt. 26:26-28). On one occasion Jesus spoke of the Son of Man giving His life as a ransom for many (Mark 10:45). He compared Himself to a grain of wheat which dies in the ground before it can reproduce (John 12:24). He also likened Himself to a good shepherd who gives his life for his sheep (John 10:15). Such vivid metaphors impressed themselves on the disciples' minds. There could be no doubt that for Jesus the path to glory lay through suffering.

In His comments on His coming passion, Jesus never suggested that His death was something imposed upon Him by circumstances beyond His control. He claimed that Pilate could have no power over Him except as it was given from above (John 19:10, 11). He referred to His death as a voluntary act on His part (John 10:18). He spoke of His "hour"—that is, the hour of His passion—as part of the divine program.[30] In no sense, therefore, can His death be regarded as an unforeseen tragedy. It was essential to the accomplishment of His mission. Jesus accepted without question the insight given to John the Baptist at the commencement of Jesus' public ministry, when John identified Jesus as the Lamb of God who would take away the world's sin (John 1:29).

The full significance of the death of Christ could not be brought out until after the event, but Jesus' consciousness of its importance exercised a powerful influence on His teaching ministry. He moved resolutely toward the climax of His mission and regarded the inter-

---

30. The references to "the hour" in John's Gospel are especially noteworthy. Cf. 2:4; 4:23; 5:25; 7:30; 8:20; 12:23, 27; 13:1; 16:32; 17:1. It is impossible to remain unimpressed by the progression from "not yet" to "now come."

vening time as an opportunity to communicate spiritual truths which would later take on new significance.

Perhaps a most important key to understanding Jesus' approach to His own mission is His insistence on *faith* for the appropriation of the truths of that mission. Men were exhorted to repent and believe (Mark 1:14, 15). Jesus made it clear that righteous people had no claim on the kingdom. It was for those willing to acknowledge their need (cf. Matt. 9:12, 13; Mark 2:17; Luke 5:31, 32). In the teaching of Jesus, the exhortation to believe occurs frequently, demanding willingness to commit oneself to a new way of life. His mission requires a personal decision.[31]

Good news about the Holy Spirit. The men of Old Testament times had little idea of the activity of the Holy Spirit. But in His teaching Jesus promised the Spirit, whose work was to glorify Jesus. It was essential for men to grasp the true nature of the Spirit's activity. The teaching on this theme is mainly in the fourth Gospel, in the sayings of Jesus to His disciples in the upper room on the eve of His passion. Three times He referred to the Spirit as "the Spirit of truth" (John 14:17; 15:26; 16:13), which shows one of His dominant characteristics. Jesus Himself had claimed to be the Truth (John 14:6). His whole mission was diametrically opposed to all forms of falsehood. The Spirit was also described as the *Paraclete,* a "Counselor" or "Helper" (John 14:16). The promised Spirit would therefore be personal and intimate—in fact, closer to the disciples than Jesus Himself had been (John 14:17).

One of the Holy Spirit's main activities is tied to Jesus as a religious teacher: the Spirit would remind the disciples of all that Jesus had told them (John 14:26). Unquestionably the teaching methods of Jesus were designed to facilitate the Spirit in this work of recall. Whatever He directed the coming church to do must be in complete agreement with what Jesus had taught—the disciples were not to develop their own teaching; they were to be not originators, but bearers of the basic doctrines of Jesus.[32]

Another highly important aspect of the Spirit is His work of convicting men of sin (John 16:8). Jesus never conceded that His

---

31. Bultmann spoke of eschatological existence—a constant decision and renewal. "New Testament and Mythology," in *Kerygma and Myth,* trans. R. H. Fuller, ed. H. W. Bartsch (London: SPCK, 1953), pp. 20, 21.

32. B. S. Easton held the view that elders were functionally tradition-bearers. *The Pastoral Epistles* (New York: Scribner, 1947).

mission would be desired by all in the sense that it would make men feel comfortable. The Spirit's work in continuation of that mission was to make men aware of their spiritual responsibility. Conviction of sin is never pleasant, but it is indispensable if men are to be taught the whole relevance of the mission of Jesus.

As a foretaste of the experience on Pentecost, the risen Christ breathed on the apostles and said, "Receive the Holy Spirit" (John 20:22). Without such enabling of the Holy Spirit, they would never be able to face the tremendous challenge of the future. Their post-Pentecostal experience amply illustrates the power which the Spirit gave them for their formidable task.

Of the corroborative evidence in the Synoptic Gospels, one saying of Jesus is particularly significant: "If it is by the Spirit ['finger"— Luke 11:20] of God that I cast out demons, then the kingdom of God has come upon you" (Matt. 12:28).[33] This means that Jesus saw the Spirit's activity as evidence of the present reality of the kingdom, especially in the conflict with evil spiritual forces. The theme of Jesus' impact on the realm of demons recurs in the Gospels. The Holy Spirit through Him launched a counterattack which continues through the history of the Christian church.

Jesus conceived of all His ministry as directed by the Spirit. The descent of the Spirit upon Him at His baptism is noted by all the Synoptics, and all mention the Spirit's part in directing Him to the place of temptation immediately afterwards (Matt. 3:16; Mark 1:10; Luke 3:22). When he began His public ministry, according to Luke's account, he applied to Himself the passage from Isaiah 61:1, 2, which speaks of the activity of the Spirit. These evidences are potent reminders that behind the teaching of Jesus lay deep consciousness that the powers of darkness faced defeat through His mission. In the first-century world fear of antagonistic spiritual forces exercised a crippling effect on many people. The gospel which Jesus taught and which He inaugurated would deliver men from bondage. In the debate between Jesus and His critics, He was accused of casting out Satan by the power of Satan. Jesus not only showed the absurdity of this charge, but warned against blasphemy

---

33. The "finger of God" passage in Luke 11:20 is an example, according to Plummer, of Luke's fondness for Hebraistic anthropomorphisms. *The Gospel According to St. Luke.* J. N. Geldenhuys maintained that "Spirit of God" explains the metaphor of the finger. *Commentary on the Gospel of Luke* (Grand Rapids: Eerdmans, 1952), p. 332.

against the Holy Spirit, which was unforgivable.[34] Jesus regarded gravely any attempt to make the Spirit's activity into an agency of evil. His whole approach to men assumes that they have the power to distinguish right from wrong; and any deliberate attempt to choose wrong rather than right shows such men to be beyond forgiveness, indeed beyond the whole purpose of Jesus' mission if they persist.

Not only was Jesus conscious of the Spirit's activity in His own mission, but He also taught the need for such activity in His disciples when they were faced with the challenge of answering for their faith. When on trial before magistrates or monarchs, they could be sure of the prompting of the Spirit (Matt. 10:18). This assurance must have been particularly relevant for those whose education had not fitted them to be articulate in such circumstances (Acts 4:13).

Another aspect of the Spirit's activity which was necessary to Jesus' teaching ministry was the conviction that Scripture was inspired by the Spirit (cf. Mark 12:36 with Ps. 110:1).[35] This is particularly important in view of the widespread appeal to the Old Testament in the teaching of Jesus. He assumed that His hearers would accept the testimony of Scripture as authoritative. This assumption explains the absence of any apologetic approach. Jesus saw no need to argue for the truth of Scripture; its authority was self-evident. It was confirmed by the Spirit. This aspect of the teaching of Jesus cannot be overstressed for it presented a pattern for the subsequent preachers of the gospel.

Good news about man. As a perfect man, Jesus was primarily concerned about man and his possibilities. Although He was realistic about man's spiritual need and recognized the sinful bias of His nature, He nevertheless assumed the dignity of man.[36] Man's limitations were acknowledged. He pointed out that man cannot

---

34. Cf. Matt. 12:32. P. Bonnard rightly restricted the reference here to the attitude of Jesus' adversaries to His ministry of exorcism. *L'évangile selon Saint Matthieu* (Neuchatel: Delachaux and Niestlé, 1963), p. 182.

35. On the general theme of the inspiration of Scripture, cf. R. Pache, *The Inspiration and Authority of Scripture*, trans. H. I. Needham (Chicago: Moody, 1969); and J. I. Packer, *Fundamentalism and the Word of God* (Grand Rapids: Eerdmans, 1958). For a nonconservative view, cf. also G. W. H. Lampe, "The Bible Since the Rise of Critical Study," in *The Church's Use of the Bible Past and Present*, ed. D. E. Nineham (Naperville, Ill.: Allenson, 1963), pp. 125ff.

36. H. W. Robinson, *The Christian Doctrine of Man*, 3rd ed. (Edinburgh: Clark, 1926), pp. 76ff.

increase his physical stature at will, neither can he make his hair white or black by an act of will (Matt. 5:36; 6:27; cf. Luke 12:25). Yet He called upon man to do the impossible: to be perfect as the heavenly Father is perfect.[37] No more exacting task could ever have been placed before man, in view of the prevalence of greed, cruelty, violence, and utter selfishness. Jesus had faith in the possibilities of human nature only because He knew that His mission was to transform man's natural tendencies. He had come to provide a new nature, wholly different from man's natural disposition.

The possibilities facing man are limitless, but they involve a person wholly dedicated, ready to put the noblest ideals before his personal interests. Such a man will not seek to advance himself, to attain the highest positions at the expense of others. He will even turn the other cheek when an enemy smites him. Teaching like this is revolutionary.[38] It challenges the universal belief that every man must look after himself. It is no wonder that such a view of man has aroused opposition from those whose philosophy of life makes man central. The idea that man finds his true dignity in taking up his cross and following Jesus is too unpalatable to be popular (Mark 8:34; 10:21). And yet Jesus seriously advocated this as man's only hope. Those who have put it to the test have found His claim to be true.

Life in Christ was to be joyous; it was to be characterized by blessedness. It was to involve purity of mind, a persistent quest for righteousness, a true spirit of humility. It would demand allegiance to a new law which must be applied to man's motives as much as, if not more than, to his actions. The climax of Jesus' demands was for a new kind of love, a love wholly superior to the dictates of passion. Indeed, it reaches fullest expression when man learns to love his enemies. No one will dispute the truth that if all men learned the way of Jesus, strife and bloodshed among men would immediately cease. But many write off such teaching as too idealistic to be practical.

---

37. Cf. Matt. 5:48. J. C. Fenton wrote, "His 'Law' is impossible because it puts before us perfection and love which are beyond our capabilities." *The Gospel of St. Matthew* (Baltimore: Penguin, 1963), p. 95. Neither E. P. Blair nor F. C. Grant took perfection in the sense of absolute sinlessness, but of inward goodness. *Jesus in the Gospel of Matthew* (New York: Abingdon, 1960), p. 136; *The Earliest Gospel* (New York: Abingdon-Cokesbury, 1943), pp. 218ff.

38. This kind of revolutionary teaching is diametrically opposed to the methods of political revolutionaries like the Zealots. Some, such as Brandon *(Jesus and the Zealots)*, have tried to maintain some connection of Jesus with that movement, however.

Good news about fellowship. Not even the briefest summary of the most important aspects of Jesus' teaching would be complete without mentioning His idea of the Christian community. It was not simply that Jesus spoke of His church, but that He implied the necessity of fellowship among believers. When sending the disciples on a mission, He did not send them singly but in pairs (Luke 10:1). He promised that His presence would be felt when two or more were assembled in His name (Matt. 18:20). He commissioned His disciples to make other disciples and to baptize and teach them. He clearly envisaged a continuous and developing fellowship of like-minded people who had committed themselves in faith to Him. It is essential to take full account of this in estimating Jesus as a religious teacher. The continuity between His work and the work of the Christian community was a vital factor in the success of His mission. In a sense every person who came to believe in Him was to reproduce the ministry of Jesus in announcing the message of deliverance. Those schools of thought which deny this essential continuity can see little relevance in the historical Jesus. But the present survey is based on the assumption that some knowledge of the historical Jesus, especially in His teaching ministry, is indispensable to account for the origin and development of the Christian community which He founded. It is equally assumed that that community ceases to function effectively as soon as it departs from the basic methods of Jesus. The greatness of any teacher may be gauged by the continuing influence which He leaves behind, and in this respect Jesus has no equal.

His Educational Principles

Consideration is given in this section to the reaction of Jesus toward those He taught. To what extent was He dominated by the desire to indoctrinate His hearers? Or, to what extent was He swayed by the felt need of His pupils? To answer these questions some research into the various types of audience is necessary.

The relationships which Jesus sustained with His audiences as reflected in the Gospels may be summarized under three groupings: His relationship to the disciples, to the general populace, and to the religious leaders.

When dealing with *the disciples,* He used a different technique, especially at the close of the ministry, from what He used to teach the multitudes.[39] On occasions He responded to specific requests, such as "Lord, teach us to pray" (Luke 11:1), or "Why do you speak to us in parables?" (Matt. 13:10). Here the teaching is in response to the felt need of the audience. There can be no doubt that questions of this kind reveal inquiring minds which predisposed the hearers to pay attention. But in most cases Jesus Himself prompted the inquiry by His own example or method. When, for instance, a rich young ruler came with a question about inheriting eternal life, Jesus used the opportunity to teach about wealth, which was no doubt necessary but was certainly not a felt need on the young man's part (Matt. 19:16-22). The Gospels do not gloss over the dullness of the disciples' understanding (Mark 4:13, 40). On many occasions they were baffled by the words of Jesus, yet He did not hesitate to tell them what He knew they could not yet grasp. Many of His basic teachings could be understood only in the future light of the resurrection. For instance, the injunction to the disciples to take up the cross and follow Jesus (Luke 9:23) would gain a deeper significance after they had witnessed Jesus' passion. He taught His disciples, therefore, not what they thought they needed but what according to His own perfect insight they really needed.[40]

It was no different with *the general public*. Jesus regarded them as sheep without a shepherd (Matt. 9:36). They were in need of counsel. It was not His policy to pander to popular taste in His teaching. Although at first He did gain popularity, it was not long before He caused offense because of His sayings (cf. John 6:59ff.). Popular reactions tend to be fickle, and response to the teaching of Jesus was no exception. Men were prepared to listen until His words became too challenging. Yet he did not cease to challenge. He came with a mission which He knew would never be popular because it was too demanding. His approach was authoritarian rather than accommodating.

The relation of Jesus to *the religious leaders* was mainly one of tension. To them His approach was not only unorthodox but revolutionary. It constituted a direct challenge to the establishment, and it is not surprising, therefore, that it produced opposition. Even so there was response from some more amenable officials, like Nicodemus and Joseph of Arimathea. While Jesus

---

39. For a study of audience reactions, cf. J. A. Baird, *Audience Criticism and the Historical Jesus* (Philadelphia: Westminster, 1969).
40. Cf. John 2:24.

welcomed members of the ruling party, He never compromised to ingratiate them. Indifferent to their authority, by way of contrast He demonstrated his own. The common people could not fail to note that the teaching of the scribes lacked the authority of Jesus' teaching (Matt. 7:29). The scribes mainly repeated what others had said, whereas Jesus spoke as One sent directly from the Father. The teaching of Jesus to the religious instructors of His day concentrated on their abuses. Invariably He drew attention to a need which He saw only too clearly, but of which His hearers appear to have been unaware.

Is the approach of Jesus relevant as a pattern for the present? To assume that it is, one must show that the modern outlook is identical with that of the first century. The crux of the matter lies in the attitude toward authority. In Jesus' time on earth, children learned to respect the authority of their elders, and pupils the authority of their teachers. In the modern age, when authority has been so widely overthrown, educators are faced with a different problem. Yet it cannot for this reason be assumed that the approach of Jesus is obsolete. The modern rejection of authority is due to a lack of respect for its source, rather than a rejection of authority itself. In any age and among all peoples, there has always been a readiness to heed those whose stature is sufficient to command respect. Twentieth-century man, with all his technological achievements, is not different in his moral needs from first-century man. The methods of Jesus are not irrelevant. In this respect He is unique among those who have sought to educate people in the religious sphere. The superlative greatness of Jesus among all others is the timelessness of His approach. If it was true in the first century, as His contemporaries acknowledged, that no one taught as authoritatively as He, it is no less true today. Truth carries its own authority.

Selected Bibliography

Curtis, W. A. *Jesus Christ the Teacher*. London: Oxford University, 1943.
Davies, W. D. *The Setting of the Sermon on the Mount*. 2nd ed. Cambridge: University Press, 1964.
Denney, J. *Jesus and the Gospel*. New York: Armstrong, 1909.
Dodd, C. H. *The Parables of the Kingdom*. New York: Scribner, 1961.
Gerhardsson, B. *Memory and Manuscript*. Translated by E. J. Sharpe. Copenhagen: Munksgaard, 1961.

Hunter, A. M. *Interpreting the Parables*. Philadelphia: Westminster, 1960.
Jeremias, J. *The Parables of Jesus*. London: SCM, 1963.
Linnemann, E. *Parables of Jesus*. London: SPCK, 1966.
Marshall, I. H. *Eschatology and the Parables*. London: Tyndale, 1963.
Montefiore, C. G. *Rabbinic Literature and Gospel Teachings*. London: Macmillan, 1930.

2

Richard N. Longenecker

Paul

When the Christian speaks of "the Teacher" par excellence, he invariably has Jesus Christ in mind. But the apostle Paul is also presented in the New Testament as a teacher. The Book of Acts begins its account of Paul's Gentile ministry by referring to his teaching at Antioch in Syria (Acts 11:26; cf. 13:1; 15:35); goes on to mention explicitly that during his missionary travels he taught in such cities as Corinth and Ephesus (Acts 18:11; 20:20); and closes with the statement that while imprisoned for two years in his own rented house at Rome, he was able to continue "preaching the kingdom of God and teaching about the Lord Jesus Christ quite openly and unhindered" (Acts 28:31). Paul wrote that he had taught the traditions about Christ "everywhere and in every church" (I Cor. 4:17; II Thess. 2:15) and to "every man" with whom he came in contact (Col. 1:28). He spoke of having been called by God to be a preacher and an apostle, but also a teacher (I Tim. 2:7; II Tim. 1:11). He urged Timothy, his "true child in the faith," to include teaching in his pastoral duties at Ephesus (I Tim. 4:11; 6:2), and he instructed that a church leader should be an apt teacher (I Tim. 3:2; II Tim. 2:24). On one occasion Paul even ranked teaching as third in the hierarchy of gifts given by the Holy Spirit for the strengthening of the church, placing it directly behind apostles and prophets (I Cor. 12:28, 29)—though elsewhere he listed it as coordinate with all the other God-given gifts (I Cor. 12:4-11; Eph. 4:11).

Clearly, in Paul's view, teaching the gospel is of major significance in the Christian ministry. This involves reducing it to its simplest essentials, analyzing it point by point, fixing its meaning by positive and negative definition, showing how each part of the message links up with the rest, indicating its major implications, and explaining it until one is sure that his listeners have grasped it. "No study of St. Paul's writing," as W. Edward Chadwick observed, "can be done without noticing the immense stress which he laid, both directly and indirectly, both by precept and example, upon the teaching function of the Christian ministry."[1] Yet little place has been given the apostle in the history of education, possibly, as Howard T. Kuist suggested, because "men have been so interested in his teachings that they have missed the pedagogy of the teacher. St. Paul did not display his art."[2]

The great teacher lives for his students and the truth he has to impart, not calling attention to his methods or unduly projecting himself. Nonetheless, the great teacher makes an immediate impression upon those who hear him and a far-reaching impact upon the world of thought. By these criteria alone Paul was a great teacher, and we can learn much from the pedagogy latent in his writings.

Educational Background

In an appendix to what is probably the oldest rabbinic tract now extant, the following program for the Jewish male is laid out: "At five years old one is fit for the Scripture, at ten years for the Mishnah, at thirteen for the fulfilling of the commandments, at fifteen for the Talmud, at eighteen for the bride-chamber, at twenty for pursuing a calling, at thirty for authority, at forty for discernment, at fifty for counsel, at sixty for to be an elder, at seventy for gray hairs, at eighty for special strength, at ninety for bowed back, and at a hundred a man is as one that has already died and passed away and ceased from the world."[3] Josephus, the

---

1. *The Pastoral Teaching of St. Paul*, p. 7.
2. *The Pedagogy of St. Paul*, p. 146.
3. Mishnah, Aboth 5:21.

first-century Jewish historian, related that the Scriptures and the traditions were taught in every city to Jewish boys "from our first consciousness,"[4] and that he personally was so precocious as to be highly versed in both by the age of fourteen.[5] And Philo, the Alexandrian Jewish philosopher and statesman of Paul's day, spoke of such instruction in the Torah taking place "from earliest youth."[6]

In the home. The education of the Jewish boy took place, first of all, in the home. There he was circumcised on the eighth day, marking his union with the covenant people of God (cf. Gen. 17:9-14). There he learned that the "weightiest" commandment of all is that of filial piety: "Honor thy father and thy mother" (Exod. 20:12). This commandment was taught to be as weighty as that of honoring God, and more, since "God makes more of it than of honoring Himself."[7] There he was exposed to a series of object lessons as every festival, symbol, and ceremony in the family observance exerted an educational influence. For example, Passover *(Pesach)* in the spring of the year was celebrated in the home for all unable to make the pilgrimage to Jerusalem. The father presided, and the oldest son asked the meaning of the rite. With joy and gratitude the family recalled God's deliverance from Egypt and bound themselves to Israel's hope for the future. The Feast of Tabernacles *(Sukkoth)* in the fall, with its symbolism of the booths, taught about Israel's wilderness wanderings and God's provision in the land. The extrabiblical Festival of Dedication *(Hanukkah)* in the winter had profound lessons to impart regarding freedom of conscience, nationalism, and the strength of minorities when God enables them. Likewise *Rosh Hashanah* (New Year), *Yom Kippur* (Day of Atonement), and *Purim* (Lots), by their ceremonies and symbolism, called forth innumerable questions and gave opportunity for Jewish parents to teach their children the meaning of life as they saw it.

The minimal obligations of a Jewish father to his son are defined: he must circumcise him, redeem him (cf. Exod. 13:15; Num. 18:16), teach him Torah, teach him a trade, and get him a wife. Jewish sentiment asserted the nobility of manual labor and advised that intellectual prowess and physical activity go hand in hand.

---

4. Contra Apion 2.178.
5. Life 9.
6. Legatio ad Gaium 210.
7. Jer. Talmud, Peah 15c.

Rabbi Gamaliel II is credited with saying: "Excellent is Torah study together with worldly business, for all Torah without work must fail at length and occasion iniquity."[8] An early Jewish tractate insisted: "Whosoever does not teach his son work, teaches him to rob."[9] In such a home Paul not only learned the traditions and ideals of his nation, but he was also initiated into the skills of tentmaking (cf. Acts 18:31). Jewish education sought to produce a man would could both think and act, one who was neither an egghead nor a clod. Paul's later life indicates how greatly he profited from such training.

At the schools. Although elementary instruction was left to the parents and provided by them or by tutors employed by them, Pharisaic Judaism in the time of Paul stressed the need for every Jewish community to maintain a secondary (or more advanced) school *(Beth Midrash)*, either in connection with the synagogue or adjacent to it.[10] Our detailed information about the schools comes only from the second century A.D., but it seems that Jewish communities frequently maintained an elementary school *(Beth Sefer)* as well, the elementary school given over to reading and writing, with the secondary school stressing the interpretation of Holy Writ. Studies in the secondary school were carried on in the ancient Hebrew of the Bible and the Mishnaic Hebrew of the scholars, and students were required to know how to read and write their ancestral language prior to enrolling. The course of study began with the Book of Leviticus and its interpretation, moved on to encompass the whole of the Pentateuch, progressed to the Prophets, and finally included the so-called Writings in the third portion of the Hebrew canon. Not every boy, of course, finished the entire curriculum, but those who did were expected to be able to read and comment upon the entire Hebrew Bible.

At thirteen a Jewish boy became a *bar mitzvah* ("son of the commandment"), when he took upon himself the full obligation of the Law. Most Jewish boys of that age either were beginning or were fully immersed in their studies at the *Beth Midrash*, with more promising lads sent off to rabbinic schools under abler teachers. It was probably at this age that Paul came to Jerusalem to further

---

8. Mishnah, Aboth 2:2.
9. Bab. Talmud, Kiddushin 99a.
10. On these schools see G. F. Moore, *Judaism in the First Centuries of the Christian Era,* vol. 1 (Cambridge: Harvard University, 1927), pp. 314-22.

his training, perhaps living with the married sister spoken of in Acts 23:16. And it is some indication of Paul's youthful ability, as well as perhaps his family's importance, that he was selected to study under Rabbi Gamaliel I, one of the greatest rabbinic teachers of the first century (Acts 22:3).

Rabbinic education focused on the Hebrew Bible and its traditional interpretations. But it also exposed neophyte rabbis to the "wisdom of the Greeks." The Talmud reports that Rabbi Simeon ben Gamaliel II, a second-century teacher, implemented a dual curriculum by having five hundred students study the traditions of the Hebrews and another five hundred the writings of the Greeks, midpoint in their program reversing the relationship.[11] Despite its antagonism to all Hellenistic systems of thought, Judaism was not averse to borrowing ideas and forms from the Greek world if it could press them into service for the God of Israel. Rabbinic Judaism, in fact, was sufficiently permeated by Hellenism in this manner to account for most, if not all, of Paul's knowledge of Gentile literature and habits.[12] What Paul knew of authentic Grecian philosophy was probably meager and secondhand, stemming entirely from his rabbinic training or his casual observance. His four quotations from Greek writers (found in Acts 17:28; I Cor. 15:33; Titus 1:12), for example, are little more than "the common property of popular philosophers."[13] He employed terms and forms which were current in the Greek world, but he used them in accordance with what he had known and experienced in Judaism and Christianity. He used them to convey his meaning without primary reference to what they necessarily denoted in Grecian thought. As C. A. Anderson Scott rightly said: "The elements in his thinking to which parallels have been found in non-Jewish literature, in Greek religion or in pagan mysteries, are obviously secondary. They belong to the surface rather than to the core of his thought and teaching."[14]

Paul's educational background, in its own way, was both intensive and broad. He was highly trained in the traditions of his fathers, but he also had rubbed shoulders with Grecian culture

---

11. Bab. Talmud, Sotah 49b.

12. Cf. W. L. Knox, *Some Hellenistic Elements in Primitive Christianity* (London: Oxford University, 1944), pp. 30-34.

13. M. Dibelius, *Paul,* trans. F. Clarke (New York: Longmans and Green, 1953), p. 31.

14. *Christianity According to St. Paul* (Cambridge: University Press, 1927), p. 10.

and inherited Roman citizenship (Acts 16:37, 38; 22:25-29). As such, he was able to speak easily within every sector of the Roman world, whether Hebraic or Hellenistic in orientation.

Philosophy of Education

It would be difficult to assert that the apostle Paul had a consciously and precisely formulated philosophy of education. Indeed, the very expression would have sounded foreign to him, but a system of educational approach is found in his writings. As a Hebrew, Paul thought more theologically than philosophically, and his teaching was more a declaration of faith than the proposal of a theory. He worked from the events and the literature of revelation rather than from the categories of the human mind or the distillation of human experience. In contrast to the Greek mentality, he tended to think more in functional and relational terms than in static or speculative fashion. Nonetheless, he was conscious of certain factors and objectives which shaped his ministry, and there are elements inherent in his teaching which may be spelled out into something of a philosophy of education.

On the unity of life. From his Hebraic background Paul inherited a strong sense of the unity of life.[15] This meant for him that there exists a vital union between knowledge and practice. He saw that enlightenment of the mind was also character education, and he faulted the pagan world for not realizing this (e.g., Rom. 1:21ff.; Eph. 4:17ff.). Paul also assumed the unity of the "sacred" and the "secular." To the devout Jew, religion was not just one factor in life but the center of his whole existence, permeating and informing all of life. Thus, the revelation of God in Jesus Christ and in the ancient Scriptures made up the core of Paul's curriculum, since what God did in history on behalf of man relates to all of life.

Similarly, there is in Paul's thought a unity of the material and the immaterial, of the natural and the supernatural, and of the visible and the invisible. Contrary to Hellenistic religious philosophy generally, the apostle did not set the material per se against the immaterial or disparage the visible as a defiled reflection of the invisible. He recognized distinctions between the two (one cannot

15. Cf. H. Mueller, *A Critical Analysis of the Jewish Educational Philosophy in Relationship to the Epistles of St. Paul* (Sieberg: Steyler, 1967).

speak of a "unity" without noting varying elements comprising that unity), and he acknowledged that sin has invaded the material realm. But he rested too heavily upon the teaching of the Old Testament to postulate that the natural world of matter and sense perception stands intrinsically opposed to all that is supernatural, invisible, and immaterial. Paul's educational philosophy, therefore, is "wholistic." His teaching concerns not just aspects or areas of man's life, but all of man's spiritual, ethical, and social relationships—all that was created by God, all that has been affected by sin, and all that God has redeemed through Jesus Christ.

Paul also exhibited in his life and teaching the Jewish ideal of combining study and physical labor. The aristocracy of Greece denied laborers the right of citizenship because they believed that manual labor debases and dulls man's appreciation for the higher things of life. Paul, however, worked to support himself that he might present his message "free of charge" and without offense at Corinth (I Cor. 9:6-23), and he commanded the idlers within the church at Thessalonica to follow his example (II Thess. 3:6-15). Although he may very well have taken pleasure in the physical exertion and creative artistry of tentmaking, he did not look upon his manual labor as an end in itself; rather, as William A. Beardslee pointed out, he seems to have thought that "because work may express the motive of love, because it may prevent one's becoming a burden to others, because in it one may dispel misapprehensions of non-Christians, work is necessary and meaningful."[16]

On the nature of God. Of great importance in determining Paul's philosophy of education is a consideration of his understanding of God and man. "Show me what concept of human nature you have, and I will tell you what educational philosophy you espouse" is an underlying maxim of all education; or, as John S. Brubacher said more prosaically, ". . . the philosophical conception of the nature of man and the world in which he lives is a potent determinative of all educational method."[17] Yet, unlike the Greeks and most modern educators, who reflect upon man as man, Paul as a Jew and as a Christian "looked to God first and then considered man as he stood in divine light."[18]

---

16. *Human Achievement and Divine Vocation in the Message of Paul*, p. 62.
17. *A History of the Problems of Education* (New York: McGraw-Hill, 1947), p. 165.
18. W. D. Stacey, *The Pauline View of Man*, p. 144.

Paul inherited a great and noble conception of God from his Jewish forefathers and through the Hebrew Scriptures. By means of divine direction in history, the prophetic Word, and the exile to Babylon, Judaism came to possess an unalterable conviction regarding the oneness of God, all local and national deities being swept into nothingness. God is One, the Creator, Maker of heaven and earth, the Judge of all mankind, the sole Ruler over human life and history. The God of Hebrew prophecy, the one true God, is both transcendent and immanent. While never entrapped by history, He has involved Himself in the course of human affairs generally and in the experiences of His people Israel in particular.

It was God as thus conceived who was in the background of all Paul's thinking and teaching. Yet there are differences between his Christian understanding of God and that which we find in the Judaism of his day. Confronted by the exalted Christ on the way to Damascus. Paul could not escape the conclusion that Jesus of Nazareth was to be associated intimately with the God whom Israel worshiped. Despite his superior credentials, his ardent zeal, and a personal assurance of doing God's will (cf. Rom. 9:4, 5; 10:2-4), Paul's life and activity in Judaism lay under the rebuke of God, for a voice from heaven had corrected him and vindicated Jesus, and nothing more could be said.

On the nature of man. Paul's doctrine of man, like that of his Jewish forefathers, was more synthetic and relational than analytic or speculative. Man had been created in "the image of God" (Gen. 1:27), in moral affinity with God and capable of knowing God and having fellowship with Him. Herein lies man's essential dignity and worth. But man lost this moral likeness to God through disobedience and opposition to God, thus breaking the relationship of dependence and trust (Gen. 3:1-24; Ps. 14:2, 3; IV Ezra 7:116-26; Rom. 5:12-14). Yet man possesses something of the original image of God and can be appealed to as a responsible creation of God. Through obedience to God's law, and finally in the Messianic age, that glory and likeness will be restored. Such, broadly, was Paul's understanding of man.

As a Christian, Paul retained the basic structure of his Jewish anthropology, but his understanding of how the image of God in man and man's relationship with God were to be restored became altered through his conversion. Experiencing the powers of the Messianic age through commitment to Jesus Christ, he found that "if any one is in Christ, he is a new creation" (II Cor. 5:17) and that believers in Christ, "beholding the glory of the Lord, are being changed into the same image from glory to glory" (II Cor. 3:18). Man's reconciliation with God is "through Christ" and "in Christ" (II Cor. 5:18-21), with the Christian life lived by the guidance of the Spirit in obedience to Christ (Gal. 5:16-26; Phil. 2:6-11).

With this view of man, Paul was both pessimistic and optimistic in his educational philosophy: pessimistic regarding every endeavor to externalize man's basic problems or to solve them simply by the increase of human knowledge. Reinhold Niebuhr pertinently observed: "The most persistent error of modern educators and moralists is the assumption that our social difficulties are due to the failure of the social sciences to keep pace with the physical sciences which have created our technological civilization. The invariable implication of this assumption is that, with a little more time, a little more adequate moral and social pedagogy and a generally higher development of human intelligence, our social problems will approach solution."[19] For Paul, man's basic problem is an internal one—the old problem of egoism, stemming from man's rebellion against God. His dilemma is at the core of his life, not on its surface. "It concerns his fundamental commitments, not his incidental acts; the quality of the ends he pursues, not the efficiency of the means he commands in pursuing them."[20]

Education today is dominated by the humanistic assumption that, while human nature is perfectable, it is basically unchangeable. The truth of such a philosophy lies in the fact that man as he is in history is capable of both a certain degree of altruism and extensive debauchery. Although Paul realized that by common grace man retains the possibilities for much good, he did not center his hope there. Much more optimistic, he was convinced that by divine special grace man may become far more than he is or could naturally become. Being "in Christ," a man becomes a son of God and a new creation—far beyond what education could produce—and, as a new creation in Christ, he presses on to Christian maturity (Phil. 3:12-16). With confidence, therefore, the apostle, "striving with all the energy which he [God] mightily inspires within me," engaged in his ministry of "warning every man and teaching every

---

19. *Moral Man and Immoral Society* (New York: Scribner, 1934), p. xiii.
20. J. F. A. Taylor, "The University and the Moral Frontier," *The Educational Forum* 21 (1962): 422.

man in all wisdom, that we may present every man mature in Christ" (Col. 1:28, 29).

Pedagogical Methods

The perennial problem in education is to define the relationship between philosophy and practice—or, as in religious education, between theology and methodology. There is evidence in the Pauline letters that the apostle felt this need and gave attention to the problem. Although he stressed the content of his message, Paul considered his function of transmitting that message of great importance as well. David M. Stanley rightly said: "His own mediatorial role is highly necessary. He is not merely a mouthpiece through which the Gospel is handed on mechanistically to other men. Not only what he says, but how he says it, as well as what he is, have a part to play in the Christian formation of those he evangelizes. The Gospel of Christ which he preaches is also his Gospel in a real, if subordinate, sense."[21] One cannot, of course, find in Paul a formal discussion of his pedagogical methods. Nonetheless, latent in the Acts account of his ministry and in his pastoral letters are certain features that may be legitimately noted in this regard.

As an evangelist. Two things immediately stand out when we study the missionary preaching of the apostle Paul as recorded in Acts.[22] In the first place, he had the gift of beginning where his hearers were. That Paul possessed this ability may be seen particularly in his three sermons recorded in Acts: in the synagogue at Antioch of Pisidia (13:16-41), to the people of Lystra (14:15-17), and before the Court of Ares in Athens (17:22-31).

These three sermons were completely different in approach. In the synagogue at Antioch, the apostle preached to Jews, Jewish proselytes, and God-fearing Gentiles, all vitally interested in Jewish history and the Scriptures. Therefore he structured his presentation along the lines of Jewish history and supported his argument with texts from the Old Testament. At Lystra, to those in the hinterland of Asia Minor where little of Jewish tradition or Greek culture

---

21. "Become Imitators of Me," *Biblica* 40 (1959): 874.
22. Cf. W. Barclay, "A Comparison of Paul's Missionary Preaching and Preaching to the Church," in *Apostolic History and the Gospel*, ed. W. W. Gasque and R. P. Martin (Grand Rapids: Eerdmans, 1970), pp. 165-70.

had penetrated, he started from nature, from the "rains and fruitful seasons." At Athens, however, he began from the local religious worship and quoted the Greek poets (Acts 17:28). He never mentioned Jewish history, the Hebrew Scriptures, or the witness of nature. "In his approach," as William Barclay pointed out, "Paul had no set scheme and formula; his approach was completely flexible. He began where his audience was."[23]

Second, Paul's preaching was not just a monologue; it also involved dialogue. His preaching was proclamation, but not a take-it-or-leave-it proclamation. It was the declaration of the gospel *plus* explanation and defense. The characteristic word of Paul's missionary preaching in Acts is *argued*. At Damascus, Athens, Corinth, and Ephesus he argued the gospel, remaining in each city as long as he had a hearing. He proclaimed and defended the faith, being sure to satisfy the mind as well as the heart.[24]

As a pastor. In Paul's pastoral ministry as reflected in his letters, the pedagogical principle of beginning on common ground with his hearers again comes to the fore. In I Corinthians 9:22 he spoke of being "all things to all men," and it is in that letter particularly where his method is most adequately exhibited.[25]

In treating the problem of immorality within the church, Paul censures it in I Corinthians 5:13 and interacts with his converts' mistaken idea of Christian liberty in 6:12-20. But the interesting thing is that in dealing with their thought, he begins by agreeing with them: "All things are lawful to me," and "Food for the stomach and the stomach for food" (I Cor. 6:12, 13). Trite maxims the pagan world used in defense of life apart from external restraint, these sayings had been taken over by the believers in defense of "Christian libertarianism." But Paul agreed with them—up to a point. In effect he said to these libertine Christians that if the gospel proclamation were only that Christ has freed us for our full expression, then even immorality could be classed as proper. But he went on to insist that the question of Christian liberty is not settled simply by considering what is lawful or what is created. These facts must be constantly tempered by the realization that not all things are profitable, the determination that we will not be enslaved by anything, and the dedication of the body unto the

23. Ibid., p. 166.
24. Ibid.
25. R. N. Longenecker, *Paul, Apostle of Liberty*, pp. 230-44.

Lord (I Cor. 6:12-20). Paul is dealing with believers whose outlook is so warped that they can call moral perversion an exercise in spiritual liberty and ecclesiastical guidance a fleshly function. Yet even here he is "all things to all men" in order to lead them on to a truer understanding and expression of their faith.

It is also instructive to note in I Corinthians 8-10 how Paul approached the issue of eating meat that had been offered to idols. He did not quote the Jerusalem decree, even though the first element of that enactment spoke directly to the situation at hand (cf. Acts 15:20, 29), for here were individuals who prided themselves on their supraspirituality and who were not at all prepared to accept ecclesiastical authority. The apostle, rather, began by agreeing with his supposedly "strong" converts that: "All of us possess knowledge," "An idol has no real existence," and "There is no God but one" (I Cor. 8:1, 4). But he went on to insist that in their refusal to condition their liberty by love for their weaker brothers, they were giving offense to those outside of Christ, working havoc within the church, and not glorifying God in the exercise of their Christian freedom (I Cor. 8:7-13; 10:24-32).

He also followed this approach in I Corinthians 12-14 and II Corinthians 12 when dealing with the misuse of spiritual gifts. He agreed that the gift of tongues was a genuine supernatural charisma (II Cor. 12:10, 28) and that revelatory visions possessed real value (II Cor. 12:1-4). In fact, he declared, "I thank God that I speak in tongues more than you all" (I Cor. 14:18), and told of a time "fourteen years ago" when he had been "caught up into Paradise" and given an "abundance of revelations" (II Cor. 12:2ff.). Such assertions were not manufactured, for Paul was a true ecstatic. But he mentioned these experiences here only to gain a hearing for his main thesis that spiritual gifts are given by the Spirit "who apportions to each one individually as he wills" and "for the common good" (I Cor. 12:4-11). Hence his plea was for believers at Corinth not to exalt the gift of tongues out of all proper perspective, but to make love their aim, to seek spiritual gifts as the Spirit gives them, and to use such gifts for the upbuilding and edification of the church. In order to win his ecstatically minded addressees, he approached them as an ecstatic.

In all these instances it cannot be said that Paul was merely opportunistic if we mean by that, taking advantage of a situation without regard for principles or consequences. He was attempting no deception. In every case he recognized his converts to be real

Christians, but Christians who, in grasping one aspect of the gospel proclamation, had perverted the truth into error. He worked from the one element of truth grasped to a fuller understanding and expression of their freedom in Christ. Far from disregarding ultimate consequences, his purpose was to strengthen his converts and the church. By beginning at the point of common agreement and omitting arguments that would needlessly cause offense, he exhibited his pastoral principle of being "all things to all men." Here is legitimate flexibility of approach and elasticity of attitude that should characterize every Christian pastor, teacher, missionary, scholar, and statesman.

As an example. While a proper emphasis should be placed upon philosophy and methods, it must be recognized that in education generally and Christian education in particular, "the single most important factor that influences learning is the life and personality of the teacher."[26] Paul had a healthy self-awareness of both his distinctive assets and his personal weaknesses (II Cor. 12:1-10; Phil. 3:12-16). He knew that Christ had made him His own (Phil. 3:12) and that, as a result, he was "blessed in Christ with every spiritual blessing in the heavenly places" (Eph. 1:3). Yet he also was keenly conscious that he needed to "press on" to make all that was his in Christ Jesus his own in experience (Phil. 3:12-16). He possessed a firm conviction regarding the truthfulness, power, and life-changing quality of his message, yet had genuine humility. He also urged all who would think themselves "mature" Christians to "be thus minded" and to "join in imitating me and mark those who so live as you have in us an example" (Phil. 3:15-17).

A number of times Paul urged his converts to follow his example. He commended the Thessalonians for imitating the lives of the apostolic band (Paul, Silas, and Timothy) and "of the Lord," and in turn becoming examples for other believers in Macedonia and Achaia (I Thess. 1:5ff.). In speaking of the problems at Corinth, he wrote: "Be imitators of me, as I am of Christ" (I Cor. 11:1; cf. 4:16). And his final exhortation to the Philippians was: "What you have learned and received and heard and seen in me, do; and the God of peace will be with you" (Phil. 4:9). As Paul viewed it, there is a chain of witness and example originating with Jesus, mediated through the apostles, and extending out into the world

---

26. F. Edge, *Teaching for Results* (Nashville: Broadman, 1956), p. 223.

through the succession of converts to Christ. Without minimizing the supremacy of his Lord, he yet urged an imitation of his own life and ministry.

Although conscious of his unique calling as "a minister of Christ Jesus to the Gentiles in the priestly service of the gospel of God," he was also vitally aware that it was Christ who was working through him and the Holy Spirit who was enabling him (Rom. 15:15-19). He placed prayer uppermost in his consideration of methods and means, and he repeatedly asked the churches to pray for him (e.g., Rom. 15:30; Eph. 6:19, 20; Col. 4:3, 4; I Thess. 5:25; II Thess. 3:1, 2). He also had a deep conviction regarding the mutual dependence of believers in "the body of Christ" (I Cor. 12:4-31). Christians have been called into "the unity of the Spirit," and they are to maintain that unity and express it in service to God (Eph. 4:1-6). The apostle himself recognized the legitimacy of Christian endeavors other than his own Gentile mission (e.g., I Cor. 9:5; Gal. 2:7-10) and of other ministers within that mission (e.g., I Cor. 3:5ff.; 9:6). Rather than egotistically viewing his ministry as exclusive, he was keenly conscious of his utter dependence upon God and of the mutual dependence of all God's ministers. To the Corinthians, for example, he said: "I planted, Apollos watered, but God gave the growth" (I Cor. 3:6).

In many ways Paul stands as almost a unique figure in the annals of Christian history. He combined the fervency of an evangelist, the compassion of a pastor, the perception of a scholar, the pedagogical skill of a teacher, and the diplomacy of a statesman. He was able within the context of their appreciation to minister meaningfully to Jews in their synagogues, to Gentiles having some contact with the teachings of Judaism, and to Gentiles entirely devoid of any Jewish preparatory instruction. He was prepared to correct and instruct his converts by beginning at a point of common agreement and then leading them on to a more profound appreciation and a proper expression of their Christian faith. He was a preacher and teacher to the Gentiles, an interpreter of postresurrection Christianity, and he used all of the tools and skills at his disposal to accomplish his mission.

Selected Bibliography

Beardslee, W. A. *Human Achievement and Divine Vocation in the Message of Paul.* Naperville, Ill.: Allenson, 1961.

Chadwick, H. *The Enigma of Paul.* London: Athlone, 1969.

Chadwick, W. E. *The Pastoral Teaching of St. Paul.* Edinburgh: Clark, 1907.

Kuist, H. T. *The Pedagogy of St. Paul.* New York: Doran, 1925.

Longenecker, R. N. *Paul, Apostle of Liberty.* New York: Harper and Row, 1964.

———. *The Ministry and Message of Paul.* Grand Rapids: Zondervan, 1971.

Niebuhr, R. *The Nature and Destiny of Man.* Vol. 1. London: Nisbet, 1941.

O'Connor, J. M. *Paul on Preaching.* New York: Sheed and Ward, 1964.

Stacey, W. D. *The Pauline View of Man.* London: Macmillan, 1956.

Whiteley, D. E. H. *The Theology of St. Paul.* Philadelphia: Fortress, 1964.

3

Howard Grimes

Augustine
(354-430)

Augustine, the greatest of the early church fathers in the West if not in the entire church, was born in 354 in Tagaste (now Souk-Ahras, Algeria). His father, Patricius, was converted only shortly before his death in 372, but Augustine's mother, Monica, was a devout Christian and an important influence on his life. He was educated at Madaura and Carthage, after which he became a teacher of rhetoric, first in Tagaste, then in Carthage. In 383 he went to Italy, where he stayed for about five years and where the direction of his life changed radically.

Although he had been raised in the church, he was converted to the pursuit of philosophy in 373 while reading Cicero's *Hortensius*. By the time he left North Africa for Rome, he was a Manichaean, a position from which he was liberated by the Neoplatonism of Plotinus and Porphyry. In 384 he went to Milan to resume his teaching career, and there he heard the preaching of Ambrose, under whose ministry Augustine was converted in 386 and by whom he was baptized in 387.

Augustine soon abandoned his professorial career and in 388 returned to North Africa. Three years later he entered the priesthood, performing such duties as preaching to candidates for baptism and establishing a monastery which included a training school for clergy. He also was launching a prolific writing career. In 395 Augustine was consecrated as the successor to Valerius, bishop of Hippo, and one year later Valerius died. Augustine held that post until he died in 430.

The two primary sources for Augustine's views on educational philosophy and methods are *The Teacher (De magistro)*, probably written about 389, and *The First Catechetical Instructor (De catechizandis rudibus)*, written in 400 or shortly thereafter. The former, cast in dialogue form, is reputedly based on a conversation between Augustine and his natural son, Adeodatus. It is essentially a nontechnical discussion of epistemology,[1] or in more modern educational parlance, of "how we learn." The latter, however, is more a practical treatise concerned with the preliminary instruction given to the *accedentes* (that is, those about to be admitted to the catechumenate).[2] It is addressed to Deogratias, a friend of Augustine and a deacon in Carthage. While *The Teacher* bears a stamp of Socratic informalism, *The First Catechetical Instructor* is more formal. The first is the more fruitful source for uncovering Augustine's educational philosophy, the second for his educational methods.

His Educational Philosophy

Augustine believed that the learner already possesses an inner apprehension of truth. "He is taught not by my words but by the things themselves which inwardly God has made manifest in him."[3] This statement does not mean, as John H. S. Burleigh reminded us, that truth is subjective. Rather, "it comes from God, whose eternal Truth, Christ, dwells in minds prepared to receive him."[4] In a sense this is a restatement of Augustine's distinction between faith and reason—we must believe before we can understand the

---

1. J. H. S. Burleigh, "Introduction to *The Teacher*," in *Earlier Writings*, p. 65.
2. This is in contrast to *The Catechetical Lectures* of Cyril of Jerusalem, which were given to those preparing for baptism. See W. Telfer, "General Introduction," in *Cyril of Jerusalem and Nemesius of Emesa*, Library of Christian Classics, vol. 4 (Philadelphia: Westminster, 1955), pp. 30-33; and J. Christopher, "Introduction," in *De catechizandbis rudibus*, Patristic Studies, vol. 8 (Washington, D.C.: University of America, 1926), pp. 1, 2.
3. *The Teacher* 12.40, in *Earlier Writings*.
4. "Introduction to *The Teacher*," p. 66.

nature of, or reasons for, our belief.[5] Although Augustine never put these two ideas together, he apparently meant that the human mind, with its innate knowledge of divine truth, being confronted with such truth from the outside, believes ("has faith"), and then explains this faith by employing the ability to reason.

Augustine also held that words are, in themselves, inadequate instruments of teaching, of communicating what one feels and knows inwardly.[6] Words, he said, "... bid us look for things,"[7] or again, "... by means of words a man is simply put on the alert in order that he may learn...."[8] Signs other than words (gestures, for example) also may help in teaching, or in modern terms, teaching occurs through relationships. The significance of this point in Augustine cannot be appreciated unless we look at it apart from our contemporary knowledge of the significance of nonverbal and noncognitive factors in learning. To be sure, Augustine did not fully appreciate these factors, but at one point he did approach a theory of the unconscious.[9]

Learning, according to Augustine, involves considerably more than verbal assent; it involves as well a change in attitude and behavior. He directed the teacher to make love an "end to which you may refer all that you say," and to "give all your instructions [so] that he to whom you speak by hearing may believe, and by believing may hope, and by hoping may love."[10] Belief, hope, love—all three are included in the teacher's purpose.

"Our real Teacher," wrote Augustine, "is he who is ... said to dwell in the inner man, namely Christ, that is, the unchangeable power and eternal wisdom of God."[11] This obviously presupposes that man possesses an innate capacity for truth. But it is also related to Augustine's insistence upon self-knowledge as the beginning of certain knowledge in any field.[12] One does not learn religious truth through its being "poured in," as it were, by someone else; one learns it in the fullest sense only by apprehending it inside. To put this in modern terminology, credulity—mere ac-

---

5. Cf. *Confessions* 6.5.7; and *The Usefulness of Belief* 14.31, in *Earlier Writings*.

6. *The Teacher* 1.1-2.3, in *Earlier Writings*.

7. Ibid., 11.36.

8. Ibid., 14.46.

9. Cf. *The Trinity* 14.9.

10. *The First Catechetical Instructor* 4.8. Christopher's translation here is an adaptation and revision of his translation in the Patristic Series.

11. *The Teacher* 11.38, in *Earlier Writings*.

12. *Enchiridion* 7.20. Cf. *Confessions and Enchiridion*, p. 351 (n. 38).

ceptance of truth second hand—is not enough; an inner response, however it may be explained, is necessary, and the beginning of this response is the realization that we are created to respond positively to God:

> . . . thou hast made us for thyself and restless is our heart until it comes to rest in thee.[13]

Finally, Augustine insisted that belief (faith) is necessary over and beyond that which we can know from sense experience and reason.

> What I know I also believe, but I do not know everything I believe. All that I understand I know, but I do not know all that I believe.[14]

So central is Augustine's doctrine of grace that it cannot be separated from his educational theory. It is only by God's gift to man that man is able to take what more recently has been called "the leap of faith."

How then does God "present" himself, as it were, to man? Here it is tempting to consider Augustine's doctrine of predestination his only answer, but in at least one place he seemed to hint at another way. In *The Spirit and the Letter,* after discussing at some length the meaning of faith, he said:

> . . . God works for our willing and our believing through the inducement of impressions which we experience: whether the impressions be external, as in the exhortations of the Gospel, or internal, as in the ideas which enter the mind willynilly. . . . In these ways does God work upon the reasonable soul to believe. . . .[15]

This appears to be a key to what Augustine promised at the end of *The Teacher* to discuss later: the usefulness of words.[16] And it also appears to explain how man is first prompted to respond in faith. The function of the teacher, then, is to provide the external impressions to which the learner *may* respond in faith.

His Teaching Methods

How is the teacher to put into practice this philosophy of education? Augustine gave several recommendations.

First, the teacher must be genuinely interested in and enjoy what

---

13. *Confessions* 1.1.1, in *Confessions and Enchiridion.*
14. *The Teacher* 11.37, in *Earlier Writings.*
15. 60.34, in *Later Works.*
16. 14.46.

he is teaching, for only in this way can he overcome the inadequacy of words to communicate all that he should. The catechist, Augustine wrote in *The First Catechetical Instructor,* must recognize the importance of his work; apparently busy pastors then, as now, considered catechizing an interruption of their daily schedules. Further, the catechist must not allow anything to trouble him and detract from his teaching. If he is troubled by someone who has defected from the faith,

> let him . . . who comes to be admitted as a candidate wipe away our sorrow at another's defection, in the hope we cherish that he will make progress in the faith.[17]

Whatever the distraction which would keep the teacher from doing his best work, he must seek to overcome it.

Second, the teacher must genuinely respect the student. ". . . we must temper his shyness by introducing the idea of brotherly fellowship."[18] Perhaps Augustine was recalling his own experience as a catechumen with Ambrose, an experience which he related in his *Confessions:*

> That man of God received me as a father would. . . . And I began to love him . . . not at the first as a teacher of the truth, for I had entirely despaired of finding that in thy Church—but as a friendly man.[19]

Third, the teacher must vary his language and approach as his students vary. This requires knowledge of the student's status in life. Thus Augustine explained in one chapter of *The First Catechetical Instructor* "how to deal with the educated," and in another how to deal with students from schools of grammar and rhetoric (the "secular" schools of the day). The teacher should seek an understanding of each student's particular problems by questioning him about himself.

Fourth, the teacher must draw out his students and encourage them to express themselves. Augustine wrote in *The First Catechetical Instructor* that

> we must drive out by gentle encouragement his excessive timidity, which hinders him from expressing his opinion. . . .[20]

The Teacher implies even greater student participation.

---

17. *The First Catechetical Instructor* 14.21.
18. Ibid., 13.18.
19. 5.13.23, in *Confessions and Enchiridion.*
20. *The First Catechetical Instructor* 13.18.

Augustine even devoted a section in *The First Catechetical Instructor* to the physical comfort of the student. He suggested, contrary to much popular practice, that the teacher offer the student who appears tired a chair. Augustine added that "doubtless it is better that he [the student] should listen seated from the first...."[21]

It seems fair to say that Augustine would approve a theory of religious education which thinks of it as fundamentally a life of dialogue—dialogue between teacher and learner, between learner and learner, between both learner and teacher and the Biblical faith, but most of all between God and man. The human vehicles— the teacher and his ideas—by which God's mighty acts become known to the learner are earthen vessels, but they are still one of the means by which God impresses the learner. However, unless teaching transcends all of these exterior means (including words), it is less than Christian.

Selected Bibliography

Augustine. *Basic Writings of Saint Augustine.* Edited by W. Oates. New York: Random, 1947.

———. *Confessions and Enchridion.* Edited by A. Outler. Library of Christian Classics, vol. 7. Philadelphia: Westminster, 1955.

———. *Earlier Writings.* Edited by J. Burleigh. Library of Christian Classics, vol. 6. Philadelphia: Westminster, 1953.

———. *The First Catechetical Instructor.* Edited by J. Christopher. Ancient Christian Writers, no. 2. Westminster, Md.: Newman, 1946.

———. *Later Works.* Edited by J. Burnaby. Library of Christian Classics, vol. 8. Philadelphia: Westminster, 1955.

———. *Sancti Aurelli Augustini hipponensis episcopi: Opera omnia.* Patrologie cursus completus, vols. 32-46. Paris, 1841-1842.

Bourke, V. *Augustine's Quest of Wisdom.* Milwaukee: Bruce, 1945.

D'Arcy, M. C., et al. *A Monument to Saint Augustine.* New York: Sheed and Ward, 1930.

Kevane, E. *Augustine the Educator.* Westminster, Md.: Newman, 1964.

Papini, G. *Saint Augustine.* Translated by Mary Agnetti. London: Hodder and Stoughton, 1930.

---

21. Ibid., 13.19.

Part Two

A.D. 500-1500

The next one thousand years of church history, from 500 to 1500, saw a number of significant external developments, many of them related to the founding of Islam in Arabia in the early seventh century and to Islam's challenge to Christianity. Islamic armies occupied much of the Mediterranean world, including Palestine, during its first century of existence. The Crusades in the twelfth and thirteenth centuries were devoted primarily to freeing the Middle East from Islamic control, but the Ottoman Turks re-established Islamic control in the fifteenth century. The most significant ecclesiastical development during this period was the division between Western and Eastern Christendom in 1054, and the exacerbation of that division during the Crusades.

The British Isles were largely untouched by these developments, and it was on the island of Iona that an Irish monk, **Columba** (521-597), established a significant educational center which was at once a monastery and a training ground for foreign missionaries.

Even more important theologically were the Scholasticism of **Thomas Aquinas** (1225?-1274) and the mysticism of **Geert Groote** (1340-1384).

Scholasticism attempted to support Christian theology and to stem rising intellectual doubts about it with Greek—and particularly Aristotelian—philosophy and science. It attempted to bring Christianity into harmony with modern civilization. Scholasticism reached its apex in Aquinas, whose emphasis on reason as the interpreter of truth had a lasting impact on the course of Christian education.

Groote's followers formed the Brethren of the Common Life and established several hundred schools, one of which enrolled over two thousand pupils. The Brethren divided students by grades and were aware of such educational influences as attention span and dormitory life. Brethren schools were to influence such men as Thomas à Kempis, John Calvin, Martin Luther, and John Sturm.

4

John Woodbridge

Columba
(521-597)

Following the example of Renaissance men, interpreters of European history have often cited the collapse of the Roman Empire as the debut of a dismal and backward epoch of human experience, the early Middle Ages, or the "Dark Ages."[1] Within recent decades, however, the historiography of late antiquity and the early Middle Ages has been revolutionized by well-documented studies which, though not glossing over the misery and confusion of the period (A.D. 450-750), do portray it in a much more favorable light. In his volume *Origins of the Medieval World*, William Carroll Bark argued persuasively for the new perspective. He contended that the early Middle Ages "were a time of innovation and discovery, and that the regression of civilisation in the West from the Roman level was a fortunate occurrence."[2] Moreover Bark argued that early medieval society was marked by a pioneer spirit which pushed back not only geographical frontiers but intellectual ones as well.

---

1. F. Lot, *The End of the Ancient World and the Beginning of the Middle Ages* (New York: Harper, 1961), p. 406.

2. *Origins of the Medieval World* (Stanford: Stanford University, 1958), p. 41. The noted historian Richard Sullivan also painted a more favorable picture of the early Middle Ages in *Heirs of the Roman Empire* (Ithaca: Cornell University, 1960).

In the advances against these frontiers, Christians often played determinative roles. An outstanding example of such a Christian was Columba, who founded the famous center of Christian learning, the monastery of Iona, on an island one mile off the coast of northern Britain. It was Columba's purpose to brighten at least his corner of the British Isles with the light of Christian culture and witness. Significant success crowned his efforts, as church historian Johann Neander noted: "In Iona, he [Columba] founded a monastery which under his management during thirty years, attained the highest reputation, a distant and secluded seat for the pursuit of biblical studies and other sciences."[3] We shall here analyze Columba's contributions as a religious educator at Iona.

Untangling historical realities from legends is a major difficulty for the historian interested in Columba's life. Furthermore, the paucity of primary data is troubling. The historian has recourse to only a limited number of sources: a few of Columba's extant works, Adamnan's *Life of St. Columba,* and Bede's *Ecclesiastical History of the English People.*[4] Undoubtedly Adamnan's book is the most extensive and valuable account of Columba's life. Ostensibly this volume is a reliable history if we are to believe Adamnan's own preface: "Let no one imagine that I either state a falsehood regarding so great a man, or record anything doubtful or uncertain. Be it known that I will tell with all candour what I have learned from the consistent narrative of my predecessors, trustworthy and discerning men, and that my narrative is founded either on written authorities anterior to my own times, or on what I have myself heard from some learned and faithful seniors, attesting facts the truth of which they had themselves ascertained."[5] And yet Adamnan, himself an abbot at Iona in the seventh century, tended to glorify Columba's deeds to such an extent as to cast doubts on their authenticity. Indeed the work has been described as an outstanding piece of medieval hagiography.[6] Consequently the historian is obliged, sometimes without other criteria than his own

---

3. Cited in W. Cathcart, *The Ancient British and Irish Churches* (Philadelphia: American Baptist, 1894), p. 206.

4. For an example of an extant piece of writing attributed to Columba, see *The Cathach of St. Columbia. The Life of Columcille Compiled by Manus O'Donnell in 1532* has not been used in this study because much of its content is legendary.

5. P. 4.

6. A. Plummer, *The Churches in Britain Before* A.D. *1000,* vol. 1 (London: Scott, 1911), p. 87.

insights and critical judgments, to distinguish historical reality from the legend and romance that surround this remarkable figure. He can also gather scraps of information from Bede's scattered allusions to Columba in *Ecclesiastical History of the English People*.

In Ireland

Columba was born in Gartan, situated in the wild hills of Donegal, Ireland, on 7 December 521. His baptismal name, *Colum*, was Latinized to *Columba*, meaning "the dove." According to an old Irish source he was also known by contemporaries as *Columb-kille*, "Columba of the cell or church," for frequently he would come from the church where he had read Psalms to neighboring children, and they would say among themselves: "Has our Little Dove [*Colum*] came to-day from church [*cille*]?"[7] As we shall see, however, until his forties Columba's character sometimes lacked the pacific characteristics of a dove.

Perhaps because he was of royal stock, Columba received an excellent education. He studied with reputable scholars at the leading monastic schools of his day: at Moville with Finnian, at Clonard with another Finnian, at Glasnevin with Mobhi, and in Leinster with an elderly bard named Gemman.[8] He acquired a working knowledge of Latin and Greek as well as a general appreciation for both history and jurisprudence.[9] Moreover the saint cultivated a keen interest in music and poetry, writing poems in both Irish and Latin, most of which have unfortunately disappeared with the passing of time.[10] Consequently, with his exceptional education and his varied interests, Columba stepped on the shores of Iona in 563 as a mature scholar and one well acquainted with the best culture available in his native Ireland.

But why did he leave his work in Ireland, which included planting monasteries (Durrow and Derry among others), for an evangelistic and educational mission to northern Britain? Several traditions, sometimes with conflicting strains within them, are propounded by biographers of the monk. It is possible that he decided to move to Britain simply because he wanted to go

---

7. J. A. Duke, *The Columban Church*, p. 59.
8. Ibid.
9. Cathcart, *The Ancient British and Irish Churches*, p. 185.
10. L. Menzies, *Saint Columba of Iona*, pp. 170-77.

on a "pilgrimage for Christ," as explained his ardent admirer, Adamnan. However, another tradition points to a more complex motivation—remorse. The story is recounted that Columba became extremely depressed when the battle of Cuil Dreimhne (561), which he himself had precipitated with a certain King Diarmain, ended in the slaughter of some three thousand combatants. For his role in instigating the conflict, he was excommunicated by the Irish church. Although this excommunication was later revoked, it evidences the church's dismay with the activities of the pugnacious monk whose name meant "dove." The tradition continues by noting that Columba, now repentant, took as his penance work for Christ in a foreign land, away from his beloved Ireland.[11] Thus, the saint's deep remorse furnished the impetus for his migration to the island of Iona with twelve followers.

It is difficult to ascertain how much of this tradition is true. But it is safe to assume that he experienced some type of religious transformation in his early forties, so that Adamnan's general remark concerning his "pilgrimage for Christ" does explain in some degree his journey to Iona. At the island he established a monastic community which became a center for Christian education and missionary witness for the British Isles.

At Iona

The monastery at Iona rather quickly gained preeminence over its counterparts. Bede wrote that the "monastery was for a very long time chief among all the monasteries of the northern Irish and the Picts, exercising supervision over their communities."[12] But why did it prosper so significantly? An explanation of its success is related to Columba's strategy for propagating Christianity. The saint was committed to the thesis that Christian education should be linked to evangelism; that is, he hoped to make Iona a model Christian community of culture and humane concern which would make the life styles of neighboring pagan cultures pale into insignificance by comparison. Thus it was not surprising that within two years after he arrived at Iona, Columba himself was on missions of evangelism. When in the community of Iona, however, he set the example of rigorous scholarship coupled with a life of austerity

---

11. Ibid., pp. 292-307.
12. *Ecclesiastical History of the English People,* ed. B. Colgrave and R. A. B. Mynors (Oxford: Clarendon, 1969), p. 221.

and humble piety. Indeed Columba lived what he preached, and thereby he won deep admiration from his followers and an interest in his religion by pagans with whom he came in contact. The saint's strategy of linking Christian education with evangelism, therefore, was largely responsible for the success of Iona.

Columba followed at least three pivotal principles as he structured the community at Iona. The participants in the monastery were to: (1) submit to the authority of the abbot and obey the dictates of the Scriptures, the focal point of studies; (2) combine their religious occupations, such as meditation and Bible study, with manual labor and the development of manual skills; and (3) support the missionary work of Iona, if not go themselves as missionaries into nearby lands. A closer consideration of these principles would be helpful at this point.

In regard to the first, Columba organized the community with a chain of command, headed by the abbot who was particularly responsible for administrative and educational policies. A bishop usually directed the spiritual life of the community, but the abbot, although his ecclesiastical rank (always a presbyter) was inferior to the bishop's, possessed more real power.[13] Bede indicated that the abbot would gather a council of monks to advise him on matters of great importance; but otherwise he guided the affairs of Iona and, for that matter, the Columban church which depended upon Iona. Members of the community submitted to the abbot and followed the admonition of Columba that they observe obedience, celibacy, caution and reason in speech, humility, hospitality, and kindness to animals. Having no personal property, the monks held the goods of the monastery in common. Moreover, they were to follow the example of Columba in making the Scriptures the source for their understanding of the world and their relationship to God. Interestingly enough, it appears that the pope at Rome had no authority over Iona, for the Columban monastic and ecclesiastical organization functioned independently from the rest of Christendom.

Columba's second principle stressed the joining of the monk's religious endeavors with manual labor. The first abbot divided the population of the monastery into at least three categories: (1) the Seniors, generally older men, who spent much of their time mem-

---

13. Although he was to stamp what became known as the Columban church with the imprint of his personality, Columba (the first abbot at Iona) never gained the rank of bishop. Duke, *The Columban Church*, p. 59.

orizing Scriptures (particularly the Psalms) and copying and illustrating the text of the Scriptures; (2) the Working Brethren, who
did much of the manual labor for the monastery as well as teaching
and missionary work; (3) the Juniors, or novices, who were pupils
learning the life of Christian devotion and mission.[14] But no matter
what their station, all members of the community were to do at
least some manual work. Adamnan observed that the monks spent
time in plowing, sowing, reaping, building with wood, working in
metals, and so forth. Thus, although religious concerns constituted
the major fare of daily life, manual labor was not despised.

The program in Christian education on the island consisted of
instruction in Christian worship and piety, memorization of large
segments of Scripture, and study of the Scriptures in Latin.
Columba served as the master teacher, teaching by example and
precept. He not only talked about humility but demonstrated it
by kneeling before strangers and washing the feet of monks returning from their work. He probably led the monks in hymns, for
Adamnan spoke of "a book of hymns for the seven days of the
week." Columba urged the memorization of Scripture, particularly
the Psalms. With his own hand he wrote perhaps as many as three
hundred copies of the Gospels, distributing them to the many
churches he founded.[15] And, being a Latinist, he trained the monks
so that they could better study the Scriptures and copy the sacred
text as well. In sum, the program of Christian education at Iona
was based on the instruction of pious teachers who served as
examples for their students. These teachers attempted to avoid any
dichotomy between their pronouncements and their actions.

The third principle of Columba was that the monks of Iona
should support missionary expeditions in neighboring lands. For
some of the monks Christian education served as preparation for
service in evangelism. During Columba's lifetime Iona sent missionaries to Northumbria, the Isle of Man, and even southern
Britain.[16] The fruit of the missionary effort was the creation of a
church described in an admirable monograph by John A. Duke,
The Columban Church. The motivation for this missionary interest
was Columba's commitment to spread the Christian message. Al-

---

14. W. D. Simpson, *The Historical Saint Columba,* pp. 11, 12. There were
some laymen at Iona as well. They devoted themselves to manual labor.

15. Ibid., p. 5.

16. J. M. Flood, *Ireland: Its Saints and Scholars* (New York: Kenedy, n.d.),
p. 25.

though he and his followers were not directly related to Christian communities on the Continent, they did not stray from orthodoxy as it was generally conceived in the sixth century. Even some of Columba's critics, such as Bede, conceded that the saint believed all the major doctrines of the Christian faith as outlined in the creeds.[17] Columba wanted the gospel of Christ to penetrate the British Isles, and he perceived that Iona could be a relay station for this penetration.

Columba's Legacy

What then were Columba's contributions as a religious educator? In the first place, the saint's example as a Christian who was an educator should rank high in any evaluation of his influence. Adamnan described Columba, the Christian scholar, in these terms: "Angelic in appearance, elegant in address, holy in work, with talents of the highest order and consummate prudence, he lived a good soldier of Christ during thirty-five years in his adopted island [Iona]. He never could spend the space of even one hour, without study, or prayer, or writing, or some holy occupation, and so incessantly was he engaged night and day, in the unwearied exercise of watching and of corporal austerities, that the weight of his singular labour would seem beyond the power of all human endurance. And still he was beloved by all, for a holy joy ever beaming on his face, revealed the ecstacies with which the Holy Spirit filled his inmost soul."[18] Second, Columba's stress on the study and copying of the Scriptures was largely responsible for the preservation of the Christian message in Ireland and Britain during the early Middle Ages. And third, his joining of Christian education to evangelism proved a successful strategy for the penetration of pagan cultures near Iona. Even after attempting to separate the legends and romance from the historical realities about the founder of Iona, the historian finds him to be a remarkable figure of early medieval church history.

Our study of the saint's career should caution us not to label the early Middle Ages as the "Dark Ages." Admittedly the disaggregation of the Roman Empire brought hardship and confusion to many peoples of the Continent, but Columba's initiative in

---

17. Menzies, *Saint Columba of Iona*, p. 79.
18. *Life of Saint Columba*, p. 5.

establishing a center of Christian education and his dedication to the preaching of the Christian gospel graphically point out that rays of light continued to keep the darkness of total cultural anarchy away from the West. Indeed, it could be argued that Columba was a precursor of the Christian culture which would dominate Europe during the Middle Ages.

Selected Bibliography

Adamnan. *Life of Saint Columba.* Translated and edited by D. MacCarthy. Dublin: Duffy, n.d.

Columba. *The Cathach of St. Columba.* Edited by H. J. Lawlor. Proceedings of the Royal Irish Academy, vol. 33. Dublin: Hodges and Figgis, 1916.

Duke, J. A. *The Columban Church.* Edinburgh: Oliver and Boyd, 1957.

Godfrey, J. *The Church in Anglo-Saxon England.* Cambridge: University Press, 1962.

Menzies, L. *Saint Columba of Iona.* London: Dent, 1920.

O'Kelleher, A., and Schoepperle, G., eds. *Life of Columcille Compiled by Manus O'Donnell in 1532.* Urbana: University of Illinois, 1918.

Simpson, W. D. *The Historical Saint Columba.* Aberdeen: Milne and Hutchison, 1927.

5

Joan Ellen Duval

Thomas Aquinas
(1225?-1274)

Born near Naples about 1225, Thomas Aquinas began his formal education at age five when his parents sent him to the Benedictine Abbey of Monte Cassino. At fourteen he matriculated at the Faculty of Arts in the University of Naples.[1] During this time Thomas entered the Order of Preachers, commonly called the Dominicans. His parents, being of noble lineage, had greater aspirations for their seventh son than the life of a simple mendicant. While journeying to Paris he was kidnapped by his brothers and held prisoner in the family castle for more than a year. All types of persuasion failed to dissuade him from his chosen vocation and, assisted by his mother, he finally escaped.

After this experience Thomas enrolled at the University of Paris, the center of theological inquiry. Here he became a student and protégé of Albert the Great. Exposure to the encyclopedic learning of Albert as well as to his already developing Aristotelian thought, influenced the development, style, and direction of Thomas's intellectual activity. Except for brief periods at Cologne, the Papal Court, and Naples, the University of Paris was the location of his

---

1. M. C. D'Arcy, *St. Thomas Aquinas*, pp. 25-40; K. Foster, trans. and ed., *The Life of Saint Thomas Aquinas: Biographical Documents.*

study, teaching, and writing, of his public defense of Aristotelianism and his attacks on heresies and false Aristotelianism.

In 1274 Pope Gregory X summoned Thomas to a church council in Lyons. During this journey to the council, Thomas died in the monastery of Fossonuove. He was canonized by Rome in 1323. His legacy to theologians and philosophers is contained in thirty volumes.

Theological Presuppositions

With the exception of Question 11 ("The Teacher") of *Truth*, Thomas never really concerned himself directly with teaching and learning. Even here he was not primarily concerned with that, focusing instead on the entire range and nature of truth and knowledge, and on how man acquires knowledge. Question 11, then, is but one of twenty-nine questions. Many educators, and in particular Catholic educators, who have written on Thomas's philosophy of education imply that Thomas wrote directly on the subject, but he did not.

This is not to say that a philosophy of education cannot be constructed from Thomas's writings. Indeed it can, if education be defined as man's development of his nature, his acquisition of knowledge, and his realization of his potential. In Thomas's metaphysics, psychology, epistemology, and moral philosophy, he developed principles that are in fact the first principles of education, and specifically of intellectual, rather than moral and religious, education. These principles are not without significant implications for the latter, however.

The entire thought of Thomas is permeated by a theocentric view of man. His concept of hierarchy, with God the Creator, the Source, and the End of all beings other than Himself, ties together his educational thought. It permits an understanding of how each operation and disposition of finite existence participates in the infinite and is ordered with respect to other finite beings by its proximity to the infinite. Man's place in the hierarchy makes him the noblest of all creatures, for he not only possesses all the powers of other creatures but also possesses an intellect and will that make him a reflection of the Source of all being. His dignity flows from this capacity to know truth and love good, and herein he participates in the essence of the Supreme Beings, who is Truth and Good and who knows and loves Himself most perfectly.

To penetrate the meaning and ramifications of theology and revelation, Thomas utilized Aristotelian principles of causality and potency-act relations. God is the first efficient cause of all creation, and man can participate in the causality of God as a second efficient cause of potency being moved to act. God is the end toward which all being is directed, the ultimate cause. And, inasmuch as within the teleological nature of being there are intermediate ends, man can participate in the creation of these ends.

Educational Philosophy

The pupil. To grasp the nature, end, and operations of man as pupil one must comprehend man's metaphysical, psychological, and physiological make-up. Thomas treated this in great detail. The student of Thomas, however, must be cautioned against the tendency to maintain an analytical view of man which compartmentalizes him; Thomas rigorously analyzed man, but he maintained a synthesized, unified view.

In "The Teacher," as has been pointed out, Thomas limited his analysis to man's intellectual powers and the manner in which the learner acquires knowledge either by himself or with the aid of a teacher. The metaphysical and psychological character of man as an intellectual being are the essential content of the inquiry. Through the activity of the First Cause (God), man has as part of his nature the active potency, or agent intellect, that acts on the imagination derived from sensible knowledge and makes it intelligible. Also, the first concepts of understanding that are the embryo of all scientific knowledge preexist in man and are known immediately through the light of the agent intellect.[2]

> Knowledge ... pre-exists in the learner potentially, not, however, in the purely passive, but in the active, sense. Otherwise, man would not be able to acquire knowledge independently. Therefore, as there are two ways of being cured, that is, either through the activity of unaided nature or by nature with the aid of medicine, so also there are two ways of acquiring knowledge. In one way, natural reason by itself reaches knowledge of unknown things, and this way is called *discovery;* in the other way, when someone else aids the learner's natural reason, and this is called *learning by instruction.*[3]

Thomas also described this process of discovery as follows:

---

2. *Truth* Q. 11, A. 1, reply.
3. Ibid.

Now, in discovery, the procedure of anyone who arrives at the knowledge of something unknown is to apply general self-evident principles to certain definite matters, from these to proceed to particular conclusions, and from these to others.[4]

Learning through discovery is in one sense the more perfect way to acquire knowledge because it is an indication that the learner is skillful in the acquisition of knowledge. In another sense, since the teacher knows the whole science explicitly, he can teach it more readily than the pupil can learn it by himself. Therefore, it is more perfect to acquire knowledge through instruction.[5]

Although Thomas's exposition of the two ways of acquiring knowledge are interwoven in Question 11, they will be treated separately for the purpose of highlighting the nature of the pupil and the activity of the teacher. Before turning to a consideration of the teacher, however, one other topic has particular relevance to understanding the pupil as conceived by Thomas—namely, the intellectual virtues, or good habits, of the intellect.

Human virtues for Thomas, as for Aristotle, are acquired qualities that dispose man to act habitually in a manner befitting the goal.

Virtue denotes a certain perfection of a power. Now a thing's perfection is considered chiefly in regard to its end. But the end of power is act. Wherefore power is said to be perfect, according as it is determined to its act. . . . But rational powers, which are proper to man, are not determinate to one particular action, but are inclined indifferently to many: and they are determinate to acts by means of habits. . . . Therefore human virtues are habits.[6]

These virtues, or dispositions to act in a particular, stable, and adequate manner, are modifications of the personality which are acquired through repetition.

There are five intellectual virtues, three of the speculative intellect and two of the practical. The speculative virtues deal with the acquisition and possession of particular levels of knowledge: namely, understanding, science, and wisdom.

The virtues of the speculative intellect are those which perfect the speculative intellect for the consideration of truth: for this is its good work. Now a truth is subject to a twofold consideration—as known in itself, and as known through another. What is known in itself, is as a *principle,* and is at once understood by the intellect: wherefore

4. Ibid.
5. Ibid., A. 2, a. 4.
6. *Summa Theologica* Ia-IIae, Q. 55, A. 1, c.

the habit that perfects the intellect for consideration of such truth is called understanding, which is the habit of principles.

On the other hand, a truth which is known through another, is understood by the intellect, not at once, but by means of the reason's inquiry, and is as a *term.* This may happen in two ways: first, so that it is the last in some particular genus; secondly, so that it is the ultimate term of all human knowledge. And, since *things that are knowable last from our standpoint, are knowable first and chiefly in their nature* (Phys. i. 2, 3); hence that which is last with respect to all human knowledge, is that which is knowable first and chiefly in its nature. And about these is *wisdom,* which considers the highest causes, as stated in *Metaph.* i. 1, 2. Wherefore it rightly judges all things and sets them in order, because there can be no perfect and universal judgment that is not based on the first causes. But in regard to that which is last in this or that genus of knowable matter, it is *science* that perfects the intellect. Wherefore, according to the different kinds of knowable matter, there are different habits of scientific knowledge; whereas there is but one wisdom.[7]

The virtues of the practical intellect have to do with reason rightly applied to doing things and making things. Art is the virtue of making, prudence of doing. Since Thomas limited his consideration of learning to intellectual learning, these virtues will not be discussed. The virtue of art, however, has particular relevance to the nature of teaching.

The pupil has the capacity to acquire both knowledge and intellectual virtues. The latter help free him from whatever deters him from deepening his knowledge, and they help direct him with a certain rectitude toward its acquisition and unification. Simply stated, these virtues are acquired by repeating the act of the virtue and eliminating contrary acts. To acquire these virtues their acts must be performed with a certain intensity. Students, then, should perform as neophyte scientists, metaphysicians, artists, and the like.

Some excerpts from a letter that Thomas wrote to a Dominican novice on the conditions of study illustrate his thinking on the appropriate method:

Since you have asked me in Christ, dear John, to tell you how you must study to attain a treasury of knowledge, I shall mention the following points of advice. Prefer to arrive at knowledge over small streamlets, and do not plunge immediately into the ocean, since progress must go from the easier to the more difficult. . . . I exhort you to be chary of speech, and to go into the conversation room sparingly. . . . Love to be diligent in your cell, if you would be led to the wine-cellar of wisdom. . . . Consider not from whom you hear any-

---

7. Ibid., Q. 57, A. 2, c.

thing, but impress upon your mind everything good that is said. Make an effort thoroughly to understand whatever you read and hear. In all doubt seek to penetrate to the truth. Try always to store away as much as possible in the chambers of your mind. What is too far above, strive not after for the present.[8]

In conclusion, the learner is the person in quest of knowledge. He can acquire knowledge through his own discovery or through instruction. This quest for knowledge is aided by the conscious acquisition of intellectual virtues.

The teacher. Thomas restricted teaching, as he did learning, to intellectual activity. It is essential that the teacher explicitly understand the body of knowledge he teaches. He must hold that knowledge with certitude, meaning that he can reduce it to the first, self-evident principles of his discipline. It is within this context that the teacher is said to teach truth. Further, truth is rooted in the existence of things and not in the mind of the teacher.

> He who teaches does not cause the truth, but knowledge of the truth, in the learner. For the propositions which are taught are true before they are known, since truth does not depend on our knowledge of it, but on the existence of things.[9]

Although Thomas never specifically stated it, we can presume that as the learner grows not only in knowledge but also in intellectual virtue, so too the teacher manifests rigorous intellectual discipline. The acquisition of intellectual virtue is never complete, but it can be presumed that the teacher approaches his area of knowledge with the appropriate disposition. So the teacher of metaphysics should manifest the virtue of wisdom; the teacher of mathematics, the virtue of science, or mathematics; and so forth.

The first mandate for teaching is that the teacher be guided by the nature of the learner, who, learning by discovery, proceeds to a knowledge of the unknown by relating it to his present knowledge in terms of whether it affirms or denies principles that he already holds with a degree of certitude. The teacher, in a demonstration of new knowledge, builds upon the knowledge of the student and reduces this new knowledge to a state where the first, self-evident principles are called into play by the learner.

> But he [man] does in a sense cause knowledge in another man as regards the new knowledge which is caused by self-evident principles.

---

8. In D'Arcy, *St. Thomas Aquinas,* pp. 28, 29.
9. *Truth* Q. 11, A. 3, a. 6.

He does this, not as one who gives knowledge of the principles, but as one who shows certain sensible signs to the external senses, and thus brings into actuality that which was contained in the principles implicitly and in a certain sense in potentiality. . . .[10]

Teaching, like medicine, is an art. The teacher does not cause, as efficient cause, knowledge in the learner, just as the doctor does not cause health in the patient. Both ply their art by imitating and perfecting nature.

In effects which are produced by nature and by art, art operates in the same way and through the same means as nature. For, as nature heals one who is suffering from cold by warming him, so also does the doctor. Hence, art is said to imitate nature. A similar thing takes place in acquiring knowledge of things he does not know in the same way that one directs himself through the process of discovering something he does not know.[11]

The product of the art of teaching is not knowledge, per se, in the student, but that which the teacher presents to the intellect of the student. The sensible signs, their selection, arrangement, and presentation become the objects for the intellect of the learner.

One person is said to teach another inasmuch as, by signs, he manifests to that other the reasoning process which he himself goes through by his own natural reason. And thus, through the instrumentality, as it were, of what is told him, the natural reason of the pupil arrives at a knowledge of the things which he did not know. Therefore, just as the doctor is said to heal a patient through the activity of nature, so a man is said to cause knowledge in another through the activity of the learner's own natural reason, and this is teaching.[12]

When the teacher is not guided by the nature of the learner and presents ideas or conclusions not contained in these seminal, self-evident principles, he does not teach but indoctrinate. In such instances, a teacher presents his own opinion or that which is held on faith.

But, if someone proposes to another things which are not included in self-evident principles, or does not make it clear that they are included, he will not cause knowledge in the other but, perhaps, opinion or faith, although even this is in some way caused by inborn first principles, for from these self-evident principles he realizes that what necessarily follows from them is to be held with certitude, and that what is contrary to them is to be rejected completely, and

10. Ibid., A. 3, reply.
11. Ibid., A. 1, reply.
12. Ibid.

that assent may be given to or withheld from whatever neither follows necessarily from nor is contrary to self-evident principles.[13]

The style of teaching as reflected in the writings of Thomas is a perfect example of his application of these principles. The Disputed Questions, of which *Truth* is but one series, are worthy of study for this alone. A question is posed, difficulties are raised that tend to deny an affirmative answer, a reply is presented that develops the correct answer, and finally the difficulties are answered. This was not a style of writing, but rather a style or method of teaching. Only after the "live presentation" was the matter refined and set down in writings. Intellectually, free inquiry was characteristic of the Scholastic period. No source was summarily dismissed because it represented a different religious persuasion, time, or culture. In *Truth* alone over 232 sources are utilized, ranging from Plato to contemporary, thirteenth-century thinkers. Nor is consideration restricted to the Greco-Roman philosophers and Catholic theologians; Moses Maimonides the Jew and Arabs Averroës and Avicenna are included. All that is consonant with Thomas's first principles, or able to be made so, is embraced, and all that is contrary is proven to be so by recourse to these same principles.

In conclusion, in "The Teacher" Thomas developed the nature of teaching as an artistic endeavor that is guided by the nature of the learner and the manner in which the teacher himself learns.

The curriculum. Thomas never specifically addressed himself to questions of curriculum. Certain principles can be inferred, but it must be remembered that Thomas was writing for and teaching students who were quite advanced. They had already passed through the liberal arts curriculum and were pursuing an advanced degree in theology.

One would do well to examine the educational program at the University of Paris. We know from Thomas's life and, in particular, from his association with Albert the Great, that he was well grounded in the arts and sciences of his day. As noted above, his writings show that he was well acquainted with the history of ideas. Finally, he wrote the "Office of Corpus Christi" and, some of his biographers contend, at least one poem. All of this background, however, simply tells us that Thomas himself was a man of wide interest and great intellectual—and perhaps artistic—talent.

---

13. Ibid.

Nowhere do we find Thomas arguing that the education of all should be as wide or as varied as his. Nonetheless, since his writings presuppose a fund of knowledge on the part of the student, we can safely assume that he accepted the curriculum of his day.

The sciences, as divided and ordered in the Middle Ages, and the appropriate method of inquiry of each are set forth in Questions 5 and 6 of Thomas's *Commentary on the "De Trinitate" of Boethius.* He based the division and hierarchical ordering of the sciences on metaphysical principles, and the methods of the several sciences on epistemological principles. He made the following comment concerning the seven-fold division of the liberal arts:

> The seven liberal arts do not adequately divide theoretical philoso-
> phy; but . . . seven arts are grouped together, leaving out certain
> other ones, because those who wanted to learn philosophy were first
> instructed in them. And the reason why they are divided into the
> trivium and quadrivium is that "they are as paths introducing the
> eager mind to the secrets of philosophy." This is also in harmony
> with what the Philosopher [Aristotle] says in the *Metaphysics,* that
> we must investigate the method of scientific thinking before the
> sciences themselves. And the Commentator [Averroës] says in the same
> place that before all other sciences a person should learn logic, which
> teaches the method of all the sciences; and the trivium belongs to the
> domain of logic. The Philosopher further says in the *Ethics,* that the
> young can know mathematics, but not physics [natural philosophy],
> which requires experience. So we are given to understand that we
> should learn mathematics, to whose domain the quadrivium belongs,
> immediately after logic. And so these are as paths preparing the mind
> for the other philosophic disciplines.[14]

For the purpose of clarification, *science* in the Middle Ages referred to a knowledge of things through their causes, and in today's context it would more properly be called philosophy of science. The sciences as we know them today were in their embryonic stages in the thirteenth century, and Thomas called them intermediate sciences.

The order in which the sciences should be learned is derived from the facts that scientific knowledge is interdependent, man's knowledge of reality is rooted in the existence of things, and his way of knowing reality must begin with sensible things.

> Although divine science is by nature the first of all the sciences, with
> respect to us the other sciences come before it. For, as Avicenna says,
> the order of this science is that it be learned after natural sciences

---

14. *The Division and Methods of the Sciences* Q. 5, A. 1., reply 3.

which explain many things used by metaphysics. . . . It should be learned after mathematics. . . . Moreover, in the beginning the sensible effects from which the demonstrations of natural science proceed are more evident to us.[15]

On the relation between mathematics and natural sciences, Thomas wrote:

Although we should learn natural science after mathematics because the extensive data it is grounded upon require experience and time, still, since natural things fall under the senses, they are naturally better known than the mathematical entities abstracted from sensible matter.[16]

The tools of learning and the general intelligence of the student are developed by means of the seven liberal arts. Only after this groundwork has been laid is the student ready for philosophy and, in particular, "first philosophy," or metaphysics. Although mathematics should be learned before natural science, the latter comes easier because it involves sensible data and is more readily knowable to man, whose intellectual knowledge begins with sense knowledge. After the student has developed the intellectual facility and basic intellectual knowledge that permit him to distinguish form from matter—that is, to conceive mathematical entities—he is in a position to begin studying form separated from matter, or pure forms, the object of metaphysics.

To summarize Thomas's philosophy of education, he held that the learner has the active potency to arrive at a knowledge of the unknown through discovery. All teaching must be guided by this principle. The signs and symbols that the teacher presents to the student must enable the latter to relate them to first principles which support what he already knows. The teacher, then, must possess explicit knowledge of what he is teaching and be able to reduce that knowledge to those first principles. As for curriculum, since the learner's intellectual knowledge is rooted in sense knowledge, he must acquire a knowledge of the material world before advancing to the world of abstraction, such as mathematics, and the world of metaphysics, which considers beings that exist apart from matter—that is, pure forms. Truth is rooted in the existence of things, and therefore the path to truth is the order of existence as it is apprehended by man.

---

15. Ibid., reply 9.
16. Ibid., reply 10.

Selected Bibliography

Aquinas, T. *The Division and Methods of the Sciences: Questions V and VI of His Commentary on the "De Trinitate" of Boethius.* Translated by A. Maurer. Toronto: Garden City, 1953.

———. *Summa Theologica.* Translated by the English Dominican Fathers. 3 vols. New York: Benziger, 1947.

———. *Truth.* Translated by R. W. Mulligan. 3 vols. Chicago: Regnery, 1952.

Copleston, F. *A History of Philosophy.* Vol. 2. Westminster, Md.: Newman, 1959.

D'Arcy, M. C. *St. Thomas Aquinas.* Westminster, Md.: Newman, 1955.

Foster, K., trans. and ed. *The Life of Saint Thomas Aquinas: Biographical Documents.* Baltimore: Helicon, 1959.

Hart, C. A. *Thomistic Metaphysics.* Englewood Cliffs, N.J.: Prentice-Hall, 1959.

Maritain, J. *Education at the Crossroads.* New Haven: Yale University, 1943.

6

Julia S. Henkel

Geert Groote
(1340-1384)

Geert Groote, a native of Deventer, Netherlands, who lived in the fourteenth century, is best known as the founder of the Brethren of the Common Life, or the *Devotio moderna*. This was not a monastic order; in fact, its organization was a radical departure from the medieval concept of the monastery. The Brethren practiced piety, fed the poor, sheltered the homeless, cured the sick, worshiped, studied, wrote books, copied (and eventually printed) sacred texts, and founded and taught schools.[1] Although they were neglected for years by historians, their far-reaching influence is now coming into prominence.

His Life

Groote was born in 1340 when Deventer was a flourishing member of the Hanseatic League. Just ten years later the Black Plague invaded the city, and among its victims were Geert's father—a wealthy member of the municipal council—and mother. The youth's uncle, Johannes Ockenbroeck, became his guardian.

---

1. J. van Ginneken, *Geert Groote's Levensbeeld*, pp. 62-78.

Little else is known of Groote's early life. He attended the school attached to the St. Lebwin church, and he probably also attended schools in the German cities of Aachen and Cologne.[2] He entered law school in Paris and obtained the M.A. degree at the age of eighteen. During 1358 and 1359 he studied theology, returning to Deventer in 1359 to lecture and teach. Later he taught at the University of Prague.[3] In 1362 he was appointed canon of the Church of St. Mary at Aachen, for which he began receiving a prebend in 1369. Two years later the pope granted him another prebend in Utrecht. About three years after that he returned to Deventer and gave up his positions, real estate holdings, and elegant mode of life.[4]

This remarkable renunciation was a result of Groote's conversion. The first step toward his conversion had occurred when a mystic stopped him on the street and admonished him to give up empty things. Later, while at Deventer, he became critically ill. When he appeared to be near death, he was persuaded by his uncle's pastor to burn his books on magic and receive the sacrament. At this point, according to Lynn Thorndike, Groote became a changed man.[5] Jacob van Ginneken indicated still a third incident, a conversation at Utrecht between Groote and his friend Henry of Calcar, after which Groote gave up his prebends and property.

Though Groote was a layman, he began to preach. His magnetic personality and sincere religious fervor and zeal drew enrapt listeners. Groote felt keenly the emptiness of his early life and was distressingly aware of the widespread need for moral and religious reform. E. F. Jacob said of him: "The successful master of Paris and Prague, with his taste for science . . . and his prospects of preferment . . . , left the world to return to it in a new missionary guise. Such a man inevitably draws friends."[6] Groote helped some pious women organize as the Sisters of the Common Life by donating

---

2. A. Hyma. *The Brethren of the Common Life,* p. 16.

3. P. Horn, "Vita Gerardi Magni," ed. W. Kuhler, *Ned. Ar. voor Kerkg,* N.S., 6 (1909): 333, 334. About 1500, Badius Ascensius, famed humanist and printer, and former Ghent pupil of the Brethren, described the Brethren and their founder. He placed Groote's study of magic at this point in his life.

4. R. R. Post, *De Moderne Devotie, Geert Groote en Zijn Stichtingen,* pp. 11, 12, 154; Hyma, *The Brethren of the Common Life,* pp. 17, 18.

5. L. Thorndike, *A History of Magic and Experimental Science,* vol. 3 (New York: Macmillan, 1934), pp. 511, 512.

6. *Essays in the Conciliar Epoch,* 2nd ed. (Manchester: Manchester University, 1953), p. 123.

some of his property and writing their constitution. He also gathered a band of twelve disciples about him at Deventer. One was young Florentius Radewijns, who had given up his prebend in Utrecht to be closer to Groote, and who would lead the Brethren after Groote's death. Some of Groote's followers lived with Radewijns, others itinerated with Groote. Groote's male followers could not organize officially during his lifetime because they would be accused by the mendicants of establishing a new order. When they did finally organize, they emphasized their lay status.

Groote and his followers were affected to some extent by the mysticism of the age. Some mystics lost faith in reason and attempted to reach God only through faith, meditation, and prayer. There were extravagant sects, sometimes called the "lunatic fringe" of mysticism, such as the quietists, or negativists. The latter were preoccupied with contemplation and, except for their writings, had little influence. But there were also mystics like Groote and the Brethren of the Common Life who remained in touch with society, and their activities bore fruit in both religious and educational reform.

It cannot be doubted that Groote was deeply impressed by such great mystics as Meister Eckhart and Jan Ruysbroeck—especially by Ruysbroeck,[7] some of whose work Groote translated. It should be clearly understood, however, that Groote opposed false mysticism and antiintellectualism.

Though he had initiated a great religious and educational revival which was to spread far beyond the boundaries of the Low Countries, Groote probably considered himself a defeated man when he died prematurely from the Black Plague. The mendicant monks, secular clergy, and some heretics had strenuously objected to his itinerant preaching. They asked the bishop of Utrecht to silence Groote, and the bishop ordered that no deacon in his bishopric preach in public. Groote obeyed but appealed to Pope Urban VI. The pope rescinded the injunction, but news of his action failed to reach Groote before he died.

His Educational Activity

Groote's dynamic preaching attracted large numbers, but still he was reaching only a small percentage of the population. He felt a

---

7. Van Ginneken, *Geert Groote's Levensbeeld*, p. 223.

heavy personal responsibility for the common man who slumbered through a mediocre existence, totally unaware of spiritual and intellectual realities. The New Testament suggested the plan of teaching men who would be able to teach others also, and Groote resolved to do this by carefully instructing his disciples and by laying plans for schools for the young. School conditions in northern Europe called for reform, and Groote set out to improve the quality of instruction for the young, to inspire them with the principles of the *Devotio moderna,* and to urge them to go out and teach others. Thus educational reform would be a means of religious reform.

Groote invited schoolboys to his house where they copied books for him and talked about their schoolwork and their aims and ideals. While encouraging these boys in their learning, he made plans to help boys in Deventer who were homeless and friendless. The Sisters began to shelter, feed, and clothe them as their own children. Groote sought for the boys capable and godly teachers— university men if possible, intellectual men of character who would win their pupils' love and refrain from punishing them until all friendly forms of admonition had failed.[8]

Groote's closest friend was John Cele, the young school administrator at Zwolle. From time to time Groote shared with Cele his dreams and aspirations. Then, shortly before Groote's death, he unfolded before Cele a more concrete plan for educational reform.[9] Cele implemented Groote's policies in Zwolle and made the school there at least as important historically as the Brethren school in Deventer.

Eventually the Brethren founded or reformed several hundred schools. Among their more famous students were Erasmus, who studied in two of their schools for twelve years; Thomas à Kempis, who was educated at Deventer; John Calvin, who spent four years in Paris in the Brethren dormitory of Montaigu; and John Sturm, who studied at Liege. Also influenced strongly by the Brethren educational effort were Wimpheling, Bucer, Beatus Rhenanus, Agricola, Gansfort, Pope Adrian VI, Dringenberg, and Cardinal Nicholas of Cusa.

---

8. T. à Kempis, *Vita Gerardi Magni* 18.5, 6; and M. Schoengen, *Die Schule von Zwolle* (Freiburg: Des Werkes vom heiligen Paulus, 1898), p. 76.

9. Hyma, *The Brethren of the Common Life,* pp. 22-26; K. De Beer, *Studie over de Spiritualiteit van Geert Groote* (Brussels: N. v. standaard-boekhandel, 1938), pp. 126-35. De Beer discussed Groote's attitude toward education.

His Educational Goals

The Brethren schools, whose policies and practices were firmly grounded in Groote's ideas, sought to make their pupils, above all else, good Christians, disciples whose primary desire was to imitate Christ and His apostles. Having a religious goal in education was not a new thing, but such a goal had usually been limited to the education of the clergy. The Brethren's concept of educating the common man, and of giving him a religious education at that, was unique. The burden of their teaching (and preaching) was more purity, more charity, more tolerance, more enlightenment, and more respect for human faculties. Their concern for the common man was behind their use of the vernacular—even to the point of translating parts of the Bible into Dutch, a move that was attacked by many in the Roman church. But the Brethren, despite their mystical orientation, did not limit their educational goals to the central religious one; they were also concerned about the intellectual, physical, and social lives of their pupils.

The intellectual goal of Brethren education was limited by the fact that the Brethren confined themselves to elementary and secondary schools. But somehow they gave an impetus to higher learning and productive scholarship. They reflected the great wealth, the artistic flowering, and the outburst of humanistic literature that marked the culture of the Low Countries. While the interest of the Brethren in the classics would not have been unusual in southern Europe, it was in northern Europe. Some of the Brethren taught Hebrew in addition to Latin and Greek.

Concern for the students' physical well-being varied in Brethren schools. Generally, however, the Brethren honored Groote's teaching that bodily neglect does not necessarily bring piety. Murmellius was a Brethren teacher who patterned physical education after that of the ancient Greeks and strove to weave it into the curriculum.

Socially, the Brethren aimed for a democratic society within their schools. By seeking to educate the common man, they had renounced the concept of supremacy of one man over another because of wealth, position, or other endowment. They recognized that some pupils are more highly endowed intellectually and financially than others, but they did their best to provide equal opportunity for all.

His Educational Practices

Brethren teachers did not always possess even master's degrees, but many were well educated and most were dedicated and excellent teachers. Some of them settled for traditional, standard textbooks, but the more thoughtful and aggressive teachers wrote texts which were more in accord with their educational philosophy and methods. The texts which they wrote weaved the principles of the *Devotio moderna* into the entire curriculum. The latter incorporated the *quadrivium* and *trivium*, but these subjects were frequently given a rather modern interpretation. In this connection, the ideas of such men as Agricola were used. The Brethren did introduce some unusual subjects into the curriculum, but the most distinctive thing about their curriculum was that religion was not a separate subject; it was woven into the program in a more natural way.

Many of their teaching methods were innovative. They explained the lessons before drilling, tiring students less and heightening their interest. Teachers recognized the limited attention span of children. They realized the need to understand and have rapport with their students. Teachers tried to motivate pupils by arousing their interest and sometimes offering prizes. And teachers considered kind warnings superior to harsh punishments.

Recognizing the value of small groups and individualized instruction, teachers organized students into grades. And rather than promoting students by grades, they promoted them individually, as the students were ready.

Finally, the Brethren discerned that much education and much moral and religious help could be given students in dormitories by qualified supervisors.

Although the Brethren schools died out after only about two centuries, their influence was great. In northern Europe such important cities as Utrecht, Liège, Brussels, and Chelmno gave the Brethren a local monopoly on secondary education. And many cities, such as Amersfoort and Zwolle, gave them substantial help and privileges.

Their influence even reached the shores of America through such groups as the Puritans and the Dutch Calvinists. Why, then, has so little been heard about the Brethren, Groote their founder, and their schools? They cared little for fame and glory; they were not trying to build lofty personal or organizational reputations. They only wanted to change the course of men's lives, to effect a religious reform, and this they did largely by means of educational reform.

Selected Bibliography

Groote, G. *Gerardi Magni epistolae.* Edited by W. Mulder. Tielt: Lannoo, 1933.

Henkel, J. S. "An Historical Study of the Educational Contributions of the Brethren of the Common Life." Ph. D. dissertation, University of Pittsburgh, 1962.

Hyma, A. *The Brethren of the Common Life.* Grand Rapids: Eerdmans, 1950.

———. *The Christian Renaissance: A History of the Devotio Moderna.* Grand Rapids: Reformed, 1924.

Post, R. R. *De Moderne Devotie, Geert Groote en Zijn Stichtingen.* Amsterdam: Van Kampen and Zoon, 1950.

Van Ginneken, J. *Geert Groote's Levensbeeld.* Amsterdam: Noord-Hollandsche, 1942 .

Part Three

A.D. 1500-1750

Various attempts to reform the church characterized the period from 1500 to 1750, and each movement contributed something to the development of Christian education. Reformers ranged from Christian humanists to pietists, and from Protestants to Counter-Reformation Catholics.

Erasmus (1466?-1536), the most eminent Christian humanist, wanted to restore the Roman church, which had lost its spiritual moorings, to its ancient purity. But he also had a decisive influence on European education, encouraging better teaching methods and a greater understanding of the student.

Erasmus was educated in a school in Deventer operated by the Brethren, part of the heterogeneous pietist movement that was to produce a number of significant educators. Among them were **John Amos Comenius** (1592-1670), **August Hermann Francke** (1663-1727), and **Nikolaus Ludwig Zinzendorf** (1700-1760). The pietists emphasized a return to devout living, personal Christianity, and serious yet practical Bible study.

Comenius was a German Brethren pastor who was forced to leave his homeland during the Thirty Years' War. His emphasis on universal education and his scientific approach to the education of the young make him in a real sense the precursor of much modern educational theory and practice. He influenced, at least indirectly, such notables as Rousseau, Pestalozzi, and Herbart.

Francke founded the famous orphanage and school at Halle, which served as a pattern for later educational institutions. He advocated such things as small classes, instruction in manual skills, and scientific demonstrations in the classroom, and he was the first to establish an institution for the training of teachers. His influence is apparent in the writings of, among others, Wesley and Zinzendorf.

The latter became a Bohemian Brethren after giving refuge on his estate at Berthelsdorf to the remnant of that group which survived great persecution. Zinzendorf, who soon became the Brethren's leader, entertained views on education which were revolutionary for his day. Children should be taught not as adults but on their own level, understanding and enjoying what they learn. The Brethren educational system organized by Zinzendorf stressed two things: the head must never outrun the heart, and outward compulsion can never produce inner religion.

The Protestant Reformation in Europe had a significant impact on all aspects of society, including education. Its primary leaders were **Martin Luther** (1483-1546) and **Philip Melanchthon** (1497-1560) in Germany, **Huldreich Zwingli** (1484-1531) and **John Calvin** (1509-1564) in Switzerland, and **John Knox** (1505-1572) in Scotland. The Protestants repudiated the authority and corruptions of the papacy, recognizing as their sole authority the Bible.

Luther, who was a teacher throughout his career, wrote more about education than any of the rest. He helped to strengthen and establish schools, and to set up new curricula. He encouraged secular authorities to take an active role in the education of their constituency, and both secular and spiritual leaders from all of Germany sought his advice on educational matters. He was assisted by Melanchthon, who eventually became known as the "teacher of Germany." Melanchthon organized, developed, and refined Luther's ideas, including those concerning education.

The educational efforts of Zwingli at Zurich and Calvin at Geneva were integral to their religious reforms. Zwingli was concerned with the education of all the people, seeing it as something to be conducted within a community of caring individuals. Calvin's gymnasium was a product of his experience at Strasbourg and became a training ground for young ministers. It was grounded in the principles of Calvin's *Institutes of the Christian Religion* and was organized just as logically and methodically. Calvin's academy became the pattern for Reformed education.

For Knox all education was fundamentally religious education; there was a dynamic interaction between the culture of his day and his religious message. His scheme of education, which made provision for the poor, identified the talented, and stressed the parents' responsibility to instruct their children, has had a lasting impact on Scotland.

The Roman church responded to the Reformation by purifying itself of much corruption and vigorously combating Protestantism. One of the leading figures of this Counter-Reformation was **Ignatius of Loyola** (1491-1556), founder of the Society of Jesus and its system of schools. Using his genius for organization and adapting the best educational theories and methods then available, he created an integrated curriculum which was graded but which also provided for the individual advancement of brighter students. He stressed the educational value of self-activity. His aim was to instill in students a Christian outlook on life and thus to influence society for good.

7

Robert Ulich

Erasmus
(1466?-1536)

One might call the Renaissance and its humanism an individual self-assertion against tradition, a new and more empirical testing of the values and depths of human existence, and a search for new forms of verification. All this is true only in part, for in some respects the humanists believed more in authority than the scholastics; though no longer Aristotle, it was now Plato, Cicero, and Quintilian. There were humanists who were more or less pagan within a church that itself had lost its spiritual moorings, but several among the greatest humanists had no more urgent purpose than to restore it to its ancient purity. Desiderius Erasmus, for example, worked during his whole life for reform without revolution.

Nevertheless, a new era began when the humanists entered the historical scene. The world had widened. Some of the new men envisioned a natural and immanent, not merely a transcendental order of the cosmos. They had a sense of the beauty of life and the preciousness of the person even here on earth; doubt and curiosity about things so far unknown were for them no longer a vice, but a virtue. But the spirit of the time had become unfriendly to liberal minds. Humanism became caught between the fighting armies of Protestantism and Catholicism. Its attempt at reconciliation of the tradition and the new mode of life was frustrated. Luther was bitter against Erasmus for his desertion of the cause of the Reformation, while the Catholic church distrusted him in spite of all the honors he received for his loyalty and scholarship. Pushed from the religious arena, humanism became philosophical and aesthetic, but also the seed ground of modern science.

His Life

Erasmus was born in Rotterdam, Holland, then a province of the Holy Roman Empire of the German nation. He pursued his studies in Latin and Germanic countries, but his most intimate friendship he found in England. The stimulus to occupy himself thoroughly with the schoolmaster's craft came to Erasmus from his English friends. And as is the case with so many northerners, the country of his innermost longing was Italy—where "one enjoys sweet liberty, rich libraries, the charming friendship of writers and scholars, and the sight of monuments."[1]

He had neither fatherland nor vernacular in which to take root, and he had no family. He was one of the two sons springing from the liaison of his father and a widow. He was thus despised by his relatives; in order to get rid of him and his brother, they pressed them to enter the monastery. So Erasmus became a monk, not out of his own decision but under force; it was probably the boy's love of letters which made him yield. He despised most of his colleagues, and they disliked him and called him a heretic.

Neither his family, country, nor the church could become the real abode of Erasmus. He was at home exclusively in the spiritual world of letters which had originated in Greece, Rome, and Palestine. It was certainly by virtue of the very rootlessness of his life that he developed his deep feeling for Christ. Christ was for him the mystical source of inner consolation, the Savior of man from unrest, and the eternal center of history. But this feeling was enlightened and undogmatic, and it was as far from Catholic institutionalism as from Luther's new theology.

Throughout his life he defended his intellectual friends. In spite of all conflicts and vacillations, he remained true to himself. He never sold himself, not even for the purple of a cardinal, and even on his deathbed he showed his independence by devoting his

---

1. A letter from Erasmus, quoted in P. Smith, *Erasmus: A Study of His Life, Ideals and Place in History* (New York: Harper, 1923), p. 115.

soul to God without asking for the customary assistance of a priest. Therefore Luther may have been right from his point of view, but he was nevertheless essentially wrong when in one of his Table Talks he accused Erasmus of sophistry, ambiguity, and lack of seriousness.[2]

Much of Erasmus's character and thought is reflected in his educational theory. We find in it the religious and moral reformer, the advocate of peace, the satirical critic of the follies of man, the man who hopes for the reconciliation of faith and reason, the liberal and tolerant personality endowed with a fine understanding of human nature, the admirer of classical letters, the scholar of the literary, not the experimental, type, and the wanderer without a vernacular or a nation.

Whatever Erasmus wrote expressed in one way or another his concern with a humanistic reform of Christian civilization, whether he was dealing as a theologian with the New Testament and the fathers of the church or as a philologist with ancient languages. In spite of his satire against the church, his religious attitude appears in all his utterances. In this respect Erasmus definitely distinguished himself, as a northern humanist, from his sometimes cynical and paganized Italian friends.

His Theology

Intellectuals considered Erasmus the umpire in theological matters by the beginning of the sixteenth century. He and Luther were first believed to be companions in the common cause of ecclesiastical reform, yet later they became bitter enemies because they represented two fundamental contrasts in human attitude. Luther drew on metaphysical sources of life which kindle in a person the fire of a missionary, the disdain of death and danger, and the courage of a fighter who must win his battle, irrespective of what may come later. The center of Erasmus's personality, on the other hand, was the intellect. This does not mean that Erasmus was one of those narrow talents in whom the functions of the brain have absorbed all the other qualities we expect from a fully developed personality. His intellect was nourished by an emphatic moral sense, an intense—though more sensitive than vigorous—emotional life, an unusual humor, and a vivid desire for form and

---

2. E. Korder, ed., *Luthers Tischreden der Mathesischen Sammlung* (Leipzig, 1903), p. 283.

beauty. Nevertheless, it is primarily through reason that his talent expressed itself.

Luther appreciated the antiquities only to the extent that they would do no harm to religious devotion, whereas for Erasmus the goal of culture is the union of antiquity and Christianity. This union, in his opinion, would resolve the conflict between reason and faith, work and grace, revelation and inquiry, self-assertion and authority. For Luther, history and philosophy are great sources of information about human affairs, but there is only one thing sacred, the Christian revelation. To call Jesus' teaching "philosophy" would have offended Luther. Erasmus spoke of the "philosophy of Christ" as the greatest and most divine, to be sure, but mentioned also the philosophies of Plato, Aristotle, Cicero, and Augustine.

Erasmus had not yet advanced far enough to apply modern historical criticism to the Bible, but the idea as such was not foreign to him. Together with such men as the philosopher Pico della Mirandola and the French philologist Lefèvre d'Etaples, Erasmus differentiated the true meaning of the Bible from its merely historical form. "The Gospel has its own flesh, [and] its own spirit," he said in the *Manual of the Christian Knight (Enchiridion militis Christiani).*[3]

In the controversy over the freedom of the will, Luther, arguing that the will is in bondage, was certainly more consistent than his adversary.[4] Yet, generally speaking, Erasmus appeals to more modern men than do most of his theological contemporaries when he said, "The sum of our religion is not to be found in one or other dogma, but is peace and concord."[5] Erasmus may seem to us more rational because he rejected the theory of predestination and gave every man a chance to come to Christ. Throughout his lifetime he attacked the identification of religion and hierarchy as the central evil in Christendom and declared mechanical routine in the office of the clergy to be the main danger to the spirit of love and religious edification.

On the other hand, it was the very same rationalism which, paradoxically enough, eventually kept him on the side of the traditional church. However much he attacked the vices of the clergy,

---

3. *The Enchiridion*, p. 108.
4. Luther's standpoint must not be confused with modern determinism, which is based on an entirely different premise. Luther denied free will with reference to God's omnipotence and Adam's fall.
5. *Opera omnia,* 3:694.

ridiculed the futile disputations of the scholastics, and felt the dawn of a new period, he hoped it would be a rational and liberal era. With disgust he observed the irrationalism of the Protestant preachers, iconoclasts, and rioting masses who followed the wake of the new movement. So he was, after all, inclined to condone much of the luxury and paganism of the Renaissance popes, for they were more broad-minded in questions of research and culture. In a letter to Pope Leo X of the House of Medici, one of the great representatives of Renaissance paganism within the hierarchy, Erasmus wrote:

> As from the Trojan horse there have come from your family within a few years excellent masters in all arts, so many Ciceros, Virgils, Platos, and Hieronymi, that this alone should encourage all lovers of the arts to hope that you, Pope Leo, have been given to the world by divine providence, that under you all excellent virtues and all liberal arts will thrive anew.[6]

It is true that the scholar of Rotterdam was sometimes too much of a diplomat, at least for such a man as Luther, but it was always in the interest of peace and culture. Much as he hated radicalism in religion and thought, because it excluded reason and tolerance, he equally hated war, using every opportunity to display its barbaric nature. He wanted a political organization with peace and justice for all, resembling the ideals of a modern democratic state, and an educational system that would both train an intellectual elite and enlighten the people as a whole. He hoped to achieve the mentality necessary for such a society by restoring the simplicity of Christ's teaching and by opening minds to the wisdom and beauty of the classics—in this respect following Origen, Clement, and his friend Louis Vives.

His Educational Theory

The state's role. About the relationship between the state, civilization, and education, Erasmus expressed his opinion in *On the Education of a Christian Prince*, published in 1516. Only three years earlier Machiavelli's famous *The Prince* had appeared, symbolizing the complete emancipation of a Renaissance humanist from Christian ethics and the enthronement of *raison d'état* as the highest principle of action for a prince. Erasmus was on the oppo-

---

6. *The Epistles of Erasmus, from His Earliest Letters to His Fifty-first Year,* 2:198.

site side of the fence. Like all the progressive people of his day, he considered a limited absolutist monarchy the best form of government. In his time this political organization promised, more than the others, an ordered and effectual society. But if one lays more stress on the spirit than on the external form of government, one can call *On the Education of a Christian Prince* the first learned manifesto of a democrat.

In this treatise Erasmus insisted that the prince and his consort should live in close contact with their subjects; they should regard themselves, and be regarded, as part of their people. Law should serve no other purpose than the welfare of the nation; every subject, irrespective of wealth or birth, should be allowed to grow up and live with a sense of honor; crime should be fought, not so much by punishment as by preventive economic and political measures; class differences and exploitation ought to be abolished; the government ought to develop the wealth of the country by a program of building and agricultural reform; the Christian prince should know that a war which is not necessary for the defense of human rights is against lasting warfare and the spirit of Christ. It is characteristic of European political morale that Machiavelli's *The Prince* has become a "classic" in the history of European government and that Erasmus's *Christian Prince* is almost forgotten.

Erasmus intended *On Christian Matrimony* (1526) to bring about a moral reform of Christian society. It is of particular interest for the historian of education because it contains an extensive chapter on the education of girls. Erasmus himself felt the refinement of the social atmosphere radiating from educated women in the homes of his beloved friend, Englishman Sir Thomas More, and of the German patrician Willibald Pirckheimer. The Erasmian sentence "Education causes my husband and me to hold each other more dearly"[7] expresses better than anything else his belief in the value of intellectual culture.

The pupil. According to Erasmus the aim of education is to lead men toward knowledge, honesty, and independent judgment.

> To dumb creatures Mother Nature has given an innate power of instinct.... But providence in granting to man alone the privilege of reason has thrown the burden of development of the human being upon training. Well has it been said that the first means, the second,

---

7. *Opera omnia*, 3:746; W. Woodward, *Desiderius Erasmus Concerning the Aim and Method of Education*, p. 150.

and the third means to happiness is right training or education. Sound education is the condition of real wisdom.[8]

This Aristotelian praise of wisdom is combined with the Christian idea that man as a rational being is potentially the image of God. He must never, therefore, be subjected to slavery, and he must be allowed to develop all of his qualities in order to realize this sublime destiny. If he fails to do so, he may sink below the animal.

It is beyond dispute that man not instructed through reason in philosophy and sound learning is a creature lower than a brute, seeing that there is no beast more wild or more harmful than a man who is driven hither and thither by ambition or desire, anger or envy, or lawless temper.[9]

The gift of reason is what unites men in a spiritual community. There exists no essential difference among nations and races as such; there are only individual differences according to the degree of man's participation in the achievements of culture. Nor must man be subjected to unquestioned authority; even the opinions of the ancients must be doubted.

Besides the humanistic ones, Erasmus's works on education also include a group which aims at general spiritual reform of Christian life, for example, the *Manual of the Christian Knight (Enchiridion militis Christiani)*, published in 1503 and first translated into English in 1533. It pictures the *Imitatio Christi* as the continual effort toward self-discipline which alone allows us to enter into the region where man and God may meet.

The teacher. The most mature of Erasmus's works on education was his *Liberal Education of Boys* (1529). Together with *The Method of Right Instruction* it presents a rather coherent system of humanist education, full of a genuine feeling for the responsibilities of a good teacher and far superior to the educational literature of the early humanists of the fifteenth century.

His sense of the dignity of the individual made Erasmus one of the strongest enemies of cruel schoolmasters. For Erasmus, the battle against maltreatment of children was a kind of holy war, the only war he was glad to enter. He was concerned with awakening the pupil's interest and his love for the teacher. The school should be a place children enjoy because they are understood, and it

---

8. *De pueris instituendis* 4; Woodward, *Desiderius Erasmus,* p. 183.
9. *De pueris instituendis* 7, 24; Woodward, *Desiderius Erasmus,* pp. 186, 207.

should prepare their minds for the cultivation of good style in speaking, writing, and living.

A poor master, we are prepared to find, relies almost wholly upon fear of punishment as the motive to work. To frighten one entire class is easier than to teach one boy properly; for the latter is, and always must be, a task as serious as it is honorable. It is equally true of States: the rule which carries the respect and consent of the citizens demands higher qualities in the Prince than does the tyranny of force.... Do schoolmasters consider how many earnest, studious natures have been by treatment of this type—the hangman type—crushed into indifference?[10]

In order to educate without the rod, the teacher must understand the nature of the child and the laws inherent in the educative process; in other words, he needs psychological insight and a workable method. In the investigation of these requisites of education, Erasmus largely followed Aristotle, Plutarch, and Quintilian. But the influences from these men were intimately interwoven with Erasmus's own experiences.

Three conditions... determine individual progress. They are Nature, Training, and Practice. By *Nature,* I mean, partly, innate capacity for being trained, partly native bent towards excellence. By *Training,* I mean the skilled application of instruction and guidance. By *Practice,* free exercise on our own part of that activity which has been implanted by Nature and is furthered by training. Nature without skill Training must be imperfect, and Practice without method which Training supplies leads to hopeless confusion.[11]

In consequence of these three "conditions," as Erasmus rather vaguely called them, education must include both the intellectual and the physical development of the child. But like most German humanists, he was more interested in pursuits of the mind than in exercise of the body.

Among teachers of Latin Erasmus became famous for his *Colloquies.* They represent a widespread type of humanist literature: namely, fictitious dialogues, destined to introduce the student to conversational Latin. Erasmus began to jot down the first of these dialogues when as a young man he had to support himself through giving private instruction. During his lifetime the *Colloquies* appeared in several ever-larger editions. It gives a clear picture of Erasmus's desire to restore pure and genuine piety in the catechetical style of Augustine. Erasmus had to defend himself against

---

10. *De pueris instituendis* 24; Woodward, *Desiderius Erasmus,* pp. 205, 206.
11. *De pueris instituendis* 11; Woodward, *Desiderius Erasmus,* p. 191.

the reproach of "childishness" because of his interest in teaching youth.

> ...if any one shall cry out that it is an unseemly thing for an old man to sport himself thus childishly, I care not how childishly it be, so it be but profitable. And if the ancient teachers of children are commended who allured them with wafers, that they might be willing to learn their first rudiments, I think it ought not to be charged as a fault upon me that by the like regard I allure youths either to the elegancy of the Latin tongue or to piety.[12]

The curriculum. As long as Erasmus viewed intellect as the center of man, the classics and the writings of church fathers were of equal importance. His curriculum was one-sidedly centered on the classics and on expression. The vernacular receives no attention, nor do the sciences. The latter had not yet become a molding influence on the life of man. The Copernican theory had not yet shattered the old Ptolemaic-Christian cosmology nor had Galileo's and other scientists' experiments reversed Aristotle's theory of the fall of bodies. Erasmus disdained the primitive experience of his more empirically-minded contemporaries. Yet in principle he was not against the study of nature; he always wished to lead the student toward a better understanding of life. Language was for him a door toward experience, not a barrier to shut it out. His *Colloquies* prove this sufficiently for they are filled with bristling actuality, combining the teaching of Latin with the teaching of the elements of worldly life and conduct.

His Educational Methodology

From 1509 to 1514 Erasmus was professor of divinity at Cambridge. Common interests with the humanist John Colet, who had just started his school at St. Paul's, led Erasmus to write the *Method of Right Instruction* (1511). There he gave an account of his ideas on the right ways of instruction in the classics, on the interpretation of authors, and on the techniques of composition. In contrast to so many of his modern followers in the liberal arts, he was deeply aware of the importance of methodical teaching.

> Such weight do I ascribe to right method in instruction—and I include herein choice of material as well as of modes of imparting it—that I undertake by its means to carry forward youths of merely

---

12. *The Whole Familiar Colloquies,* trans. N. Baily (Glasgow, 1877), p. vii.

53619

average intelligence to a creditable standard of scholarship, and of conversation also, in Latin and Greek, at an age when, under the common schoolmaster of today, the same youths would be just stammering through their Primer. With the foundations thus rightly laid a boy may confidently look forward to success in the higher range of learning. He will, when he looks back, admit that the essential condition of his attainment was the care which was devoted to the beginnings of his education.[13]

No wonder that Erasmus became one of the first advocates of a systematic training of teachers.

Erasmus believed that man is endowed with certain dispositions which the teacher must know in order to utilize. The human being possesses imagination and other inborn or potential urges, such as self-preservation, imitation, ambition, and the desire for attachment. In appealing to these qualities, the teacher can motivate the child voluntarily to undergo, and even to enjoy, the many inconveniences connected with the educative process. Therefore good education is to a large extent encouragement; to mix patience and understanding properly with severity is the criterion of the good teacher. He will also know that play for a child is not only a relaxation or pleasure but a part of his life and learning. Erasmus recommended also the use of visual aids, for education must make use of the senses in order to help the mind grasp the reality behind the words.

The good teacher respects individual differences in the child, but not to the extent that he allows him to develop only some of his qualities at the expense of others. Respect for specific talents and the cultivation of "many-sidedness of interest," as Herbart phrased it later, do not exclude each other.

The German theologian and biographer Melchior Adam wrote around 1600 that Erasmus's satire against ecclesiastical corruption (expressed particularly in his *Praise of Folly*) had done more harm to the papacy than Luther's direct attack. Erasmus's influence reached from England to Italy and from Spain to Hungary and Poland. But Erasmus died a lonely man. For his contemporaries he had become the symbol of a man incapable of decision because he had refused to take sides in the religious struggle. For Luther, Erasmus was an enemy of Christ. The Catholics disclaimed Erasmus; at the Council of Trent (1545-1563) they put his name on the

---

13. *Opera omnia*, 1:530; Woodward, *Desiderius Erasmus*, p. 178.

Index librorum prohibitorum and tried to suppress his influence in the universities.

Yet, few men have molded European education as decisively as Erasmus. He encouraged a better method of teaching and a more understanding and tolerant attitude toward the pupil, and he infiltrated classical studies with the spirit of exactness, historical criticism, and international perspective. This allowed ancient philosophy to dominate the humanities until the beginning of the nineteenth century.

Selected Bibliography

Allen, P. *The Age of Erasmus*. New York: Oxford University, 1914.

Erasmus, D. *The Enchiridion*. Translated by R. Himelick. Bloomington: Indiana University, 1963.

——. *The Education of a Christian Prince*. Translated by L. Born. Records of Civilization: Sources and Studies, no. 27. New York: Columbia University, 1936.

——. *The Epistles of Erasmus, from His Earliest Letters to His Fifty-first Year*. Translated by F. Nichols. 3 vols. New York: Longmans and Green, 1901-1918.

——. *Opera omnia*. Edited by J. Aerici. 20 vols. Lugd. Bat., 1703-1706.

——. *Opus epistolarum*. Edited by P. Allen. 12 vols. Oxford: Clarendon, 1906-1958.

Froude, J. *Life and Letters of Erasmus*. New York: Scribner, 1899.

Huizinga, J. *Erasmus*. New York: Scribner, 1924.

Mangan, J. *Life, Character and Influence of Desiderius Erasmus of Rotterdam*. 2 vols. New York: Macmillan, 1927.

Woodward, W. *Desiderius Erasmus Concerning the Aim and Method of Education*. New York: Columbia University, 1964.

8

Harold J. Grimm

Martin Luther
(1483-1546)

The Reformation era was one of momentous changes, not only in religious but also in political, economic, social, and cultural history. The rise of the territorial state, the emergence of a capitalist economy, the growth of an increasingly active bourgeois class, the development of self-confidence among the peasants, and the flowering of culture in all its forms made adjustments necessary among all classes and caused all thinking people to give attention to the role of education in society.[1] Moreover, the church, which

---

1. Luther's chief works on education are his "To the Councilmen of All Cities in Germany That They Establish and Maintain Christian Schools" and "A Sermon on Keeping Children in School." The best studies of the Reformation's contributions to the theory and practice of education are F. Paulsen, *Geschichte des gelehrten Unterrichts auf den deutschen Schulen und Universitäten vom Ausgang des Mittelalters bis zur gegenwart*, 3rd ed., 2 vols. (Leipzig, 1919-1921); Paulsen, *German Education Past and Present*, trans. T. Lorenz (London: Unwin, 1912); H. G. Good, *A History of Western Education* (New York: Macmillan, 1947); E. P. Cubberly, *A Brief History of Education* (Boston: Houghton-Mifflin, 1922). Detailed studies in English on Luther's contributions to education are G. M. Bruce, *Luther as an Educator* (Minneapolis: Augsburg, 1928); and F. Eby, ed., *Early Protestant Educators* (New York: McGraw-Hill, 1931). Both Bruce and Eby used the translations of Luther's statements on education in F. V. N. Painter, *Luther on Education*.

had dominated medieval society for centuries, was losing its control over education as well as over other aspects of life and culture. Territorial rulers were becoming aware of the importance of training officials for their courts, and townsmen were eager to develop schools in which their youth would be educated in subjects in line with their predominant interests.

Strangely enough, the impetus for far-reaching reforms came from the field of religion and proved so dynamic that it greatly influenced the entire life of Europe, particularly education. It was the Lutheran Reformation which accelerated the decline of cathedral and monastery schools, and layed the basis for much broader goals and functions of education. Henceforth education was to serve not only the church but the state and society at large. The ultimate result, the state-controlled secular education of our day, was not foreseen by Luther and the other Reformers, who were opposed to a complete secularization. Since this secularization has created many problems, it is in the area of the impact of religion, and particularly religious ethics, on education that Luther still has much of significance to say to us in the twentieth century.

It is interesting to note that Luther wrote more about education than any other Reformer of the sixteenth century, publishing tracts, sermons, catechisms, commentaries, and letters on the subject. His entire career was one of teaching. He was involved in establishing schools and setting up new curricula, partly by choice and partly by force of circumstances. His primary mission of spreading the gospel and reforming the church was essentially one of education. On the other hand, the secularization of church lands with the concomitant closing of monasteries and seizure of endowments for educational purposes by princes and cities led to the collapse of cathedral and monastery schools in many places. Moreover, a number of left-wing religious groups stressed the importance of inner revelation and minimized education. Consequently Luther found it necessary to strengthen existing schools and establish new ones. He turned for support to the secular authorities, who had appropriated much of the church property and who likewise had an interest in establishing schools on a broader foundation than those of the Middle Ages.

Since Luther first carried out his educational theories in Electoral Saxony and expressed himself vigorously on matters of pedagogy, discipline, curriculum, and support of schools, secular and spiritual leaders from all German lands and cities touched by the Reformation sought his advice. Furthermore, Luther and his colleagues had reformed the young University of Wittenberg along humanist lines, placing considerable emphasis on the languages and literatures of the ancients and embodying some of the educational principles of the humanists. The reputation of the University was enhanced and the cause of education as a whole was advanced by the addition to its faculty of Philip Melanchthon, the young humanist who eventually came to be known as the *praeceptor Germaniae,* or teacher of Germany. He had the happy faculty of making the Reformation movement intellectually respectable and devoted considerable time and effort to organizing ideas as they developed in the fertile brain of his friend Luther.

A lively correspondence developed between the Wittenberg Reformers and humanists throughout Europe. Many humanists, even after they had begun to oppose Luther's cause, continued to correspond with Melanchthon and to maintain a contact with the evangelical movement. As a matter of fact, humanism and Lutheranism were both prominent in the development of education during much of the century until basic differences came to outweigh the elements which they had in common.

Wittenberg students spread Luther's theories on education as well as his evangelical doctrines. But even more important was Luther's correspondence with princes and their secretaries and with members of city councils who sought his advice on all matters concerned with the improvement and establishment of schools.

The Education of Youth

Theological presuppositions. Luther's interest in primary and secondary schools stemmed primarily from his overwhelming religious concern. Recent Luther scholarship has established that the Reformation had its origins in Luther's inner struggle concerning salvation, and not, in the first instance, in his criticism of abuses in the church.[2] It was Luther's doctrine of justification by faith alone which led him to criticize the church as an institution for obtaining the salvation of souls and ultimately led to his break with the papacy. Out of this doctrine, which proved unacceptable to the church, grew two others which proved equally heretical and constituted the basic doctrines of sixteenth-century Protestantism:

2. G. Ritter, *Die Weltwirkung der Reformation* (Munich, 1959), pp. 44, 45.

namely, the Bible as the sole and ultimate authority in matters of faith, and the universal priesthood of believers.

Luther's doctrine of justification by faith alone involved a radically new conception of man and his relation to God. Its implications with respect to education are obvious. In place of obedience to established authority, Luther emphasized the individual's responsibility to God and his fellow man. Man's relation to God, his personal faith in Him and His plan of salvation, provided a powerful dynamic and determined his relation to society in all its aspects. If man severs his relation with God, he becomes purely materialistic, self-centered, and indifferent to the common good, a matter of great concern to the princes and townsmen of the sixteenth century. This was true especially since a widespread breakdown of respect for authority was evident. Dissatisfaction was evinced in virtually every phase of man's activity and frequently took the form of rioting and even revolt. Life, Luther maintained, makes sense only when one serves his neighbor. Once man is certain of his own salvation, he is free to serve others, particularly the young, who need his guidance.

Luther's emphasis on the Bible as the sole authority in matters concerning faith made it incumbent on his followers to read and understand it. This led him to stress the need for educating all people and for encouraging the study of languages at an early age as a preparation for Biblical scholarship in the secondary schools and the universities. It is at this point that his views coincided with those of the Biblical humanists and received their wholehearted endorsement.

The Reformer's doctrine of the universal priesthood of believers changed the basic conception of education in a number of respects. It was no longer to be primarily "of, by, and for" the clergy. Just as the selection of ministers and the control of church matters in general were to be in the hands of the congregation, so the supervision of education was to devolve upon members of the congregation.

It fell first of all on the parents, to whom God, according to Luther, gave both spiritual and secular authority over their children. He warned parents against being dilatory in having their children study the catechism at home and attend catechetical sermons regularly, saying that if they were lax, he would not admit them to the Lord's Supper. Discipline in the home Luther considered to be of paramount importance.

Where father and mother rule their families poorly, permitting their children to have their own way, there no city, market, village, land, principality, kingdom, or empire are ruled well, for a son becomes a father, judge, burgomaster, prince, king, emperor, school teacher, etc. . . . God gave you children so you would educate them to the best of their ability.[3]

Parents alone, however, could not or would not educate their children adequately, and since the clergy had functions of greater priority to perform—such as preaching, administering the sacraments, and carrying out their pastoral duties—Luther placed responsibility for establishing and maintaining schools on princes and city councils. They were responsible "for the welfare and improvement of the city," which consisted "not alone in gathering treasures and providing solid walls, beautiful buildings, and a goodly supply of guns and armor," but particularly of "having many learned, wise, honorable and well-bred citizens."[4] Teachers, acting as substitutes for parents, thus became co-workers with God in leading children to faith and to an ethical life growing out of this faith.

Although Luther retained the main features of the medieval conception of church and state and maintained that there were two distinct realms, the spiritual and the temporal, the lines between them became blurred for him in actual practice. Thus princes and city councils who had appropriated church property and religious endowments upon joining the Reformation movement assumed the administrative and legal functions previously exercised by the Catholic bishops. Although Luther agreed to such an assumption of episcopal functions only as a temporary expedient in the hope that order would be restored and that these functions ultimately would be returned to the church, the exigencies of that day were such that no prince or city council would or could relinquish such authority. By the beginning of the sixteenth century the tendency toward centralized territorial states was too strong to be reversed by the Lutheran Reformers.

Moreover, by emphasizing the divine-right of all government, whether Christian or not, Luther provided a religious sanction for the growing centralization of authority in both territories and city states. That these governments should have a strong interest in educating their youth from the primary schools through the uni-

---

3. *Works of Martin Luther,* 1:502 (hereafter cited as WML).
4. Ibid., 4:iii.

versities is understandable, for they, like the church, needed educated and trained officials. Luther deserves great credit for seeing that the needs of church and state coincide, and that education for the general welfare of society and for the development of a cultured population should go hand-in-hand with education for Christian faith and life. He was the first educator in modern times to make the state aware of its great obligations to society and of its far-reaching opportunities in the field of education.

Educational goals. By insisting upon a well-rounded education which includes the study of the realities of life as well as of the spiritual and intellectual interests of man, Luther had the support of the humanists, all of whom were concerned with the development of well-rounded personalities. By making education practical and giving it to all the people, however, he avoided the extremes of the humanists in their emphasis on pure Latinity and the development of an esoteric learning. He once stated:

> True it is, that human wisdom and the liberal arts are noble gifts of God.... But we never can learn from them in detail what sin and righteousness are in the sight of God, how we can get rid of our sins, become pious and just before God, and come to life from death.[5]

Luther's foremost objective in demanding a thorough revamping of education was the inculcation of faith in God. His basic doctrine of justification by faith alone was implicit if not explicit in virtually every statement concerning education. It is significant that courses in religion were the only content courses which he advised for the primary schools, and these courses also occupied a prominent place in the curricula of the secondary Latin schools. In his "Address to the German Nobility" he stated that

> the foremost and most general subject of study, both in the higher and the lower schools, should be the Holy Scriptures.... A spinner or a seamstress teaches her daughter the trade in her early years, but now even the great, learned prelates and bishops themselves do not know the Gospel.[6]

In his letter "To the Councilmen of All Cities of Germany That They Establish Christian Schools," written in 1524, a time of great

---

5. *D. Martin Luthers Werke: Kritische Gesamt-Ausgabe* (Weimar: Böhlau, 1883ff.) 48, 78 (hereafter cited as WA—Weimar Ausgabe).
6. WML, 2:151, 152.

popular agitation which culminated in the Peasants' Revolt, he asked:

> If it is necessary, dear sirs, to expend annually such great sums for firearms, roads, bridges, dams and countless similar items, in order that a city may enjoy temporal peace and prosperity, why should not at least as much be devoted to the poor, needy youth?[7]

From the beginning of his career as a reformer, Luther placed great emphasis on the need for educating people for service to God and the church, the state and society. This was the main argument in his influential pamphlet on "The Freedom of a Christian Man," written during the critical year 1520. In 1519, in his "Sermon on the Estate of Marriage," he had called attention to the duty of educating children to God's service.

> Parents must know that they please God, Christendom, the entire world, themselves and their children in no better way than by educating their children.

In his "Sermon on Keeping Children in School" he stated:

> If you raise a son who will be a pious Christian pastor, preacher, school-teacher, [you will] have raised for God a special servant, ... an angel of God, a true bishop before God, a savior of many people.[8]

The office of pastors, he explained, like that of "teachers, preachers, lectors, priests [whom men call chaplains], sacristans, school-teachers," belongs to the ministry of the Word.

Implicit in this service to God is service to one's fellow man, for

> a Christian lives in this temporal world, builds, buys and sells, deals with people, and does everything necessary for this world, but only as a guest who does what the host wishes him to do and what is in accord with the law and customs of the land, city or inn. Therefore those people are incomprehensible fools who flee from the world into deserts and woods.[9]

Such service includes the education of youth for service to church and state. In one of his Table Talks he stated that

> learning, wisdom, and writers must rule the world. ... If God out of His wrath would take away from the world all the learned, people would become beasts and wild animals. Then there would be no wisdom, religion, or law, but only robbery, stealing, murder, adultery,

---

7. Ibid., 4:106.
8. WML, 4:146.
9. WA 21, 346.

and the doing of all kinds of evil.... Where there is no domestic and secular order, there are bears, lions, goats, and dogs.[10]

On another occasion he said,

In order outwardly to maintain its temporal estate, the world must have good and skilled men and women.... Now such men must come from our boys and such women from our girls. Therefore the thing to do is to teach and train our boys and girls in the proper manner.

He wrote Elector John of Saxony on 22 November 1526 to this effect:

Now there is no more necessary thing than the education of the people who are to come after us to be the rulers.[11]

He described the government in his "Sermon on the Duty of Sending Children to School" as

a glorious ordinance of God and splendid gift of God, Who has established and instituted it and will have it maintained as something that men cannot do without.

Without it men could not live together, for

one would devour the other, as the brute beasts do.... So it is the function and the honor of worldly government to make men out of wild beasts.

Good government, he added, cannot be maintained by ruling with the "law of the fist, but the law of the head," not by force, "but wisdom or reason, among the wicked as among the good."[12] The laws of the land cannot be upheld unless there are educated jurists and scholars. He called attention to the great need for chancellors, secretaries, judges, lawyers, notaries, and the like, and explained "that every lord must have a counsellor." Such service is much better than serving "the belly ... and living like hogs, wallowing forever with noses in filth."

Still another important goal in education, according to Luther, is the development of character. He was well aware of the tendency of youth to ignore laws and disobey those in authority. From a psychological point of view, he considered this a consequence of self-will, a perversity which harms all people. To develop an ethical Christian character in the young, he considered it necessary

---

10. WA 25, 44; WML, 4:121.

11. In P. Smith and C. M. Jacobs, eds., *Luther's Correspondence* (Philadelphia: Lutheran Publication Society, 1918), 2:383, 384.

12. WML, 4:158-60.

first to destroy their self-will and then, largely by example, to give them inner direction and stability. Accordingly he admonished teachers and preachers to train themselves

> by studying, reading, meditating, and praying to be able in tempta-
> tion to teach and comfort your own conscience as well as the con-
> sciences of others and to lead from the law back to grace, from active
> justice to passive justice.

Furthermore, Luther believed with the humanists that the young should be given as broad an acquaintance with culture as possible, that people should know literature, history, music, and science as well as the Bible and the languages. He did not consider culture an end in itself, however, but another aspect of service to God.[13] It is Christian faith as a creative force implanted by God which, when operative in cultural pursuits, gives a person a dynamic character. All schools which ignore this divine force must be avoided.

Finally, education should help young people lead a prayerful life. All good education, according to Luther, should lead to communion with God and recognition of the fact that learning, like every other advantage, is a free gift of God for which the individual must give thanks in prayer.

The curriculum. It is generally recognized that Luther's contributions to modern education are many, particularly in the field of theory, and that he laid the foundation upon which we build even now. When one studies in detail his statements concerning education, one is amazed by the originality of his program, the breadth of interest evinced in his proposed curricula, and his imaginative approach to child psychology.

Luther was the first educator in modern times to see the need for universal. compulsory education, not only because the basic principles of the Reformation made it necessary that all persons be able to read the Bible, but because both church and state required trained personnel. In a letter to Elector John of Saxony, Luther stated that his prince had the power to compel a town or a village to support schools, just as the prince had the power to force it "to contribute and to work for the building of bridges and roads, or any other of the country's needs."[14] In his "Sermon on Keeping Children in School" Luther specifically stated that

---

13. WA 35, 475.
14. In Smith and Jacobs, eds., *Luther's Correspondence*, 2:383, 384.

it is the duty of the government to compel its subjects to keep their children in school.... For it is truly its duty to maintain the [spiritual and temporal] offices and classes that have been mentioned, so that preachers, jurists, pastors, writers, physicians, schoolmasters, and the like may continue.

He argued,

If the government can compel citizens fit for military service to carry pike and musket, man the walls, and perform other military services in time of war, how much more can it and ought it compel its subjects to keep their children in school.

He urged gifted boys to continue beyond the elementary schools in preparation for the professions and services in church and state. "If the father is poor," he stated, "let it [the government] help him" with income from sequestered church property. "Let the rich make their wills with this work in view."[15]

In a letter to Margrave George of Brandenburg dated 18 July 1529, Luther advised the establishment of a kind of territorial system of schools, with primary schools at the bottom and one or two universities at the top. He advocated a surprisingly broad curriculum of studies for all schools. Not content with the narrow curricula of the late medieval schools, which concentrated largely on reading, writing, and religious study, he urged the teaching of the Biblical and other languages, grammar, rhetoric, logic, literature, poetry, history, music, mathematics, gymnastics, and even nature study, to be preceded by the inculcation of a knowledge of the vernacular and the catechism. He said before his marriage,

If I had children and could accomplish it, they should study not only the languages and history, but singing, instrumental music and all the branches of mathematics.[16]

He stressed the great value of the liberal arts as a whole, stating their founders were "learned and outstanding people, even though they were heathens." These liberal arts are

serviceable and useful to people in this life, noble and precious gifts of Christ who used and uses them according to His good pleasure for the praise, honor and glory of His holy name.

Yet the principal subject of study, in both the higher and the lower schools, must be the Holy Scriptures.[17]

15. WML, 4:177, 178.
16. Ibid., p. 123.
17. Ibid., p. 106.

The most comprehensive statement of Luther's views concerning the curricula of the schools is found in "Instructions for the Visitors of Parish Pastors."[18] Although written by Melanchthon, the contents were endorsed by Luther and he wrote the preface. In this work the schools were divided into three divisions, or classes.

The first division consisted of children who were beginning to read. They were expected to read the primer containing the alphabet, the Lord's Prayer, the Creed, and prayers for various occasions; to study the *Ars grammatica* of Aelius Donatus (fourth century B.C.) and a work by Publius Valerius Cato (first century B.C.), two popular textbooks of the Middle Ages; to learn to read and write; and to learn music.

The second division consisted of those who could read and were ready for a more detailed study of grammar. They were taught music, *Aesop's Fables,* the *Paedagogia* of Peter Mosselanus (A.D. 1493-1524), selections from the *Colloquies* of Erasmus, the writings of Terence (190?-159? B.C.), some fables of Plautus (254?-184 B.C.), Christian doctrine, and parts of the Bible.

The third division consisted of those bright students who had learned their Latin grammar well. They were taught music; Vergil, Ovid, and Cicero; composition; dialectics and rhetoric. And they were expected to speak Latin as far as possible.

Luther made much of the study of languages, not only for a better comprehension of the Bible but also for the practical use of future lawyers, statesmen, and merchants. In his letter "To the Councilmen" he stated that,

> although the Gospel has come and daily comes through the Holy Spirit alone, we cannot deny that it has come by means of the languages, by which it was also spread abroad and by which it must be preserved.

God, he maintained, gave the languages for the purpose of spreading the gospel, and "by means of the Roman Empire" He made Greek and Latin the languages of many lands, "that His Gospel might the more speedily bear fruit far and wide." He called the languages

> the sheath in which this sword of the Spirit is contained, ... the casket in which we carry this jewel, ... the vessel in which we hold this wine.[19]

18. See especially pp. 314-20.
19. WML, 4:113, 114.

He attributed the amazing spread of the Reformation to the linguistic accomplishments of the new learning which enabled man to study and preach the gospel in a form almost as pure and unadulterated as it was at the time of the apostles, and much purer than it was in the days of Jerome and Augustine.

> How often does not St. Augustine err in the Psalter and in other expositions! Likewise St. Hilary, and indeed all of them who attempted to expound Scripture without [knowing] the languages.[20]

Although Luther advocated the continued study of logic and rhetoric, since by means of them "people are wonderfully fitted for the grasping of sacred truths," he opposed the use made of logic by many of the scholastics and the use made of rhetoric by many of the humanists.

> Logic teaches, rhetoric moves and persuades. The latter pertains to the will, the former to the intellect.... *Dialectic* says, "Give me something to eat." *Rhetorica* says, "I have had a hard road to go all day long, am tired, sick, hungry, etc., and have eaten nothing; dear fellow, give me a good piece of meat, a good fried chicken, and a good measure of beer to drink."[21]

True eloquence, he pointed out, does not consist of flamboyant language but of clear and simple words which, like a beautiful painting, throw light on the subject at hand.

The Reformer was particularly fond of history and was well ahead of his time in advocating its inclusion in the curriculum. Since he considered world history the story of divine providence and a practical guide for life, he praised historians for aiding the understanding of events of this world and "noting the wonderful works of God."[22] He urged that all important rulers have records made of their actions and have histories of all kinds preserved for later use.

> It would be most beneficial to rulers if from youth on they would read and have read to them history, both in sacred and profane books, for in them they would find more examples of the art of ruling than in all the books of law.[23]

> It is unfortunate that so many important deeds go unnoticed because no one makes a record of them. Only the Greeks and Romans had their historians.[24]

---

20. Ibid., p. 116.
21. WA TR 2, no. 2199a.
22. WML, 4:128, 129.
23. WA 6, 261.
24. WA TR 3, no. 3616b.

But he cautioned that history must be written objectively and that the reader should bear in mind the motives of the less reliable historians.

> Historians are most useful people and the best teachers, whom we can never sufficiently honor, praise, and thank.... An excellent man is required [for the writing of history], a man with the heart of a lion, fearless in presenting the truth. The majority write in such a way that they keep silent about the vices or evils of their time in order to please their rulers or friends ... or to favor their fatherland and place foreigners in a bad light.[25]

Since Luther himself greatly enjoyed music in his home as well as in church services, and considered it "an outstanding gift of God and next to theology" in importance, he insisted that it be retained and expanded in the curriculum. He encouraged the employment of cantors in all the Lutheran schools and urged princes and city councils to maintain outstanding organists and choirs in their churches. Music enlarged and brightened the spiritual life of Lutherans not only in church but in home, school, and even places of work.

> It is right that we retain music in the schools. A Schoolmaster must know how to sing, otherwise I do not look at him. And a young man should not be admitted to the ministry before he has practiced music in school. Music is a beautiful and glorious gift of God.... I would not give up my slight knowledge of it for a very great consideration.[26]

Most unusual for Luther's day was his advocacy of the study of science. Although he himself did not accept the Copernican system, he rejoiced in the fact that men no longer relied entirely on the books of the ancients but studied nature itself.

> We are at the dawn of a new era, for we are beginning to recover the knowledge of the external world that we lost through the fall of Adam. We now observe creatures properly, and not as formerly under the Papacy. Erasmus is different, and does not care to know how fruit is developed from the germ ... and looks upon external objects as cows look upon a new gate.[27]

For the purpose of furthering the scholarship of teachers, students, and others, Luther advocated the collection of books and the founding of libraries. Well known are his tireless efforts in obtaining money for the purchase of books for the library of the

---

25. WA 50, 384-85.
26. WA TR 1, no. 968.
27. Quoted in Painter, *Luther on Education*, p. 163.

University of Wittenberg. Like princes and churchmen, the city councils of a number of cities such as Nürnberg had made promising beginnings in the founding of libraries which were made available to schools, townsmen, and gifted young people. In his letter "To the Councilmen" Luther stated that

> no effort or expense should be spared to found good libraries, especially in the larger cities, which can well afford it, in suitable buildings . . . not only that those who are to be our spiritual and temporal leaders may have books to read and study, but that the good books, the arts and the languages that we now have . . . may be preserved.[28]

He urged the use of discrimination in the accumulation and preservation of books and even suggested the kinds of books which should be acquired: the Bible in Latin, Greek, Hebrew, German, and other languages, together with good commentaries in Greek, Hebrew, and Latin; books useful in the learning of languages, regardless of whether they were written by heathen or Christian authors; works on all the arts and sciences; books on medicine and jurisprudence; and chronicles and histories of all kinds.

Educational principles. More amazing still are Luther's pedagogical principles and practices. Before his time emphasis still was placed on form, the study of grammar, and on memorization. This invariably involved rigid discipline and the use of corporal punishment as a threat for the wayward. To an astonishing degree the Reformer stressed content rather than mere form and urged that parents and teachers appeal to the natural inquisitiveness of youth, as well as to their desire to play and to participate in the learning process by means of discussions, debates, and dramas.

> By the gracious arrangement of God, children take delight in acquiring knowledge, whether languages, mathematics, or history.

Schools no longer are to be "a hell and a purgatory" in which children are "tormented with cases and tenses," and in which with much "flogging, trembling, anguish, and misery" they learn nothing.[29]

The Reformer's understanding of the psychology of children was considerable. He realized that young persons must be active, saying that a boy "is like the juice of fruits. You cannot keep it; it must ferment." He warned that young people brought up with excessive strictness and severity

---

28. WML, 4:126.
29. Ibid., pp. 122, 123.

become much worse when freed from restraint than those who have not been so strictly reared. So utterly impossible is it to improve human nature by commandment and punishment.

On the other hand,

when a child is permitted to do what it pleases and parents say, "Whatever our little daughter does is good," that girl certainly is headed for prostitution.

Children are not to be rebuked and beaten, but are to be "chastised out of love." Parents who vent their tempers on their children and try to cow them into obedience in their tender years destroy their spirit and make them so timid that they are unable to do anything.

Also those nursemaids should be stopped who, especially in the evening, frighten children with terrifying actions and gestures.[30]

To get the best results in teaching young children, Luther said, it is necessary to love, understand, and work with them instead of acting as their lords and masters.

When Christ wished to influence men, He had to become a man. Since we are preaching to children, we must prattle with them.[31]

Luther was far ahead of his time in advising the use of the oral method of teaching languages. He explained that one learns languages better by speaking them in ordinary conversations than out of books, and gave his daughter Magdalena as an example:

Although my little daughter is not yet four years old, she knows how to speak very well and, indeed, clearly about domestic matters. In ten years a boy cannot learn from a grammar or a textbook a language which an infant learns in two years. Such is the power of imitation.[32]

Another novel theory advanced by Luther was a study-work plan.

My idea is to let boys attend ... school for one or two hours a day and devote the rest of the time to working at home, learning a trade or doing whatever their parents desire, so that study and work might go hand in hand while they are young and able to do both. . . . A girl can surely find time enough to go to school one hour a day and still attend to all her duties at home; she sleeps, dances and plays away more time than that.[33]

The teacher. Finally, Luther made an outstanding contribution

---

30. WA 1, 449.
31. WA 30, 1, 143.
32. WA TR 3, no. 2882.
33. WML, 4:123, 124.

to the development of modern education by helping raise the status of the teaching profession. As co-workers with God, he insisted, teachers render a divine service. Like Christian pastors and preachers they are

> special servants of God than whom there is no dearer treasure, nor any more precious thing on earth.... A diligent and pious schoolteacher or master or whoever it is that faithfully trains and teaches boys can never be sufficiently rewarded.... If I could leave the preaching office and other things, or had to do so,... I would not be so glad to have any other work as that of schoolmaster, or teacher of boys, for I know that it is the most useful, the greatest, and the best, next to the work of preaching.[34]

The Education of Adults

The evangelical doctrines developed by Luther in his search for answers to his questions concerning salvation and in his study of Scripture constituted such a radical break with late medieval doctrines that much effort was required by him and his fellow Reformers to educate people in them. Old textbooks and manuals in theology quickly became dated, and late medieval handbooks on sermonizing became useless. Adults, as well as the young, needed educating, and the primary means used by Luther for educating them was the sermon.[35] Preaching had become exceptionally widespread and popular during the fourteenth and fifteenth centuries, as attested by thousands of printed sermons extant in the latter half of the fifteenth century alone; and as early as 1500 the pulpit had been moved into the nave and raised above the altar as a symbol of the importance attached to preaching. But medieval methods of preaching did not satisfy the needs of those who were attracted by the new evangelical doctrines. At first Luther attempted to use the prevalent scholastic form of the sermon, with its stilted divisions into many parts and the development of these parts by means of logical exposition, definitions, questions, arguments,

---

34. Ibid., pp. 173, 174.
35. Detailed accounts of Luther's preaching are W. Beste, *Die bedeutendsten Kanzelredner der lutherischen Kirche des Reformationszeitalters* (Leipzig, 1856-1858), vol. 1; A. Nebe, *Zur Geschichte der Predigt* (Wiesbaden, 1879), vol. 2; E. C. Dargan, *A History of Preaching* (New York: Armstrong, 1905), vol. 1; H. J. Grimm, *Martin Luther as a Preacher* (Columbus, Ohio: Lutheran Book, 1928); and E. C. Kiessling, *The Early Sermons of Luther and Their Relation to the Pre-Reformation Sermon* (Grand Rapids: Zondervan, 1935).

analogies, examples, and, for virtually every point, quotations from canon law, papal decretals, writings of church fathers, and lives of saints. But he soon substituted for this form the simple homily, or discourse, treating each verse of the text in its proper sequence. This form had been initiated by Origen in the third century and had been temporarily revived by Wycliffe. Luther's exposition of the text, whether pericope or free, was always simple and direct, no matter how difficult and involved the doctrine which he was teaching. He gave so little attention to form that it is often difficult to find any scheme of presentation. Johann Gerhard called his sermonizing "heroic disorder." Believing that the preacher should constantly teach the doctrines of the church, Luther touched on the most important of these in every series of sermons, repeating the fundamentals time and again.

Luther and his fellow Reformers devoted much time to preaching. In Wittenberg there were three sermons on Sundays—one on the Pauline epistles at five in the morning, one on the Gospels at nine, and one in the afternoon on the catechism or as a continuation of a morning sermon. There also were sermons every day of the week. Luther assumed a large share of this responsibility, on some Sundays preaching as many as three sermons in church and one at home.

Because of his great emphasis on the *Logos,* or the living Word, and its dynamic power, Luther made this central to his teaching and preaching. Like Paul, he constantly stressed the spoken word which comes to the speaker from the Holy Spirit; and he insisted that the Bible text should determine both the content and form of the sermon. Always reflecting the deep inner satisfaction that came to him with the discovery of the doctrine of justification by faith, he revived the apostolic *kerygma,* or proclamation, which had fallen into disuse since the days of Chrysostom in the East and Augustine in the West. Virtually every sermon was a lesson directly or indirectly concerned with God and His plan of salvation, which brought consolation to those who, like him, faced great spiritual perplexities and physical dangers. Every word he spoke was uttered with a strong conviction that he, like the apostles, was God's spokesman. He once told his congregation that

> certainly we must boast that we are your preachers. We did not set ourselves up in this office. The Word, baptism, and sermon are not

ours, but we are servants for this purpose, called to this office. We interpret the Gospel and the Psalms.[36]

Although Luther was reluctant to talk about himself in his sermons, it was his rich, inner religious experience which made his sermons personal and dynamic. This experience he universalized and imparted to others with such sincerity and fervor that people were often electrified by his message. The reciprocal relationship between him and his congregation was a very close one. He seemed to take his listeners into his confidence and to look upon himself and his audience as learners and teachers at the same time. He frequently departed from both text and outline to talk at length on a topic apparently suggested by the response of his congregation. But he never lost sight of the fact that his main purpose was to teach Christ, not simply as a great teacher, physician, or psychologist, but as Christ crucified for Hans the farmer, Georg the merchant, or little Magdalena. He made everyone aware of his personal responsibility for the salvation of his soul and of his direct relation to God. Frequently attacked by his opponents for minimizing good works as aids to salvation, Luther devoted considerable time to showing how good works were a natural consequence of faith, how the love of God was followed by the love of one's neighbor. Unlike his predecessors he laid much stress upon the correct attitude toward and confidence in God rather than upon humble obedience to established authority. Social service received constant emphasis, replacing medieval contemplation and ceremony.

To get his points across, the preacher, Luther said, must employ devices used in the graphic arts, for

> the attention of the common man is aroused by illustration and examples more readily than by profound disputations. . . . He prefers a painted picture to a well-written book.[37]

Luther was a master of this art and frequently added to an explanation of a doctrinal point a word-painting vividly and objectively portrayed and readily comprehended, as he did when he explained the ease with which a devout Christian could overcome the devil:

---

36. *Predigten D. Martin Luthers,* ed. G. Buchwald (Gütersloh, 1925-1926), 2:117. Since the 194 sermons in the two volumes of this collection, preached by Luther during Pastor Bugenhagen's absence from Wittenberg from 1528 to 1532, have been reconstructed accurately and since they were preached at a time when Luther was at his best as a preacher, they have been used almost exclusively in the preparation of this essay.
37. WA 40, 1, 548.

He [the devil] goes into his armory ... and grabs his dagger by the blade, not the hilt. If you only defend yourself, he will cut off his own fingers.[38]

Some of his illustrations he drew directly from the natural phenomena he observed and loved. In a sermon on Christ's resurrection, he likened man's resurrection to the annual resurrection of nature in spring. Nature is dead in winter, he said.

... on earth you see no blade, no leaf, no fruit, but everything is hidden in the earth. Finally there grows from the seed of grain a beautiful blade, from the leaf an apple.[39]

He often spoke of the delights of a rose garden, a picture he frequently used of Christian happiness. On one occasion he called attention to the fact that many peasants and townsmen walked in the fields and woods without seeing the many beautiful flowers and birds.

All little flowers and little birds have the gospel written on their throats and teach you what an idolatrous drip you are if you serve mammon. Every flower and every bird is more pious than you.[40]

He once likened growth in faith to the development of a child.

When a mother has her baby in her arms, it is not aware of it, for it does not know its mother as a mother knows her child. ... Therefore it cannot say, "I am your daughter, you are my mother." In time, however, the understanding of the child will develop to the point where it can say, "dear mother."[41]

Some of those to whom Luther regularly preached were themselves preparing to preach. At the beginning of the Reformation, few men were prepared to preach the new evangelical doctrines. People from virtually all walks of life became preachers, some with little education of any kind. Former priests and monks as well as many others who now filled the pulpits in behalf of the Reformation needed to learn the fundamentals of Christianity. Those who were in Wittenberg as students, teachers, and clergymen took copious notes on Luther's sermons and used them as a kind of corpus of theology. Realizing that many clergymen were too poorly educated and trained to fill their pulpits, Luther at an early date

---

38. *Predigten D. Martin Luthers,* 1:55.
39. Ibid., 2:314.
40. Ibid., 1:72.
41. Ibid., 2:330.

began to prepare for publication his postils,[42] that is, collections of sermons which could be read in the pulpit or used as models in the preparation of sermons. The qualifications Luther looked for in aspiring preachers were the ability to communicate, a good head, eloquence, a good voice, a good memory, industry, courage, and patience. "One must serve people and not expect gratitude for it," he once said, and added that a preacher who has a hundred virtues may obscure them all by one fault.[43]

> Dr. Jonas has all the virtues of a good preacher, but people cannot overlook the fact that the good man clears his throat too often.[44]

The mature Luther devoted virtually all his time to teaching. Whether he had before him his students at the University of Wittenberg, his fellow townsmen in the City Church, his family and friends at table in his home, his companions on his many travels, or his fellow Germans with whom he corresponded or for whom he wrote his works, he was a teacher with an overpowering mission. And people cherished every spoken or written word that came from him. They flocked in great numbers to hear his sermons so that he occasionally had to preach outside the church in the open; and they bought his works in such large quantities that three printers in Wittenberg alone were kept busy publishing them. Since Luther understood how to present to the people on the street in their own language religious doctrines and issues with which he had grappled in the quiet of his study, he became one of the greatest preachers and teachers of all time.

Selected Bibliography

Bruce, G. M. *Luther as an Educator.* Minneapolis: Augsburg, 1928.

Eby, F., ed. *Early Protestant Educators.* New York: McGraw-Hill, 1931.

Good, H. "The Position of Luther upon Education." *School and Society* 6:511-18.

Kaufmann, H. "Grundfragen der Erzichung bei Luther." *Luther* 25:60-76.

Luther, M. "To the Councilmen of All Cities in Germany That They Establish and Maintain Christian Schools." Translated by A. T. W. Steinhaeuser. *Works of Martin Luther,* 4:101-30. Philadelphia: Muhlenberg, 1931.

---

42. E. G. Schwiebert, *Luther and His Times* (St. Louis: Concordia, 1950), pp. 631-36.

43. *Predigten D. Martin Luthers,* 1:556.

44. WA TR 2, no. 2580.

————. "Instructions for the Visitors of Parish Pastors." Translated by C. M. Jacobs. *Luther's Works*, 40:263-320. Philadelphia: Fortress, 1958.

————. "A Sermon on Keeping Children in School." Translated by C. Bergendoff. *Works of Martin Luther*, 4:131-78. Philadelphia: Muhlenberg, 1931.

————. *Treatise on Christian Liberty*. *Works of Martin Luther*, 2:297-350. Philadelphia: Muhlenberg, 1930.

Montgomery, J. W. "Luther and Libraries." *The Library Quarterly* 32:133-47.

Painter, F. V. N. *Luther on Education*. Philadelphia: Lutheran Publication Society, 1889.

9

H. Wayne Pipkin

Huldreich Zwingli
(1484-1531)

Huldreich Zwingli, the German-Swiss Reformer and forefather of the present-day Reformed church, enthusiastically supported schools and education during his brief career. Zwingli's early education and development reveal certain strains of influence on his development as both Reformer and educator.

From the first, Zwingli exhibited a social sense characterized by patriotic feeling, and his later willingness to work within the traditional political arena (i.e., the Zurich magistracy) had its roots in his early youth. Furthermore, Zwingli's education was thoroughly humanistic; Erasmus had significantly influenced his development. This left Zwingli with the typical humanist dedication to, and faith in, truth, knowledge, education, and scholarship, as well as with a predilection toward the humanities, especially the classics and languages.

Zwingli's political sense and his dedication to the values inherent in education itself are quite apparent in his work as a Reformer. His reform could not have issued in the withdrawal of a purified church from evil society; rather, his work was directed toward reforming the whole of society. Zwingli's assumption that God works within the socio-political realm led him to split with the radicals.[1] This explains the deliberate tempo of the Reformation in Zurich and Zwingli's commitment to the education of the people. Knowledge was an essential weapon in his reforming work, and G. R. Potter correctly assessed the genius in Zwingli's approach: "Zwingli kept his feet firmly on the ground; he was content to advance slowly, to consolidate one position before attacking the next, to keep ahead of, but not too far ahead of, the public opinion of the city, to make each step appear the inevitable result of the former, and his opponents as ignorant and unpatriotic."[2] This show of patience and faith in education was not without its opposition among the radical elements, but Zwingli was not to be denied.

Walter Gut noted that, in general, Zwingli's reformation can be understood from the pedagogical perspective.[3] It was a time of educating people according to the spirit of the gospel, an education to Christian faith and affairs. One of the clearest examples of this assertion is the critical period of the acceptance of the Reformation in Zurich—the events and publications of 1523-24. The year 1523, which began with the First Zurich Disputation between Zwingli and his Catholic opponent, John Faber, brought many significant Reformation writings. The climax of the year was the Second Zurich Disputation of October and the decision of the City Council to proceed slowly and peacefully with the reform. Zwingli found himself steering a middle course between the old believers who would not welcome change and a growing group of radicals who advocated rapid change.

The final reform of the Zurich Church was not carried out until June 1524. The Council was not prepared to take final action until the people of Zurich and the other members of the Confederacy had been thoroughly instructed as to the purpose of the reform and given the opportunity to respond. It was to meet this need that the Council authorized Zwingli to write the *Short Christian Instruction,* which served as a catechism and a confession of faith for the intended reform. The treatise was to be used by the pastors both for their own edification and for instructing their parishioners. Zwingli and the Zurich Council desired unanimity. In the thinking

1. For a definitive treatment of Zwingli's efforts to reform Zurich society and of his split with the radicals, see R. C. Qalton, *Zwingli's Theocracy* (Toronto: University of Toronto, 1967).
2. E. Bonjour, et al., *A Short History of Switzerland* (Oxford: Clarendon, 1963), p. 150.
3. "Zwingli als Erzieher," p. 289.

of Zwingli, the preferable means of achieving this oneness of spirit was education.

At this point he broadened his educational base, for he sent his *Instruction* to all the pastors to use in educating all the people. Whereas Erasmus was normally concerned with an educational elite, Zwingli optimistically took his case to all the people. This faith in, and reliance on, education of the people is one of the distinguishing characteristics of the Zwinglian reformation. In this regard Oskar Rückert suggested that Zwingli's pedagogical thought was based on the ideal of a politico-religious renewal of the people.[4] The attempts to renew the whole society and individual persons according to the spirit of the gospel has significant implications for a theory of general education.

Educational Theory

The main source for Zwingli's views on education is a short essay which appeared in 1523, *Of the Education of Youth*.[5] The treatise was conceived and presented to Gerold Meyer von Knonau as a *Badenschenke,* a customary gift with which one greeted a friend or relative returning from the baths at nearby Baden. Gerold, whose father, Hans Meyer von Knonau, had died several years earlier, was soon publicly to become Zwingli's stepson when the Reformer married the youth's mother, Anna Reinhard, on 2 April 1524. Gerold later served on the Great Council and fell with Zwingli at Kappel in 1531.

The treatise is more than a private discussion on the value and principles of education, for Zwingli obviously composed it with an eye to publication. Zwingli stated in the letter which accompanied the treatise that he had been planning such a work for some time but that his "plans were hindered by the many distracting matters which came up."[6]

The treatise was not concerned with educating the very young

---

4. *Ulrich Zwinglis Ideen zur Erziehung und Bildung,* p. 30.
5. In G. W. Bromiley, ed., *Zwingli and Bullinger,* pp. 102-18. The critical Latin text is in *H. Zwinglis sämtliche Werke,* ed. E. Egli and G. Finsler (Leipzig: Schwetschke, 1905), 2:526-51. The German translation, probably done by Zwingli himself, is in 5:427-47. A recent German edition is *An den jungen Mann,* ed. E. G. Rüsch. Bromiley's translation is based on the Latin text but does not ignore the German. For a discussion of other Zwingli writings which have implications for education, see Rückert, *Ulrich Zwinglis,* pp. 4ff.
6. *Zwingli and Bullinger,* p. 103.

or those in the earliest years of school. Instead Zwingli gave directions "which are suitable for young men who have already attained to discretion and can stand on their own feet." The Reformer divided the work into three parts which correspond naturally to very basic relationships: the relation of the youth to God, to himself, and to others. This order of division is not unusual and has antecedents in the humanistic educational writings with which Zwingli was no doubt acquainted.[7]

The student and God. It begins with a few comments on the providence of God, a characteristic beginning for a Reformation theologian. Man cannot create faith in God; only God can do this. It is significant that in a treatise on education, the reader is immediately reminded of the limitations of education; it is only where the Spirit of God works that one can be brought to God.

Having established this point, the Reformer did not, however, reject the possibility of natural theology. He commented that it is "quite in keeping with Christ's own teaching to bring young people to a knowledge of God in and through external phenomena." His own youth and education must have influenced him here, for this is reminiscent of Oswald Myconius's assessment of his hero: "... he drew something of divine quality directly from the heavens near which he lived."[8] These external phenomena teach us further about the providence of God and show that it is the place to begin. The youth must learn "that all things are ordained by the providence of God." When a man learns this fact, he will then know that he depends upon God.

Zwingli next considered the nature of the gospel. The young man must first learn about man—his original state,

> how he transgressed the commandment of God and became a prey to death, how by his transgression he infected and corrupted his offspring.

The youth may then be able to come to an existential recognition of his own sin.

> And he will see that sickness, too, when he realizes that everything we do has its origin in frailty, lust and temptation.[9]

---

7. E.g., in the works of Maffeo Vegio. See Rüsch, "Die humanistischen Vorbilder der Erziehungsschrift Zwinglis," pp. 130ff.

8. "The Original Life of Zwingli," in S. M. Jackson, ed., *The Latin Works of Huldreich Zwingli* (New York: Putnam, 1912), 1:2.

9. Quoted in Myconius, "The Original Life of Zwingli," p. 2.

This condition of man prevents his coming to God on his own merit. It is for this reason that grace is necessary, and it is here that grace breaks in.

> God requires of us a perfect righteousness, but we are corrupted and full of sin and whether we will or not we can do nothing but evil. Therefore we have no choice but to give up ourselves into the hand of God, to abandon ourselves entirely to his grace. And here it is that there breaks forth the light of the Gospel, the good news proclaimed to us that Christ releases us from the desperate plight in which we were held.[10]

This perfect righteousness can be found only in Christ, yet man may appropriate it so that he may be worthy before God. Man is still man, and as such does not find himself free from temptations or entirely without sin, "but Christ himself is ours and makes good all our deficiencies."

Although man cannot merit this righteousness, it does not follow that he is to do nothing. Zwingli reminded his readers that "confidence in Christ does not make us idle." Those who are truly the people of Christ cannot remain unmoved but must engage in His service. They must endeavor to live rightly.

This is the point at which education becomes important. We must "learn the Gospel with all exactness and diligence." Whenever the occasion presents itself,

> we should study what services will be most pleasing to God: and undoubtedly these are the very ones which he himself renders to us, righteousness, fidelity and mercy.[11]

It becomes the responsibility of the young man to study, "to grow up a man of God, righteous in life and as nearly like God as possible." Education emerges as one of the goals of life; a man is to educate himself in the ways of God and is to become like God.

The student and himself. The second part of the treatise is directed toward the education of the youth in personal matters, for,

> once a young man is instructed in the solid virtue which is formed by faith, it follows that he will regulate himself and richly adorn himself from within.[12]

The place to begin is with the study of the Scriptures, and in order

---

10. *Zwingli and Bullinger,* p. 106.
11. Ibid., p. 108.
12. Ibid.

to obtain the best understanding one must know the languages: Latin, Greek, and Hebrew. One does not learn languages merely for pleasure or profit, "for languages are gifts of the Holy Ghost." After the young man has the proper tools for studying Scripture, he must be careful to approach his study with the proper attitude, "a humble and thirsting spirit." The student will then look to Christ, who is the true pattern of conduct.

And if he knows Christ fully both in his words and deeds, he will know that in all his acts and counsels, so far as human frailty allows, he must venture to manifest some part of the virtues of Christ.[13]

Zwingli then discussed a number of the characteristics befitting the young man who follows Christ, "the perfect exemplar of all virtues."

Furthermore, the young Christian is to be a paragon of moderation, avoiding all manner of extremes. The Reformer pointed to specific instances requiring moderation. In the matter of conversation, Zwingli warned against excessive talking and against inappropriate style and gestures in public speaking. As for eating and drinking, Zwingli cited the example of Galen, the famous doctor of antiquity who "lived for a hundred and twenty years because he was never satisfied when he left the table."[14] The youth should avoid both extremes, "the man who is wolf-like in his voracity" and the one who "makes himself useless for the lack of sustenance."

Zwingli's approach was not that of the narrow pedant. After warning Gerold against expensive clothes, pointing to the poor baby Jesus, who had "no more clothes in which to be swaddled than those which the Virgin Mary had taken with her,"[15] the Reformer turned to a consideration of love.

It is when the young man begins to fall in love that he must show true nobility of spirit.... That he should fall in love is inevitable. But let him be careful not to give way to despairing passion.[16]

The Christian youth should shun fame and ambition, for "once this evil takes hold of the spirit, right conduct becomes impossible." A warning is given regarding mathematics (which includes music). It is not a forbidden subject, but neither does it merit much time.

---

13. Ibid.
14. Ibid., p. 111.
15. Ibid., p. 112.
16. Ibid.

Insofar as possible the Christian should avoid practicing the way of *art,* and above all the youth should avoid all signs of idleness.

The student and others. In the third part of the treatise on education, Zwingli addressed himself to the youth's relations to others. It is an essential relationship of the Christian life. Since Christ gave himself for others,

> we ought to give up ourselves for the good of all men, not thinking that we are our own, but that we belong to others.[17]

The youth is not to seek the quiet life, withdrawn from society, but rather to become involved actively in the socio-political sphere, serving the Christian community and the common good. The Christian is to be strong; only the weak retreat from the world. At this point Zwingli revealed a strong sense of community. Man does not live alone as an isolated individual. As a member of humanity, man is a part of the fortunes and griefs of everyone else.

Zwingli did not discourage the youth from recreation. He noted that Christ Himself did not despise the wedding feast. Zwingli permitted games, "but they ought to be useful either educationally or as bodily exercise." He encouraged many physical games, such as running and wrestling, but found only limited value in swimming.

The Christian youth is to be as like Christ as possible in his personal relationships. He should guard against anger and bitterness; he should honor his parents; and if it becomes necessary to oppose his parents because they are not following the mind of Christ, he must do it as gently as possible. Furthermore, the youth's speech should be characterized by truth and consistency. In fact, "we must study to be truthful not only in our words but in all our actions."[18] This is not an exhaustive list of the characteristics of the Christian youth, for such a list is not necessary. If the young man fixes his whole attention on Christ, "he will be a rule to himself." It is in following the way of Christ that the youth will find himself becoming the person Christ wants him to be. Zwingli concluded by noting that

> the true Christian is not the one who merely speaks about the laws of God, but the one who with God's help attempts great things.[19]

---

17. Ibid., p. 113.
18. Ibid., pp. 116, 117.
19. Ibid.

Oskar Farner and others suggested that this treatise also contained Zwingli's ideas for the reform of the school program in Zurich. In retrospect one must conclude that this is partly true, a conclusion which is reinforced by the fact that, even after election to the school board in 1524, Zwingli did not find it necessary to publish any other works on education.

The writing certainly betrays a strong humanistic bias, both in the curriculum it suggests and in the abundant reference to classical authors. E. G. Rüsch studied the treatise with an eye to the humanistic forerunners of Zwingli,[20] and his study reveals that in many ways Zwingli's views on education are essentially humanistic. An analysis of the work shows that, although its author is clearly a humanist, he is also an evangelical Christian. He began with God and ended with Christ, and he defined the goal of education in this context.

The proper goal of education was to render the student as much like Christ as possible,[21] and this was seen in its broadest outline. This meant essentially that the youth would grow into a Christian gentleman, certainly modeled after Christ but well educated in the humanities and having a well-developed body. Basically, the curriculum suggested by the treatise would provide an ethical (or moral), physical, and liberal-arts education, with a strong emphasis on the classics and languages. Zwingli placed little emphasis on natural science, but his personal library, if nothing else, reveals that he maintained a lively interest in the subject. One concludes that Zwingli considered the sciences less useful than classics or languages. Education for him was more than the mere dissemination of academic information; it also taught one how to live. The student needs this education, for man needs the example of Christ in order to live the worthwhile life. Man is dependent on the work of God in Christ to obtain the end which he wishes.

Educational Practice

Zwingli was involved in education from his earliest times in Zurich. He taught in the school of the Cathedral Chapter and in a community of theologues, the *sodalitium literarium Tigurense.*

20. *"Die humanistischen Vorbilder der Erziehungsschrift Zwinglis,"* passim.
21. Rückert, *Ulrich Zwinglis,* pp. 21ff. See also K. Spillmann, *"Zwingli und die Zürcher Schulverhältnisse,"* p. 429.

In 1523 the City Council issued a mandate for the reform of the monastery and of the schools. Dated 29 September, the ordinance provided for the appointment of

> well-learned, able, and honest men . . . to give public lectures day by day in Holy Scripture, for an hour in the Hebrew, an hour in the Greek, and an hour in the Latin tongue, as is necessary for the right understanding of divine Scripture.[22]

It was almost two years before Zwingli was in a position to implement the mandate. The first problem was financial, solved largely by reducing the number of canons in the Great Minster. The other problem was the two conservative opponents to school reform, Dr. Niessli and Konrad Hofmann. Not until Hofmann left Zurich in the summer of 1524 and Dr. Niessli died in April 1525, was Zwingli able to carry out his plan.

Zwingli was elected to the school board on 14 April 1525, thereby giving him official authority to oversee education in the city. His greatest contribution to the educational program of Zurich, however, was not in the realm of the lower schools, which were responsible for the primary education of students, but in the area of the education of ministers and theologues. In essence, as has often been pointed out, Zwingli's reform of the schools began at the top and moved downward.[23] The Reformer saw to it that the church leaders were educated and left to them the education of the masses. It is in the founding of the theological institute in Zurich that one finds the creative, new educational practice of Zwingli. Of course, the lower schools were also of concern to him, and he sought to improve the quality of instruction there.

To supply a well-educated clergy which was dedicated to the new situation in the church, Zwingli set up a theological institute, a prototype of the Reformed academies and the later theological faculty in Zurich, which he called the *Prophezei*—a novel but somewhat misunderstood name. The name *prophezei*, literally meaning "prophecy," was derived by Zwingli from I Corinthians 14, especially verses 19 and 28-33. It is interesting that Zwingli apparently misunderstood the passage, thinking that Paul was

---

22. In B. J. Kidd, ed., *Documents Illustrative of the Continental Reformation* (Oxford: Clarendon, 1911), no. 194.

23. E.g., in U. Ernst, *Geschichte des Zürcherischen Schulwesens bis gegen das Ende des sechzehnten Jahrhunderts* (Winterthur, 1879), p. 45. For a brief survey of the *"Deutschen Schulen"* and the *"Lateinschulen"* in Zurich, see Spillmann, "Zwingli," pp. 431-34.

referring to speaking in known languages rather than ecstatic utterances. Yet those who understood God's message were called prophets (v. 29), hence the term *prophezei*.

Zwingli needed competent linguists to assist in the school, and Zurichers Felix Manz and Conrad Grebel would have been the logical choices had they not gone over to the radicals. But he found the scholar he needed in Jakob Wiesendanger, or Ceporinus. *Herr Ciprin,* as the Zurichers called him, had spent several months in Zurich as a language teacher and then had carried on his studies and literary activity in Basel. Ceporinus was eminently qualified for the job, having studied with Reuchlin in Ingolstadt. After Hofmann died and Zwingli was able to use the funds allotted to the canon, he brought Jakob to Zurich. On 19 June, the new study group took its place in the choir on the Great Minster, and the instruction began.[24]

Pastors, preachers, canons, chaplains, and teachers attended. Zwingli offered the opening prayer:

> Eternally omnipotent and merciful God, whose word is a lamp unto our feet and a light unto our paths, open and illumine our minds so that we clearly and conscientiously understand your prophecies, and may be transformed by that which we shall have properly understood, by which we may not in any way be displeasing to your majesty. Through Jesus Christ our Lord, Amen.[25]

The procedure followed in the *Prophezei* is unique and interesting. First, a student read a passage from the Latin Bible, then Ceporinus read the same text in Hebrew and explained the meaning of the Hebrew in Latin. After Ceporinus finished, Zwingli read the same text from the Septuagint, and explained it in Latin. Finally, a preacher, generally Leo Jud, spoke homiletically on the text in German, thereby cementing the discussion in the minds of those attending and enabling them to speak to their laymen on that text. The session concluded, as it had begun, with prayer.[26]

The *Prophezei* met daily except market day, Friday, and Sunday. Since there was not yet a suitable lectorium, the choir of the

---

24. A description of the *Prophezei* from contemporary chronicles is in J. J. Hottinger and H. H. Vogeli, eds., *Heinrich Bullingers Reformationsgeschichte* (Frauenfeld: Beyel, 1838), 1:289-91.

25. Ibid., p. 290. For an analysis of the prayer in the light of the prayer (collect) for the Holy Spirit at Pentecost, see F. Schmidt-Clausing, *"Das Prophezeigebet,"* pp. 10-34.

26. The wording of such a concluding prayer has been transmitted in the Zurich Liturgy of 1535. It is given in O. Farner, *Huldrych Zwingli,* 3:556-58.

Great Minster was used. During the lifetime of Zwingli, this particular group studied only the Old Testament. Myconius led a similar group through the New Testament in the afternoons in the choir of the Fraumünster. After Ceporinus's untimely death at Christmas, 1525, Zwingli brought to Zurich the former Franciscan, Konrad Pellikan. In 1526 Zwingli also brought there two young scholars, Johann Jakob Ammann and Rudolf Collin, who took over the exposition of the Greek, thereby allowing Zwingli to dedicate himself more to summary and conclusions. As soon as one book was completed, they would move to the next. Should the Old Testament be finished, they were to begin it again.

Although it fell to certain authorities to speak on the passages under consideration, this method of instruction was not merely a one-sided lecture. Johann Kessler pointed out that if one of the pupils understood the passage under consideration better than the lecturer, it was the student's privilege and responsibility to point that out,[27] and the lecturer was to accept such suggestions in a friendly way. This corresponds more to the present-day seminar than to the lecture. The teacher was an authority, but not an authoritarian. In fact, the use of various authorities in the *Prophezei* is a near-perfect example of team teaching. Each teacher brought his expertise to the subject, and by means of dialogue, achieved the proper understanding. The *Prophezei* was actually a community of learners dedicated to finding the truth.

This approach is consistent with the training and understanding of Zwingli. Small units of material were selected which could be reasonably treated in a day. The only text was the Scripture itself, albeit in various translations. It is a linguistic approach to understanding the Christian sources; but above all it is a study of the sources themselves. The humanist's call, *ad fontes,* was fully carried out by the evangelical party in Zurich. Once the sources are understood, then the pupils are ready to speak to the laity. The approach itself reflects respect for the pupil; it is not authoritarian in discipline or one-sided. Fully in keeping with Zwingli's appreciation for society, the learning experience was in the context of a community of caring people. Personal relationships are inescapably important, and, as the personal tone of Zwingli's educational writing reveals, such relationships are the foundation of the learning experience. It is perhaps in this sense that Zwingli is a forerunner of modern educational techniques.

---

27. Quoted in Farner, *Huldrych Zwingli,* 3:560.

Selected Bibliography

Bromiley, G. W., ed. *Zwingli and Bullinger.* Library of Christian Classics, vol. 24. Philadelphia: Westminster, 1953.

Farner, O. *Huldrych Zwingli.* 4 vols. Zurich: Zwingli, 1943ff.

Gut, W. "Zwingli als Erzieher." *Zwingliana* 6:289-306.

Meister, W. *Volksbildung und Volkserziehung in der Reformation Huldrych Zwinglis.* Zurich: Zwingli, 1939.

Rückert, O. *Ulrich Zwinglis Ideen zur Erziehung und Bildung im Zusammenhang mit seinen reformatorischen Tendenzen.* Gotha: Thienemann, 1900.

Rüsch, E. G. "Die humanistischen Vorbilder der Erziehungsschrift Zwinglis." *Theologische Zeitschrift* 22:122-47.

Schmidt-Clausing, F. "Das Prophezeigebet: Ein Blick in Zwinglis liturgische Werkstaat." *Zwingliana* 12:10-34.

Spillmann, K. "Zwingli und die Zürcher Schulverhältnisse." *Zwingliana* 11:427-48.

Staehelin, R. *Huldreich Zwingli: Sein Leben und Wirken.* 2 vols. Basel: Schwabe, 1895-1897.

Zwingli, H. *An den jungen Mann.* Edited by E. G. Rüsch. Zurich: Zwingli, 1957.

10

George E. Ganss

Ignatius of Loyola
(1491-1556)

To be properly understood, the educational work of Ignatius of Loyola must be viewed against the historical background of the fifteenth and sixteenth centuries. At that time the Roman church was full of abuses and in need of reform "in head and members"; religious unity was crumbling in northern Europe; and southern Europe, though still one in faith, was beset by appalling ignorance of that faith and neglect of its practice. In the world of culture and education, various heritages of the past, such as monastic schools, cathedral schools, court schools, and universities still existed. In fact by 1450 some 150 schools of the Brethren of the Common Life were spread throughout Flanders, France, and Germany, and John Sturm conducted his marvelously organized gymnasium at Strasbourg after 1537. Yet many towns and cities, although awakening to the value of schools, still lacked them. Illiteracy was common; scarcely five percent of the population at large had more education than a little knowledge of reading, writing, and counting. The liberal education of the fifteenth-century Renaissance was in many places passing into a training in Ciceronianism and the form of the classical languages which is known as the narrow humanistic education.

His Life and Outlook

That was the world into which Ignatius, who was to become the founder of the Society of Jesus and of its system of Christian schools, was born in 1491 in his ancestral castle of Loyola near the Basque town of Azpeitia. From the time he was about fifteen until he was twenty-six, he was trained as a court page, and after 1516 he participated in military expeditions for the Duke of Nájera.

While recovering in 1521 from wounds received in the defense of Pamplona, he read *The Life of Christ* by Lodolph of Saxony and the *Legenda aurea*, short lives of the saints by Jacobus de Voragine. The result was his conversion, and he resolved to live as a knight wholly devoted to Christ. After a year of prayer and penance (1522-1523) at Manresa, and a pilgrimage to Jerusalem, he determined to make himself capable of helping others spiritually. Hence, at the age of thirty-three he began studies for the priesthood at the universities of Alcalá, Salamance, and especially Paris (1529-1535). With nine companions he founded the Jesuits, or Society of Jesus, a new religious order which was approved by Pope Paul III in 1540. From 1546 until his death in 1556, Ignatius especially devoted himself, as its superior general, to governing it, composing its *Constitutions* and founding thirty-three "colleges," three of them actually universities. He was, as is well known, a loyal Catholic. Although his life span coincided with the early years of the Reformation in northern Europe, he devoted himself more to reforming the Catholic church from within than to combatting the Protestants.

Ignatius was a deeply prayerful man, one of Christianity's greatest mystics. It was in his native Basque environment that he first inherited the Christian outlook on life, enveloped in sixteenth-century trappings. Through extraordinary mystical experiences at Manresa, he gradually conceived a world view which was centered around the divine plan in creating and redeeming man, and he intensely desired to be intimately associated with Christ and to cooperate with Him in achieving that plan as it slowly unfolded in history. He hoped through all his activities to bring greater praise to God than would have accrued to Him without those efforts. When confronted by a choice, he habitually decided on the basis of which procedure was likely to bring greater glory to God in the long run. As a result he employed the phrase "for the greater glory of God" *(ad majorem Dei gloriam)* so frequently that it became a motto of his order.

Ignatius's desire to cooperate with Christ was focused both on the Jesus who had lived in Judea, and also prominently upon the Savior, whom Ignatius saw in his vision at La Storta near Rome, in late 1537. The Lord he saw there was the glorified Christ, who was still present and was acting both in the church, His mystical body (for Ignatius, the Roman Catholic church), and in the pope whom he regarded as Christ's representative on earth. From the time of that vision, he determined to call the order he was founding the *Compañia de Jesus,* the group or company belonging to Jesus. As he saw it, those who joined should desire to give service to their fellow men through spiritual ministries, especially preaching, missionary evangelization anywhere on earth, and teaching.[1]

That, in compressed form, is the world view or philosophy of life, which, in his mature years, Ignatius projected into everything he wrote. In his *Spiritual Exercises* (published 1548) he applied it to aiding and inspiring individual persons ("exercitants") in the discovery of how they can serve God best. In his *Constitutions of the Society of Jesus,* written chiefly from 1547-1556, he applied it to organizing, inspiring, and governing an apostolic religious order. In part 4 of the *Constitutions,* he applied it to the order's activities in training youth to become good Christian citizens.

The first of Ignatius's "colleges" was the one at Paris, which he founded in 1540. These were residences for young members of his order who went to the public university for their lectures. Often, however, these lectures were unsatisfactory and were not part of an organized sequence of courses, hence lectures by Jesuit teachers were gradually introduced into these colleges.

The occasion which led Ignatius to make the training of lay youth one of the major occupations of his order was a request from the magistrates of Messina, Sicily, in 1547. Desiring to found a *studium generale,* or university, and "to obtain the benefits to a Christian state which ordinarily followed the Jesuits' activities,"

---

1. Ignatius's chief writings are his *Spiritual Exercises (Exercitia spiritualia), Constitutions of the Society of Jesus (Constitutiones Societatis Iesu), Letters (Epistolae et instructiones),* and *Autobiography.* Ignatius's *Constitutions* is available in an English translation by G. E. Ganss (St. Louis: Institute of Jesuit Sources, 1970). For copiously documented studies of Ignatius's interior life and world view, see J. de Guibert, *The Jesuits: Their Spiritual Doctrine and Practice,* trans. W. J. Young (Chicago: Loyola University, 1964), pp. 21-73; and Ganss, "Introduction," *Constitutions,* pp. 3-33.

they requested five masters to teach theology, the arts, rhetoric, and grammar. Seeing here an opportunity for Christian service, Ignatius sent ten of his best men to open the College of Messina in 1548. Gratifying results ensued, and from that point on Ignatius enthusiastically threw the resources of his order into educational work. Between 1546 and his death in 1556, he opened thirty-three colleges and approved six more.[2] His aims and hopes are best exemplified in the Roman College, later known as the Gregorian University.

His Educational Concepts

Meanwhile this experience was aiding him to perfect his educational concepts. A letter dated 1 December 1551, urging the foundation of colleges in Spain, contains a remarkable epitome of his purposes, procedures, curriculum, and methodology. In it Ignatius revealed his desire to give advice about the procedure and advantages of establishing colleges for the purpose of increasing service to God and aid to man. A guarantee of an annual sum should be sought from some city, ruler, or zealous person. A suitable building should be acquired, and two or three priests of sound doctrine and some seminarians ("scholastics") should be sent, who by their example, conversation, and teaching could help the pupils to advance in learning and virtue. The instruction should be free. The lower faculty of grammar and humane letters would be opened first. After the students had sufficiently learned these, a course in arts or philosophy would be inaugurated. After further progress someone should be named to lecture in theology.

The establishment of schools of this type would bring advantages to the Jesuits, in that they would learn much themselves by teaching and would be encouraged by the spiritual fruit of their labors; to the lay students, in that they, though often poor, would receive free teaching and be helped to develop a virtuous Christian life; and to the nation or region where the college would be situated. Ignatius concluded a statement of the social purposes of education by saying:

> From among those who are at present merely students, in time some will depart to play diverse roles: one to preach and carry on the care of souls, another to the government of the land and the admin-

---

2. They are listed in A. P. Farrell, *The Jesuit Code of Liberal Education* (Milwaukee: Marquette University, 1938), pp. 431-35.

istration of justice, and others to other occupations. Finally, since young boys become grown men, their good education in living and doctrine will be beneficial to many others, with the fruit expanding more widely every day.[3]

That letter and other sources clearly reveal Ignatius's procedure. He appropriated the structure of the four university faculties inherited from the Middle Ages and adapted it to his own purposes and spirit, which were in vital contact with the Renaissance culture of his day. His ideal school had at least three faculties. The lower faculty of languages was usually for boys aged ten to thirteen and was designed to impart facility in speaking, reading, and writing Latin, which was necessary then for further studies in any branch. This college, or faculty of languages, became a university when the higher faculties were added: the faculty of arts or philosophy, with chairs of logic, physics, mathematics, ethics, and metaphysics, for students about fourteen to sixteen; and the faculty of theology, with instruction in scholastic theology, Scripture, the fathers, and canon law. Faculties of civil law and medicine could be added but were, in fact, rare.

In general, Ignatius appropriated the pedagogical methods common to his day. Rather than inventing new methods, he chose from others the features he deemed best and adapted them to his own objectives. Reacting against the pell-mell disorder of the lecture system in Italian schools, he arranged the branches in a curriculum with an ordered sequence from grade to grade and made provision for more rapid advancement of the brighter, more diligent students. Disapproving mere passive attendance at lectures, he stressed much self-activity on the part of the students, "according to the method of Paris, with much exercise."

Ignatius gave his educational philosophy its longest and most mature expression in part 4 of his *Constitutions*.[4] After its official approval in 1558, this treatise remained both the inspiring force and the official law in Jesuit schools. Here he was not writing a theory of education in the abstract, as Plato did in *The Republic*, but statutes for conducting schools in the concrete circumstances of the Renaissance. As a result, his large and inspiring principles were intricately woven into structures and procedures often applicable only in his own era. We here cull eight of his perennial

---

3. The complete letter, in English, is in Ganss, *St. Ignatius' Idea of a Jesuit University* (Milwaukee: Marquette University, 1954), pp. 25-29.

4. *Constitutions* 307-509; cf. Ganss, *Constitutions*, pp. 171-229.

objectives from many more which could be documented from his *Constitutions* if space permitted.

First, "the end of the Society and of its studies is to aid our fellowmen to the knowledge and love of God and to the salvation of their souls."[5] Ignatius is here treating the ultimate end of education, the "end of the worker," which extends beyond the immediate task and to which the work of teaching is a means in the hierarchy of means and ends. The educator should stimulate the students to relate all their activity in this life to that ultimate end.

Second, the students should strive to master their fields of study, both sacred and secular.[6] In this he was treating the immediate end of teaching or studying, that is, mastery of the subject matter and the skills it entails.

Third, the Society of Jesus hopes by means of education to pour capable leaders into the social order, in numbers large enough to leaven it effectively for good.[7]

Fourth, the branches of the curriculum should be so integrated that each will make its proper contribution toward the integrating goal of the curriculum as a whole: a Christian outlook on life, as carefully and even scientifically reasoned out as possible. By the whole curricular structure of a university as given in the *Constitutions*,[8] Ignatius made clear that he desired all the particular truths learned in other faculties to be viewed in the light of God's revelation whenever it throws light upon them.

Fifth, theology should be regarded as the most important branch in the university, since the light it gives is the chief means of imparting the carefully-reasoned Christian world view and of tying the other branches into a unity. The other branches are worthy of serious study in themselves, but they are also handmaids of theology.[9] This importance given to theology is a matter of emphasis and outlook rather than hours in class, of an atmosphere in which professors and students alike view temporal goods as truly goods but also as means to man's eternal interests. In the early Jesuit schools most lay students had no formal instruction in theology beyond the classes in Christian doctrine, but they studied

5. *Constitutions* 446; cf. 307, 360, 392, 622. For further documentation on this and the remaining eight principles given here, see Ganss, *Constitutions,* pp. 210, 211 (n. 3).

6. *Constitutions* 460; cf. 341, 355, 356, 361.

7. Ibid., 622e.

8. Ibid., 442-52.

9. Ibid., 447-51.

in a cultural atmosphere permeated by the theological outlook of their Jesuit teachers.

Sixth, "very special care should be taken that those who come to the universities of the Society to obtain knowledge should acquire along with it good and Christian moral habits."[10] In other words, the formation should be both intellectual and moral, providing reasoned-out motives for moral living.

Seventh, the professors should be personally interested in the intellectual and spiritual progress of their students.[11]

And eighth, the schools should continually adapt their procedure to circumstances of time, place, and persons.[12]

His Significance

Many of the clergy and Christian laity had previously engaged in teaching youth, but Ignatius's society seems to have been the first religious order whose constitution made the conducting of Christian schools one of its major ministries. The Christian educational principles expressed in his dynamic synthesis were widely appropriated by other educators after him, so that they may seem commonplace today. In his own era, however, many of them were creatively original. They also had widespread and long-lasting effects within his own order. Through the thirty-three schools he founded throughout Europe, he set up a whole educational system which soon became larger than anything the world had seen before. It was an organization of schools which, though located in different countries, were governed by common statutes, followed one curriculum, reviewed and evaluated classroom and administrative experiences, exchanged competent teachers, and provided a steady supply of them. City after city sought to obtain a Jesuit school.

The tree Ignatius planted grew steadily for centuries after his death in 1556. In the *Constitutions,* Ignatius called for a separate set of ampler directives about the procedures, schedules, exercises, and other pedagogical means to achieve his large objectives better.[13] Hence a series of educational treatises which culminated in the definitive *Plan of Studies* (1599). It is more a document of curricular organization and pedagogical procedures than of educational

10. Ibid., 481.
11. Ibid.
12. Ibid., 488; cf. 395, 466.
13. Ibid., 455.

theory, since it was a means to achieve the large objectives which were presupposed from the *Constitutions* rather than restated. But it had great merit. In an age suffering from educational disorganization and seeking greater uniformity, the *Plan* sustained the unit of procedure in the far-flung Jesuit schools of Europe, the Americas, and Asia. Thus it fostered the growth of the Jesuit school system to extraordinary proportions. Jesuit institutions of secondary and higher education numbered 372 by 1625 and 612 by 1710. Shortly before the suppression of the Society in 1773, Jesuits were also directing 15 universities and staffing 176 seminaries.[14] Since the restoration of the Society in 1814, it is still inspired by Ignatius's objectives and has devoted an equal proportion of its manpower and effort to this work. For example, in the United States during the academic year 1969-70, the Jesuits conducted 18 universities and 10 colleges with a total enrollment of 149,456 students, and also 51 secondary schools enrolling 36,982.

All this Christian educational effort which he set in motion was a strong force in the recovery of the Catholic church from the disorganization and decay which were important causes of the Reformation. Perhaps more important, however, was the enormous benefit the education brought to individual students, by imparting to them a Christian outlook on life and a deep spirituality which made their lives far more significant and satisfying for this world and the next.

Selected Bibliography

Donohue, J. W. *Jesuit Education: An Essay on the Foundations of Its Idea.* New York: Fordham University, 1963.

Ignatius. *Autobiography. Fontes narrativi de S. Ignatio de Loyola et de Societatis Iesu initiis,* 1:354-507. Rome, 1943.

———. *Epistolae et instructiones S. Ignatii. Monumenta historica Societatis Iesu,* series 1. Madrid, 1903-1911.

———. *Exercitia spiritualia S. Ignatii eorumque directoria. Monumenta historica Societatis Iesu,* series 2. Madrid and Rome, 1919 and 1915.

———. *Sancti Ignatii constitutiones Societatis Iesu. Monumenta historica Societatis Iesu,* series 3. Rome, 1934ff.

Lukács, L., ed. *Monumenta paedagogica Societatis Iesu.* Vol. 1 (1540-1556). Rome, 1965.

---

14. For a map of the schools in Europe and many illustrations, see Ganss, *The Jesuit Educational Traditions and St. Louis University* (St. Louis: St. Louis University, 1969).

11

Carl S. Meyer

Philip Melanchthon
(1497-1560)

A pedagogue all his mature life, Philip Melanchthon began teaching at the University of Tübingen during his teen years and remained in the classroom until ten days before his death. His pedagogical endeavors also included writing textbooks, founding schools, and structuring curricula. He was the teacher of famous teachers, and the authorities regarded him as an authority.

During his own lifetime Melanchthon was known as *praeceptor Germaniae*,[1] a sobriquet that still belongs to him four hundred years after his death,[2] but he would have thought of himself primarily as a Christian educator. To him education must of necessity be Christian, and a Christian philosophy of education must embody both a due regard for the humanities and an existential role for piety.

Melanchthon received his B.A. degree in 1511 at the age of fourteen. By the time he was awarded the M.A. three years later,

---

1. C. L. Manschreck, *Melanchthon, the Quiet Reformer*, p. 131.

2. In the bibliography which he compiled in 1889, K. Hartfelder noted at least eight books whose titles called Melanchthon *Lehrer Deutschlands* or *praeceptor Germaniae. Philipp Melanchthon als Praeceptor Germaniae* (Berlin, 1889; reprinted Nieuwkoop: DeGraaf, 1964), pp. 621-45 (numbers 40, 113, 135, 153, 157, 239, 269, 368).

he had already served as tutor to two sons of a nobleman and been praised as a born teacher. By the age of nineteen he had lectured on the Latin dramatist Terence and had published an edition of the works of this apt teacher of rhetoric and morals.

The Christian Humanist

Rhetoric held a dominant place in Melanchthon's thinking not only as a young lecturer in Tübingen but also as an established mentor at Wittenberg.[3] In one of his early orations, "The Liberal Arts," delivered in 1517, Melanchthon praised the traditional seven liberal arts of the *trivium* and *quadrivium*. (The *trivium* consisted of grammar, dialectics, and rhetoric.) He was not so narrow in his outlook, however, that he would confine the "liberal arts" to rhetoric; instead, he expanded them to include history and poetry.

His *Three Books on Rhetoric* appeared in 1519, and it was the first of a series of texts on rhetoric which he pressed into the service of the gospel as a sharpened tool for the kerygmatic function of the church. He wrote several treatises on the art of preaching, and his first manual on rhetoric had a section addressed specifically to those who are called to preach. Eloquence was the foundation for solid doctrine as well as for the servant of the gospel. He wrote:

> And ever since Paul opposed "peddlers of God's word," no one traffics in the Word of God more impudently than those, who neither by death or erudition can prove themselves good; they gain the favor of the impious masses by their treatment of sacred letters. How so? You see them reject our writings, by which everything good and honest, by which piety, by which public morals, indeed by which Christ Himself is spoken of.[4]

He cited himself as a promoter of things holy and of Christ Himself.

The cause of the Reformation, which to Melanchthon was synonymous with the cause of the gospel, required the promotion of learning. He felt that the seven liberal arts (especially rhetoric), history, poetry, the languages, and the Scriptures require study and mastery.

It is this program which identifies Melanchthon as a Christian humanist. Indeed Melanchthon cannot be understood as an edu-

---

3. W. Maurer, *Der junge Melanchthon zwischen Humanismus und Reformation* (Göttingen: Vandenhoeck and Ruprecht, 1967), 1:111-16, 190-98.
4. *"Encomion eloquentiae"* (1523), in *Melanchthon Werke in Auswahl*, ed. R. Stupperich (Gütersloh: Gerd Mohn, 1961), 3:58.16-22 (hereafter cited as StA). The reference is to II Cor. 2:17.

cator if he is not taken seriously as a Christian humanist. He spelled out these convictions in his inaugural address at the University of Wittenberg on 29 August 1518. In it he made a strong plea for the study of the languages.

And so because theology is partly Hebrew, partly Greek (for we drink of their streams in Latin), the foreign languages are taught not as dumb external things, when we guide theologians.[5]

Closely connected with the study of languages was the study of Holy Writ. Called as professor of Greek, he began his career in Wittenberg with lectures on Homer and on Paul's Letter to Titus.

In other contexts too Melanchthon showed his great concern for the study of the languages. In his introductory letter for the *Clarorum virorum epistolae latinae graece et hebraicae variis temporibus missae ad Ioannem Reuchlin Phorensem LL.doctorem,* Melanchthon gloried in the multilingual character of the letters.[6] In his preface to Luther's commentary on the Psalms (1519), he discoursed on theological studies and pointed out the necessity for learning the languages, paying tribute in the process to Erasmus, Reuchlin, and others for their contributions in this area. In his thinking the gospel, the church, and the doctrine of Christ gain by the pursuit of the ancient tongues. In commending a student to his friend Egerbach, Melanchthon said, "He is able to philosophize with you both in Greek and Latin." And in a poem for another friend, Joachim Camerarius, Melanchthon praised him for his command of rhetoric, Greek, and Hebrew.[7] His oration at the opening of the Latin school in Nürnberg (1526), a school devoted to humanism, praised the Florentines for supporting professors of Greek, "the unique monument of religion." It was a high compliment for the German city to have its achievement linked with the Italian center of art and learning. Melanchthon, however, reminded his German audience,

Unless you preserve letters, religion and good laws cannot endure; moreover, may God grant that you instruct your children for virtue and religion.[8]

---

5. "*De corrigendis adolescentiae studiis*" (1518), StA, 3:40.11-14.
6. *Corpus Reformatorum: Philippi Melanthonis opera quae supersunt omnia,* ed. G. Bretschneider and H. E. Bindseil (Halle, 1834-1860), 1:4, 5, no. 1 (hereafter cited as CR).
7. CR, 1:644, no. 262. He recommended Camerarius to the council of Nürnberg. CR, 1:713, no. 314.
8. StA, 3:68.34-37.

Nowhere else, however, does Melanchthon praise the study of languages more highly than in an oration on the study of Greek, prepared for Vitus Oertel. An emphasis on Greek was a relatively rare note, even in 1549. To minimize the study of Greek for Melanchthon meant to succumb to the blandishments of the devil; this *satanicus error* deserves the severest pains of hell. He saw Greek as the sweetest and most erudite of languages and worthy of study, for in it, "God, the Father of our Lord and Savior Jesus Christ, [conveyed] the immense treasure of sacred doctrine." He also said,

> For firstly God entrusted the New Testament to this language, that is His doctrine, in which He sent us a Messenger and Teacher, His eternal Son.[9]

Melanchthon had other reasons for the study of Greek (e.g., its value for mathematics), but his primary emphasis was on its usefulness in the study of pure religion. He also quoted Luther in speaking a good word for the study of Hebrew. He held that the languages were to be preserved for the sake of the light of the celestial doctrines, given by the eternal and most gracious God. Examples from Melanchthon's writings could be multiplied, but little could be added to the expressions of praise he heaped on the study of the Greek, Latin, and Hebrew languages.

The Classicist

Melanchthon's appraisal of classical authors will also give us insight concerning his stress on languages. He praised many Greek authors, but none more than Homer.

> He provides many instructions and wise exhortations by means of general and very useful rules and regulations for morals, which will prove profitable throughout life and in all circumstances. He lets drop in the most delicate manner decent and wholesome information for discretion, modesty, and other virtues. There is no better teacher than Homer for graciousness and refinement of manners.[10]

Melanchthon translated eighteen of the tragedies of Euripides into Latin, and they were meaningful to him because they provided

> the most serious examples and topics, which admonish us about many aspects of life and ... supply for writing excellent ornaments of style.

9. Ibid., 3:139.18-23.
10. *"Praefatio in Homerum,"* CR, 11:403, no. 53.

Among the philosophers he spoke of Plato as the most eloquent and Aristotle as the surest guide for morals. The fables of Aesop were of special worth because, during all periods of history and in all forms of literature, including Sacred Writ, fables had been used for the instruction of the young.[11]

Melanchthon demanded of the authors he recommended that they further the manners and morals as well as the literary accomplishments of the students. Plutarch qualified on both counts. In the preface to Plutarch he repeated a thought in his 1516 oration:

> It seems that we are advised to love the best of the classical writings, which pertain to training in the languages and the formation of a philosophy of life.[12]

Cicero, however, as a Latin author, was unsurpassed in Melanchthon's estimation: "Everybody knows that Cicero is the foremost master of style."

Melanchthon took a pragmatic approach to the classical writers when it came to ethics. Throughout his teaching career he looked to the ethical stance of the writer in the evaluation of a classical work. *Euriditio* was coupled with *emmendatio vitae* in his thinking. Along these lines he said, "For who has a place for moral philosophy, whom Demosthenes and Cicero did not influence?"

For Melanchthon, Aristotle was the outstanding writer when it came to ethics, a philosophy of truth. He wrote a commentary on Aristotle's writings, having lectured repeatedly on the Stagirite.

Credit for being the first Protestant to write a philosophical treatment of ethics must go to Melanchthon. In that endeavor he used as a model the *Nicomachean Ethics* of Aristotle. In 1538 his epitome of ethics appeared, followed by revisions in 1540 and 1546 and a third edition in 1550. In his writings he defined moral philosophy as "that part of divine law, which gives precepts about external actions."

A careful distinction between philosophy and theology marked Melanchthon's thinking. The gospel, the law of God, and philosophy ought not to be confused. He said:

> Accordingly great praise belongs to moral philosophy, which is part of the divine law and the wisdom of God, although it is not the Gospel.[13]

---

11. In his preface to a collection of Aesop's fables, in CR, 7:561, no. 4689.
12. CR, 1:74, no. 37. See also his letter to Feldkirck, in CR, 1:79, 80, no. 41.
13. StA, 3:158.30-32.

Moral philosophy is an unfolding of natural law. Combining discipline and education makes it useful for magistrates, the governing of political units, and the interpretation of laws.

Since moral philosophy is part of the law of God, as said above, precisely man's end is the same according to divine law and according to true philosophy, namely to know God and to obey Him, and to disclose and adorn His glory, and to preserve human society before God. For men are made in the image of God, that in it God is apparent and known.[14]

Recognizing both the merits and shortcomings of moral philosophy, Melanchthon examined the teachings of the Epicureans and the Stoics. The concept "virtue" *(virtus)* was of prime importance to him here; he defined it as "the condition which inclines the will to obeying right reason." The gospel and the Spirit of God, however, give a different approach to the question and raise the problem of free will. Extensive examination of the problem led Melanchthon to reject the Stoic position. An examination of the emotions of man led to the conclusion that men "do not please God without fear or faith."[15] Only Christ's doctrine can adequately set forth the cause of love, not philosophy.

Law and gospel, in Melanchthon's terminology, must be distinguished when one speaks about fear and faith. It calls for a definition of the term *iustitia,* not a simple term, differing in philosophy and theology. It is significant to note that throughout his discussion Melanchthon maintained the Christian perspective in his ethical discussions. He wrote, for instance:

Why, I pray you, Son of God, Lord Jesus Christ, were you crucified for us and risen, but that you might teach us and intercede for us before the Eternal Father, and govern us by your Holy Spirit, gather for yourself a church among us, heal our wounds and mitigate [our] penalties by your immense goodness when you testified by assuming human nature that you loved humankind most sincerely.[16]

This illustration shows how Melanchthon can use humanistic concepts and classical formulations in the service of the gospel and Christian education, viewing Greek moral philosophy as of consequence.

---

14. Ibid., 163.35-164.6.
15. Ibid., 191.17.
16. Ibid., 355.21-26.

The Historian

For Melanchthon history is closely akin to moral philosophy. We have noted that in 1517 he added poetry and history to the seven liberal arts of the schools. History meant for him a knowledge of the Greek and Latin historians of antiquity. Within a year he wrote: "Histories are examples of the wrath and grace of God, Law and Gospel."[17]

The study of history, he believed, is essential to the study of theology. Without a knowledge of history, humanity is condemned to perpetual childhood, a lasting blindness. He saw history as belonging to the *opera eloquentiae,* a vital part of the pedagogical task. Among the uses he saw for history, therefore, were the moral, theological, and practical.

"History is utterly necessary for this thing [the study of the classics]..."[18] because history instructs by examples, and many examples can be cited from the writings of the ancients. In his introduction to the revised chronicle by Carion, he pointed to the usefulness of history in providing examples for conduct.

In an oration on the life of Joseph Bugenhagen, Melanchthon cited the late pastor of the Wittenberg church as an example from which youth could learn about doctrine and life. He saw Bugenhagen as an example of a man capable of and involved in change,

> for it is of great importance to posterity to know of what kind these changes were, how the teachings of the past were changed and battered, and which princes and governments were helped by these studies.[19]

We might note that Melanchthon also stressed instruction in music. The *Visitation Articles* of 1528 provided for daily instruction in singing, and he pleaded that music be used to the praise and glory of God, for it is a gift of God.

The study of nature and history were closely connected in Melanchthon's system of thought, so closely that Wilhelm Maurer maintained he identified them. Mathematics and physics were of importance to him in the education of the Christian, and to

---

17. *"Artifitium epistolae Pauli ad Romanos a Philippo Melanchthone,"* in E. Bizer, *Texte aus der Anfangszeit Melanchthons* (Neukirchen-Vluyn: Neukirchener, 1966), p. 20. Again (1521) he wrote, "Histories are examples of the work of God pertaining to the Law and the Gospel." Ibid., p. 46.

18. StA, 3:39.13.

19. CR, 12:296.

Melanchthon must go primary credit for introducing the natural sciences into the curricula of the schools and universities. It is true that he held to the validity of astrology, believing that the stars rule men *(astra regunt homines)*, yet his commentary *De anima* is a tract that evolved from his concern for genuine physics and psychology. Wilhelm Dilthey called it "a transformation of the Aristotelian work from a theological point of view." Melanchthon used theological terms in his definitions and thus pressed psychology into the service of the church. In his discussion, free will rather than intelligence becomes the high point.

To understand Melanchthon as educator one must understand his concept of free will. *De anima* (1553) contains his mature and independent concept *de libero arbitrio*. He rejected the Stoic teachings because man is not able to do away with sin and death.

> The human will, not reborn by the light of the Gospel and the Holy Spirit, is not able to produce the true fear of God, a firm assent, trust and love of God, true patience and constancy in great dangers, and similar spiritual operations, much less is it able to take upon itself the perfect obedience of the law of God.[20]

Therefore he invoked the Son of God to gather His church and enlighten the minds and wills of His people.

Melanchthon felt that the educational task must include and be governed by the precepts of the Lord. He refuted Pico della Mirandola's contention that philosophy is superior to rhetoric, arguing that wisdom must be transmitted, not merely taught. Wisdom is the revelation of God in the Word of God, that is, in the incarnation and in the Scriptures.

> For wisdom is not only the Word of God revealed in creation, in the salvation of man in the Church, but also in the Law and Gospel.

Sapientia carnalis and *sapientia rationis* are not enough to insure man's well-being. In an autographed inscription of a Bible (1542) Melanchthon emphasized:

> We should not regard this command as insignificant, to learn, read, and consider with great earnestness the Word of God revealed by the prophets and Apostles. For without this Word the human heart is full of blindness and falls miserably into the devil's snare and error and sin.[21]

---

20. StA, 3:353.31-352.2.
21. O. Walz, "*Epistolae Reformatorum* I," *Zeitschrift für Kirchengeschichte* 1 (1877): 148, no. 26. See C. S. Meyer, "Melanchthon as Educator and Humanist," *Concordia Theological Monthly* 31 (1960): 536, 537.

The Christian Educator

In the *Visitation Articles* of 1528, Melanchthon, concerned about the betterment of the parishes, placed religious education at the core of all instruction.[22] The school plan which he proposed called for dividing the pupils into three groups or classes. The children of the first division were to use the children's manual,[23] which contained the alphabet, the Lord's Prayer, the Creed, and other prayers. He did, however, provide for a balance in his instructional directive; he knew that religious education should be imparted in both the home and the church. There would be regular attendance at the church services during the week, so he prescribed that on one day of the week (which he evidently regarded as sufficient under the circumstances) Christian instruction, based on Holy Writ, be given the children.

> For some teach absolutely nothing out of the Sacred Scriptures; some teach the children absolutely nothing but the Sacred Scriptures; both of which are not to be tolerated.[24]

Melanchthon, the humanist, favored an education that made religion an integral part of the instruction, rather than its entirety.

In the second division of the school plan for the *trivia* schools, which he set up in 1528, he provided for a review of the Decalogue, the Creed, and the Lord's Prayer. He wanted the pupils to learn some of the easy Psalms (112, 34, 128, 125, 127, 133). The Gospel according to Matthew, Paul's two letters to Timothy, the First Letter of John, and the Proverbs of Solomon were to be added to the pensum as the pupils matured. By this time some of the pupils would be in the third division. Beyond that, however, he felt that the schoolmaster should not attempt any other Scriptural writings.

---

22. CR, 26:3-27, 41-96; H. Lietzmann, *Kleine Texte für Vorlesugen und Ubungen* (Bonn: Marcus and Weber, 1912), no. 87; "Instructions for the Visitors of Parish Pastors," trans. C. M. Jacobs in *Luther's Works* (Philadelphia: Fortress, 1958), 40:263-320; "Book of Visitation School Plan," trans. H. Barnard, in F. Eby, ed., *Early Protestant Educators*, pp. 180-87; StA, 1:215-71. Only the StA will be cited in future references.

23. Melanchthon's *Enchiridion elementorum puerilium* (Wittenberg, 1524). In CR, 20:391-424; and Hartfelder, *Philipp Melanchthon*, p. 584, no. 84. See also Melanchthon's *Handbuchlein, wie man die kinder zu der geschrift und lere halten sol* (Wittenberg, 1524), in CR, 23:107ff.; and *Catechises puerilis*, in CR, 23:103-93, and in Hartfelder, *Philipp Melanchthon*, p. 620, no. 703.

24. StA, 1:269.29-31.

For it is not profitable to burden these young people with difficult and exalted books. Some [teachers] read Isaiah, St. Paul's Letter to the Romans, the Gospel according to St. John, and others of that kind, to enhance their own reputation.[25]

Melanchthon saw it as essential that "children learn the foundations of a Christian and godly life." Faith, the fear of God, and good works were to be impressed upon the pupils by the schoolmaster. His scheme for the religious education of pupils in the lower school had well-defined aims and objectives; it was life-centered and pupil-oriented in its indoctrination. The Scripture-based content of the instruction was in accord with the *sola Scriptura* principle of the Reformation and the *ad fontes* principle of humanism.

The same principles upon which the *trivia* schools were based became the basis for the Latin schools which he set up. He was much more general in the principles he advocated for the humanistic school at Nürnberg, but he intended that the will of God be a guiding principle of this school as well. He wrote in support of such schools as he had occasion,[26] and he told the Council of Nürnberg that "to found a good school in which good manners and conduct are taught is not a mean thing."

Nor did Melanchthon forsake these principles in structuring the curriculum of the colleges and universities. His role in reorganizing the University of Wittenberg should not be underestimated. His first concern was that the studies carried on at the University might conform to the doctrine "by which God calls and gathers His eternal church." The regulations called for the study of Latin, grammar, dialectics, rhetoric, philosophy, arithmetic, physics, and Aristotle's ethics. They required, moreover, that all those preparing to teach in the church must learn Greek and Hebrew, for the sources *(fontes)* of the church's doctrine lie in the Greek and Hebrew languages.[27]

It was noteworthy to this writer that Melanchthon placed great emphasis on the church! This is shown in such statements as, "God

---

25. Ibid., 270.37-271.3. See the context, 269.36-271.3.

26. See, e.g., *Ein Nutzbarliche Schone Ermanung* (1540), in Hartfelder, *Philipp Melanchthon*, p. 597, no. 348. This tract was addressed to the city of Soest. Cf. the tract published in 1533, in Hartfelder, *Philipp Melanchthon*, p. 591, no. 218.

27. *Ein Nutzbarliche Schone Ermanung*, sig. A iii[r]; see also D ii[v]. Also see *Leges Academiae Witebergensis* (Wittenberg, 1562), sig. A 4[r-v]. The latter is on microfilm in the Library of the Foundation for Reformation Research, St. Louis.

always gathers the church and does not want learning and erudition
to perish." The language is unmistakably Melanchthon's, and the
ecclesiological emphasis is his. His approach was that of the churchman with a high regard for humanistic pursuits, but with the
end in view that these serve the church and that they be maintained by God for the sake of the church, not vice versa. The
theological professors were pledged to teach in accordance with
and to defend the three ecumenical creeds (the Apostles', the
Nicene, and the Athanasian) and the Augsburg Confession (1530).

For the college of liberal arts (to use a twentieth-century term),
the statutes provided ten professorships. Besides a tutor or pedagogue, there were two professorships each for Latin, mathematics,
dialectics, and rhetoric, and one each for physics, Hebrew, Greek,
and ethics.[28] The lack of a "professor of religion" does not mean
that religion was neglected in the liberal arts curriculum, for the
rector of the University, none other than Melanchthon himself,
set forth the cause of the gospel to the students in frequent addresses and discourses.

It is impossible to present in detail Melanchthon's emphasis on
philosophy in the training of the youth at the University and the
role which reason played in his educational philosophy. It should
be noted, however, that he held reason to be necessary for theological formulations and discourse. Theologians, he wrote to Camerarius, should study logic since that was essential to anyone
who did not want to become a blockhead. Logic and order are
necessary, he held, for teaching correct doctrine. To attempt to do
theology justice without an adequate educational background is
to try to fly without feathers. He asserted that the study of philosophy is necessary to learn the right methods for borrowing materials
and integrating them into Christian theology.[29] Theology enlarges
philosophy, in his view, and philosophy completes the content of
theology. Melanchthon said that he would not have known how to
use philosophy if he had not come to faith in the gospel; he
asserted that it would be ingratitude to decline this benefit of
the gospel. He also looked at philosophy as a very pragmatic
discipline. He presented details about proper philosophizing,

---

28. *Ein Nutzbarliche Schone Ermanung*, sig. D iii2-E ir. The *Leges* also
provided for ten professorships. Sig. E iiir-v. Hartfelder discussed the structure
of the University in *Philipp Melanchthon*, pp. 436-49.

29. Manschreck, "Reason and Conversation in the Thought of Melanchthon,"
in *Reformation Studies*, ed. F. H. Littell (Richmond: Knox, 1962), p. 169.

obviously keeping in mind that there were those who denied the roles of philosophy, reason, and learning in general in Christian higher education.

The relationship and roles of logic and philosophy, as Melanchthon conceived them, were utilized concretely in the *loci* ("topics") method which followed. His definition of a *locus* reads:

> A dialectical *locus* is a *sedes argumenti* [an area for discussion], or rather, an index pointing out where the source of the material is located from which the material is to be drawn by which a proposition in question is to be confirmed.[30]

Whether Melanchthon followed Aristotle or Cicero in his concept of a *locus,* and what he owed to Agricola and Erasmus for this concept, cannot be explored here. At the very close of his life, in the preface to the 1559 edition of his *Loci praecipui theologici,* Melanchthon set down the rationale for the *loci* method.

> God has formed men in such a way that they think in terms of numbers and arrangement, and in learning one thing or another they are frequently helped by numbers and orderly arrangement. Thus in transmitting the arts special care is given the order of the divisions of the various arts; and the principles, the direction the arts take and the limitations of the study are indicated. In philosophy this manner of making things clear is called method. But the method which is employed for demonstration in the arts is different from the method used in the teaching of the Church. The demonstrative method proceeds from those things which are subject to the senses and from prime notions which are called principles. In the teaching of the Church only a proper order of arrangement is called for, not a method of demonstration. For the doctrine of the Church is not obtained from demonstrations, but from words which God has committed to our human race by means of sure and clear evidences, words through which out of His immense goodness He has disclosed Himself and His will.[31]

Certainty in the church is found in the revelation of God, not in the judgment of man.

> We become certain of the articles of faith by divine revelation which God establishes with sure and clear testimonies. . . .

Philosophical doubts should not touch matters of faith, and there-

---

30. CR, 13:659. See discussion of Melanchthon's use of terms *loci* and *loci communes,* in Q. Breen, *Christianity and Humanism* (Grand Rapids: Eerdmans, 1968), p. 102.

31. Trans. R. Preus, *Bulletin of the Library* (of the Foundation for Reformation Research) 1 (1966): 13.

fore the teachers of the church present matters of faith as given by God.

> Because simple people do not everywhere understand the nature of theological discourse and do not immediately see the arrangement of the materials, the voice of the interpreters must teach them about the nature of the language and the arrangement of the things discussed.[32]

Melanchthon himself summarized his approach:

> Let them [teachers] teach philosophy in such a way that they do not corrupt the teaching of the Gospel.

All education is to harmonize with the pure teachings of the church. By way of illustration we may look at a practical application of this principle made by Melanchthon in 1539. In the course of the visitation of Ducal Saxony for Duke Henry, he encountered a pastor at Weissensehe who, he recommended, should be deposed because he was unlearned and frivolous, and lived a scandalous life.

The Writer of Catechisms

More needs to be said about Melanchthon's catechisms, although they were overshadowed by Luther's *Small Catechism* and *Large Catechism,* published in 1529. Melanchthon published seven catechetical works before 1529.[33] In these catechisms he treated primarily the Ten Commandments, the Lord's Prayer, and the Creed. All but the first two were strongly conditioned by the fact of the Peasants' Revolt. The author seems somewhat frustrated in his attempts to communicate the gospel to an uneducated and unbridled people. He was rigoristic and even moralizing in his treatment of the law; he tended toward intellectualism in his treatment of the gospel. Nevertheless, throughout his various presentations, there was an understanding of the prior and overarching action of God, as Giver of both law and gospel.

---

32. Ibid.
33. *Supplementa Melanchthoniana* (Leipzig: Haupt, 1915), 5:i. The seven, and where they appear in this volume, are: *In caput Exodi XX Scholia*, pp. 3-19; *Enchiridion elementorum puerilium*, pp. 20-56; *Paraphrasis Domincae orationis*, pp. 57-60; *Etliche Spruche darin das ganze chrisliche Leben gefasst ist*, pp. 61-73; *Kurze Auslegung der gehn Gebote*, pp. 74, 75; *Kurze Auslegung des Vaterunsers*, pp. 76, 77; *Eine kurze Auslegung der kehn Gebote des Vaterunsers und Glauben*, pp. 78-88.

Melanchthon's most extensive catechetical work appeared in 1543 (perhaps as early as 1540) in Latin, with a German translation the same year. Called *Catechesis puerilis,* the work is fashioned according to the *loci* method. The main topics treated are law, gospel, justification, good works, preservation of faith, the sacraments (in general), baptism, confession, and the Lord's Supper. About seventy-eight percent of the space is devoted to an exposition of the law. It forms Melanchthon's clearest summary of what he regarded as the Christian position toward the socioeconomic, political, and ecclesiastical milieu. The effectiveness of the Christian position, he held, is dependent on the gospel. Throughout his lengthy exposition of the Decalogue, Melanchthon emphasized the principle that the law can be obeyed only by the followers of Christ.

Of his other catechetical writings, the *Catechism Lateinisch und Deutsch* is notable for its delineation "of the principal powers of the human nature." Here he discussed the natural law, the senses, the emotions, and free will. The last topic was not discussed in its relationship to regeneration, but in its relationship to external works.

All of Melanchthon's catechetical works show his inability to get down to the elementary levels of instruction. The last of his catechisms, however, following the basic outline of Luther's *Small Catechism,* comes closest to achieving this goal. In it he followed an approach of simple informational questions rather than the *loci* approach. Although he was always Scripture-oriented, the humanist is evident in his quotations and references. He felt that all learning is to be put into the service of the church, but he was eminently conscious of the fact that he was writing books of instruction for children in a society in which the state played a major role in directing the affairs of the church. Thus obedience to the government meant obedience to God.

The Civil Pragmatist

Melanchthon, no less than Luther, was aware of the role of the government in education. R. Freeman Butts made it clear that the stimulus of men like Luther, Bugenhagen, and Melanchthon caused the civil authorities to take hold of educational reform during the Reformation era. Butts contended that "one of the most far-reaching and profoundly important results of the Reformation was the growth of civil control of education as opposed to private and religious control."[34]

Melanchthon, like Luther, encouraged the civil powers to found and maintain schools. To him has been ascribed the paternity of the modern system of state schools. He prepared school plans for Eisleben (1525), Nürnberg (1526), Saxony (1528), Herzeberg (1538), Cologne (1543), Wittenberg (1545), Mecklenberg (1552), and the Palatinate (1556). The plans for Eisleben and Nürnberg were not different from the others. The Nürnberg school is one of the most famous which Melanchthon helped to fashion. There Jerome Baumgartner and Lazarus Spengler were influential members of the Council, and it was the Town Council which Melanchthon advised.

The universities also were regulated by the civil authorities. In the case of the University of Wittenberg, authority rested in the Elector of Saxony, Frederick the Wise, who had founded the University in 1502. The Elector's wisdom and ability are demonstrated by the fact that he invited Johann Reuchlin to be professor of Greek upon the suggestion of Melanchthon. After the Leipzig Debate, John Eck wrote to the Elector Frederick:

> I humbly pray your Grace not to take it ill nor with displeasure that I have allowed myself to debate with your Grace's professors from Wittenberg, for I did not do it to hurt your Grace's university, but, on the contrary, am much inclined to serve your Grace, as one who is renowned before other princes of the Empire *for cherishing letters and learned men*.[35]

Carlstadt and Luther were "your Grace's professors," and the University was "your Grace's university." Melanchthon knew this, and the councilors of the Elector could turn to him for information and advice. The laws promulgated for the University were promulgated in the name of the Elector, and Wittenberg's dependence on him is well known and needs no further elaboration. Less well known are the facts that Melanchthon served as advisor to Philipp of Hesse in the founding of the University of Marburg (1527), and that the University of Königsberg (1542), founded by

---

34. *A Cultural History of Western Education* (New York: McGraw-Hill, 1955), p. 207. An excellent summary of Luther's and Melanchthon's educational activities is L. C. Green, "The Reformation and Education in the Sixteenth Century," *Bulletin of Appalachian State University: Faculty Publications, 1969-70* 67 (1970): 34-49.

35. In P. Smith and C. M. Jacobs, eds., *Luther's Correspondence* (Philadelphia: Lutheran Publication Society, 1918), 1:202, 203. Italics are the editors'. The letter is dated 22 July 1519.

Margrave Albert von Hohenzollern, was erected under Melanchthonian auspices. The University of Jena was founded by John Frederick of Saxony in 1548, and it, too, was under Melanchthonian leaders in its beginnings. Ulrich von Württemberg was aided in the reorganization of the University of Tübingen by Melanchthon, and Joachim Ivon Brandenburg in the reorganization of the University of Frankfort on the Oder. Sufficient illustrations have been cited to demonstrate Melanchthon's cooperation with the civil authorities in the furtherance of education, particularly on the secondary and higher levels.

The Influential Educator

It would be futile to try to list all the educators of northern Europe whom Melanchthon influenced directly. Such a list would include almost every outstanding German educator from about 1525 to 1575. It would be equally futile to tell about his influence in other Protestant countries, especially Scandinavian and Baltic countries and England. His influence on Lutheran education was far-reaching.

Perhaps as good a summary as any of Melanchthon as educator can be found in his own words:

I apply myself solely to one thing, the defence of letters. By our example we must excite youth to the admiration of learning, and induce them to love it for its own sake, and not for the advantage that may be derived from it. The destruction of learning brings with it the ruin of everything that is good—religion, morals, and all things human and divine. The better a man is, the greater his ardor in the preservation of learning; he knows that of all plagues, ignorance is the most pernicious.... To neglect the youth in our schools is just like taking the spring out of the year. They, indeed, take away the spring from the year who permit the schools to decline, because religion cannot be maintained without them. And a terrible darkness will fall upon society, if the study of the sciences should be neglected.[36]

Selected Bibliography

Eby, F., ed. *Early Protestant Educators.* New York: McGraw-Hill, 1931.
Green, L. C. "Melanchthon." *The Encyclopedia of the Lutheran Church,* vol. 2. Minneapolis: Augsburg, 1965.

---

36. Quoted in F. V. N. Painter, *A History of Education* (New York: Appleton, 1896), p. 150.

Loffler, K. "Melanchthon." *The Catholic Encyclopedia,* vol. 10. New York: Encyclopedia, 1913.

Manschreck, C. L. *Melanchthon, the Quiet Reformer.* Nashville: Abingdon, 1958.

Melanchthon, P. *Selected Writings.* Translated by C. L. Hill and edited by E. E. Flack and L. J. Satre. Minneapolis: Augsburg, 1962.

Tillman, W. G. *The World and Men Around Martin Luther.* Minneapolis: Augsburg, 1959.

Vajta, V., ed. *Luther and Melanchthon.* Philadelphia: Muhlenberg, 1961.

12

Marshall Coleman Dendy

John Knox
(1505-1572)

John Knox was a stormy Reformer in a stormy age. By the beginning of the sixteenth century, many "Morning Stars of the Reformation" had suffered martyrdom, often by burning at the stake. Knox was to witness the death of men he loved and admired, men whose beliefs and teachings were unacceptable to the church or the state, and his own life was to be in danger on several occasions. Both the church and society at large were distressingly corrupt and in need of reform in Scotland. The nobles and the clerics, the latter controlling fifty percent of the country's wealth, vied to outdo each other in profligate living and heartless oppression of the poor. Ignorance and superstition were prevalent. With few exceptions priests and monks were illiterate. They taught, if they taught at all, what had been drilled into them by rote. Books were few, even in populous centers. "Conditions were darker in Scotland than in other parts of Europe or the British Isles at the time. If changes were to be perfected, a brave man would be required. The times would require a brave heart and a brave hand."[1]

---

1. R. C. Reed, *John Knox: His Field and Work*, p. 3.

His Life

Knox was born, probably in 1505, near the small town of Haddington in southwestern Scotland. The peasant's son, as he described himself, learned Latin grammar in a Haddington school. When about seventeen years old, he went to Glasgow to study under John Majors, "the most famous teacher of his day in Scotland" and a very progressive thinker. Majors pointed out to his students some of the regrettable fallacies in the doctrines then taught and practiced in the church, and encouraged them to critically examine those doctrines and practices. After his college education Knox taught school for about twenty years in Haddington, and "by 1543 he was known as a priest" there, being called "'Sir John Knox,' the usual designation of a priest who has not obtained a Master's degree."[2] While he was not a deep scholar, Knox had a genuine enthusiasm for knowledge and was well-read.

His preaching career began officially when he was called to preach at the castle of St. Andrews, a call which was precipitated by Knox's courageous denunciation, first of the crimes of Cardinal Beaton, then of those backers of the Reformation who murdered Beaton. But the French, angered by Beaton's assassination, captured the inhabitants of St. Andrews and made them galley slaves. Several months later, however, Knox was back in Scotland and preaching boldly again. At the invitation of Edward VI of England, Knox went south to preach, serving in Keswick, Berwick-on-the-Tweed, Newcastle, and in 1552 being one of the king's Royal Chaplains. When Mary Tudor (Bloody Mary) succeeded Edward VI, Knox fled to the Continent. Four of his years there were spent in Geneva, and under John Calvin's tutelage Knox was well grounded in the principles of the Reformation. Knox became thoroughly convinced that personal piety is not enough; there must also be civic righteousness which results in the reform of both church and state.

While still on the Continent, Knox laid the foundations for the Scottish Reformation. Through letters he was in constant contact with leaders in his native land, as well as with the Queen Regent of Scotland, seeking her consent to the people's reading the Bible in the vernacular. His letters revealed much of his views of Christian education: parents should instruct their chil-

---

2. M. Dendy, *Changing Patterns in Christian Education*, p. 38.

dren in the home as well as seeing to their attendance at church; and adults should read the Bible in groups, discussing its meaning and sharing their views with others.

Knox finally returned to Scotland in 1559. In 1560 Mary Stuart, Queen of Scots, became queen, and she was determined to restore Catholicism in Scotland. In part because of her unpopular marriage to the earl of Bothwell and in part because of Knox's bold, unflinching leadership, Knox succeeded in establishing the Presbyterian church.

His Educational Views

For Knox all education is fundamentally religious education; the guiding principles of his educational philosophy grew out of his religious faith. A fruitful source of his views is the *Book of Discipline,* authored by him and five others, and adopted by the state church.

Knox believed that God speaks in and through the Bible, and that it is therefore authoritative in all matters relating to faith and church life. This new view of the authority of the Bible and its effect on the life of the people was important for Christian education. Because all truth comes from God, who reveals Himself through His Word, real Christian education is possible only through a return to the Word, not through tradition.

The aims of education, as Knox saw them, were to enable the people to read and thus discover for themselves God's Word; to train youth in virtue and godliness, and to prepare them for daily vocations which are useful to either church or state; and generally to glorify Christ.

The education of youth is first of all the responsibility of the parents.

> No father... should use his children at his own fantasy... but all must bring up their children in learning and virtue. The rich and potent may not be permitted to suffer their children to spend their youth in vain idleness... but they must be exhorted, and by the censure of the church, compelled to dedicate their sons, by good exercise, to the profit of the church.... The children of the poor... if they be found apt to letters and learning, then may they not be permitted to reject learning, but must be charged to continue their study....[3]

3. Quoted in F. Eby, ed., *Early Protestant Educators* (New York: McGraw-Hill, 1931), p. 279.

Every master of a household must be commanded either to instruct
or else to cause to be instructed, his children, servants and family,
in the principles of the Christian religion; without the knowledge
whereof ought none to be admitted to the Table of the Lord Jesus:
for such as be so dull and so ignorant, that they can neither try
themselves, neither know the dignity and mystery of that action,
cannot eat and drink of that Table worthwhile.[4]

The parents' commitment to educating their children begins
when they present them for baptism, and parents are regularly
to renew their commitment. The family should read the Bible
together daily and memorize portions of it. Common prayers are
to be said morning and evening. Children are to be taught the
church's doctrine, the Ten Commandments, and the Psalms. Should
the parents

suffer their children and family and servants to continue in willful
ignorance, the discipline of the church must proceed against them
unto excommunication. . . .[5]

The success of this education in the home was measured annually
when every member of the household confessed again his faith
and recited the chief points of religion.

But education was not confined to the home, and Knox's most
important contribution to education was the scheme of national
education which he instituted in Scotland. It consisted of a graduated system of elementary schools, secondary schools (colleges),
and universities.[6] The elementary schools were established and
conducted by the church, which appointed the schoolmaster and
paid him. Attendance was compulsory for girls and boys, rich and
poor, for at least four years. Where people met only once a week,
the minister or reader was to take charge, teaching the youth at
least the rudiments and the Catechism. Those who finished the
elementary course and passed the final examination were compelled to attend the colleges, which were established in every
famous town. Those who completed college, passed final examination, and produced testimonials to their good character could
enter one of six universities, located in St. Andrews, Glasgow, and
Aberdeen.

The Bible was the main subject in schools of all three levels.
Additional subjects on the elementary level were grammar, Latin,

---

4. Ibid., p. 294.
5. Ibid.
6. Ibid., pp. 277, 278, 281.

and the Catechism in English; on the college level, Latin, Greek, logic, rhetoric, and the arts. Each university was divided into three colleges. Each student began in the first college and studied dialectics, mathematics, and physics for three years. Then he could continue in that college for two more years and receive a diploma in medicine, or he could go to the second college and in two years receive a degree in moral philosophy. Then he could remain there for four more years and receive a doctorate in law, or he could enter the third college and after studying Greek, Hebrew, and divinity for five years, receive a degree in theology. At the age of twenty-four he could enter the ministry.

The Book of Discipline prescribed the organization of the schools. Each was to have a principal, a superintendent, rectors chosen by the principal, a treasurer, professors, readers, and graduate students. In addition there were stewards, a cook, a porter, and a gardener, all of which were subject to the principal and the other officers. Great emphasis was placed on the qualifications of the staff, and especially on their religious and moral character; they should be faithful and submit to the principal and to God. They were elected by the people and were regarded with great honor, making them value their professions. The schools were supported by the church, with the universities also receiving support from a general collection and tuition. Financial aid was available for worthy students who needed it.[7]

His Influence

John Knox was one of "the remarkable group of religious reformers who helped to re-lay the foundations of education in the sixteenth century." His influence was greatest, of course, in Scotland, but through Scotch Presbyterianism "his influence was felt in England and more profoundly still in America...."[8]

Financial problems prevented the system for national education which Knox proposed in the *Book of Discipline* from ever being fully implemented, but "the record of the church in Scotland in promoting education is without equal and caused the Scottish peasantry to be the best educated in the world." That is the assessment of A. M. Renwick, who notes that in 1800 Oxford and Cambridge, the only universities in England, had a combined

7. Ibid., pp. 279, 287-89.
8. Ibid., p. 233.

enrollment of 1,000; the university in Edinburgh, one of four in Scotland, had an enrollment of 993.[9]

Because he emphasized the authority of Scripture and the study of it in the vernacular, stressed that conduct must accord with the creeds and discipline of the church, placed the responsibility on parents for the instruction of their children, and suggested a scheme for national education (which provided for the poor and searched out the talented), Knox must be considered an important educator of his time.

Selected Bibliography

Brown, P. H. *John Knox.* 2 vols. London: Black, 1895.

Crofton, W. "The Influence of John Knox on Formal Education in Scotland." Thesis, University of South Carolina, 1921.

Dendy, M. *Changing Patterns in Christian Education.* Richmond: Knox, 1964.

Fleming, D. H. *The Reformation in Scotland: Causes, Characteristics, Consequences.* London: Hodder and Stoughton, 1910.

Knox, J. *The History of the Reformation of Religion Within the Realm of Scotland.* Edited by W. C. Dickinson. 2 vols. London: Nelson, 1949.

———. *Works.* Edited by D. Laird. 6 vols. Edinburgh: Woodrow Society, 1846-1864.

McEwan, J. *The Faith of John Knox.* Richmond: Knox, 1961.

Melrose, A. *John Knox: A Bibliography.* London: Macmillan, 1905.

Mitchell, A. *The Scottish Reformation.* Edinburgh: Blackwood, 1900.

Reed, R. C. *John Knox: His Field and Work.* Richmond: Presbyterian Committee, 1905.

---

9. *The Story of the Scottish Reformation* (Grand Rapids: Eerdmans, 1960), p. 118.

13

Elmer L. Towns

John Calvin
(1509-1564)

Originally named Jean Chauvin, the French Protestant theologian and religious reformer was born in Noyon, Picardy, and educated at the Collége de la Marche and the Collége de Montaigu in Paris. He was appointed to the curacy of St. Martin de Martheville at the age of eighteen, and later to the curacy of Pont l'Évêque. Because of his skill at disputation, his father sent him in 1528 to the University of Orléans to study law, but after his father's death in 1531, Calvin returned to Paris to study the classics and Hebrew. His interest in the principles of the Reformation and his sudden conversion in 1533 led to his preaching Reformation doctrine in Paris. To avoid persecution Calvin traveled from city to city. In 1536 he completed his *Institutes of the Christian Religion*, which profoundly affected the course of the Reformation. In that same year he arrived in Geneva and was elected preacher of Geneva by its magistrates. He then compiled a systematic Protestant Confession of Faith which the citizens were required to confess under oath, and wrote the first Geneva Catechism, published in French in 1536 and in Latin two years later.[1]

---

1. C. Bourgeaud, *Histoire de l'Universite de Geneve*, 1:25. On Calvin's life see "Dedicatory Epistle," *Commentary on I Thessalonians*, trans. J. Pringle

His Early Educational Efforts

When Calvin began his ministry in Geneva, he was faced with a dearth of ministerial helpers and a citizenry that was, by and large, ignorant of Christianity as well as the rudiments of education. Calvin considered a knowledge of Christian doctrine fundamental to effective faith and life, and he recognized the crucial role of an educated ministry in imparting that knowledge. On 21 May 1536 Calvin proposed to the citizens of Geneva a constitution which included plans for a school that all children would have to attend, the poor paying no fees. The result was the establishment of the Collége de la Rive. In addition to instruction in reading, writing, arithmetic, grammar, and religion, Guillaume Farel, the school's principal, and Calvin were to lecture daily, Farel on the Old Testament and Calvin on the New.[2]

But Calvin's reforms alienated even many of his friends, and in 1538 he and Farel were expelled from Geneva. They went to Strasbourg, where Calvin became pastor and professor of theology. When Geneva's town fathers, after a period of disorder in the town, prevailed upon Calvin to return in 1541, he revised the city's laws to establish an autocratic government which controlled social as well as religious life.

The Reformer also radically revised his Geneva Catechism. Appearing in 1542 and about fifty-eight pages in length, the revised edition treats faith, the Commandments, prayer, the Word of God, and the sacraments.[3] Calvin's "Dedication" warned that "the world is threatened with the extremity of barbarianism" and the church with "fearful ruin." At least part of the solution was education.

Finally, Calvin called for the erection of an adequate building and the appointment of suitable teachers for both elementary and advanced education. All instructors were to be chosen and supervised by the ministers of the churches; no others would be allowed

---

(Grand Rapids: Eerdmans, 1949), p. 234; T. Beza, *The Life of John Calvin,* trans. F. Francis (Philadelphia: Gibson, 1836); and E. P. Cubberley, *A Brief History of Education* (Boston: Houghton-Mifflin, 1922), p. 143. The biography by Beza, Calvin's friend and co-worker, is perhaps the best primary source on the Reformer's life.

2. Bourgeaud, *Histoire de l'Universite de Geneve,* pp. 16ff.; Cubberley, *History of Education,* p. 175; and J. T. McNeill, *The History and Character of Calvinism* (New York: Oxford University, 1954), p. 135.

3. Calvin, *Tracts and Treatises on the Doctrine and Worship of the Church,* p. 35.

to teach in the city. Thus the Collége de la Rive was revived, and it continued its program for another eighteen years.

The education of the children was supplemented by church services—two on Sunday and one on Wednesday. They were to spend Sunday "hearing, meditating upon, and recording the sermons," and Wednesday they were to listen to the sermon and then sing Psalms for one hour.

During these years Geneva was rife with political turmoil, making it impossible for Calvin to refine his educational plans. "From 1541 to 1556," wrote W. Stanford Reid, "there was a continual battle to maintain the reformed church against the attack of the Libertines, Romanists, and politicians, so that little time could be spent in improving the schools."[4]

His Geneva Academy

In 1557 Calvin visited Strasbourg, then under Lutheran control. He was given no governmental reception, but at a university reception he discussed educational problems with his former colleagues. Upon returning to Geneva he immediately pressed for the establishment of a university. He obtained a site outside the city wall overlooking Lake Geneva, and he appealed to the city authorities to finance the project. When they pleaded poverty, Calvin turned to private philanthropy.[5]

Calvin's next problem was staff. Zwinglian authorities at Berne helped by alienating the academy faculty at Lausanne. The renowned Theodorus Beza and most of his colleagues resigned, emigrated to Geneva, and accepted appointments to the staff of its academy. Beza was rector; Antoine Chevalier, professor of Hebrew; Francois Beraud, professor of Greek; and Jean Tagant, professor of the arts.[6] At the dedication program, held 5 June 1559 at the Church of St. Peter, Beza explained to the audience that attendance at the academy would not be "solely for instruction, and less for ephemeral gains, as the Greeks were accustomed to in their gymnasia, but . . . to work for the glory of God and for their duty, to become soldiers worthy of their mission."[7] Part of the program

4. "Calvin and the Founding of the Academy at Geneva," p. 8.
5. Bourgeaud, *Histoire de l'Universite de Geneve*, pp. 38, 47.
6. P. F. Geisendorf, *Theodore de Beza* (Geneva: Labor and Fides, 1949), pp. 105ff.
7. Quoted in Geisendorf, *Theodore de Beza*, p. 107.

was Calvin's reading the laws and regulations of the academy, laws which he had written.[8]

The academy was controlled by the church. Each teacher was under strict ecclesiastical discipline, and each was appointed by the ministers. The teachers had to subscribe to the Confession of Faith, and they closely supervised their students' beliefs and lives.

The academy was divided into a *Schola privata*, for children up to about sixteen years of age, and a *Schola publica*, the university. The latter offered only the arts and theology at first, but Calvin hoped to add law and medicine.[9] The entire academy was run by the rector, who was appointed for a two-year term and whose responsibilities included admitting students and granting degrees. He personally supervised the *Schola publica*, while his assistant was principal of the *Schola privata*. Under the rector were the public professors of Hebrew, Greek, the arts, and theology. Under the principal were regents, or teachers.

The academy was in direct contrast to the schools of contemporary Europe, of which Charles Bourgeaud wrote: "The students attended classes largely according to their own particular pleasure without any supervision, and after a number of months or years, they would put forward some 'thesis' which they would defend publicly against all comers. If they did this successfully they would then be granted the appropriate degrees. There was no system of examination or promotion, nor was there any direction. Everything was haphazard and disorganized, at least to modern eyes."[10]

The Schola privata. Students in the *Schola privata* were divided into classes, beginning with class seven and finishing with class one. Class divisions were clear-cut and promotion was deliberate. Students learned first to recognize the alphabet, then to form syllables from the Latin-French alphabet, then to read French fluently, and finally to read the Latin in the Latin-French Catechism. If age permitted, the boys (girls were never considered) learned to write. Within two years students studied Vergil's *Bucolics* and *Aeneid*, Cicero's *Epistles*, Ovid's *De Tristibus* and *De Bonte*, Caesar's *Commentaries*, and Isocrates' orations. History was studied in Latin,

---

8. An apparent translation of these laws is in Reid, "The Founding of the Academy," pp. 22, 23. Future references to the Order of the College of Geneva will be taken from this source.

9. Bourgeaud, *Histoire de l'Universite de Geneve*, p. 30.

10. Ibid., p. 25.

and Cicero's speeches provided a text for dialectics. The student was expected to learn Greek within two years and then to study the writings of Seneca, Xenophon, Polybius, Herodian, Demosthenes, and Homer, in addition to the Gospel of Luke and some apostolic letters. Although the student received no mathematical or scientific training, he did learn how to read, think, and express himself.

The academic year began on 1 May and lasted for twelve months, allowing a three-week vacation at grape harvest. Classes began at 6 A.M. in summer and 7 A.M. in winter, and they ended at 4 P.M. Breaks included one-half hour for breakfast and 1½ hours for lunch. The school day was concluded with students reciting prayers and the Ten Commandments and listening to an exhortation. At the end of the school year, students wrote essays in French on the same topic and then translated the essays into Latin. Because of his strong belief in original sin, Calvin insisted that teachers remain in the classroom while students wrote. The rector corrected the essays and based promotions upon them. The best two essays in each class earned prizes.

The Schola publica. The curriculum in the *Schola publica* was not as structured. Each week, twenty-seven one-hour lectures were offered for anyone who wanted to attend.[11] Each Saturday afternoon theology students expounded a Scripture passage for one hour under the supervision of the ministers. Each month students had to defend a theological proposition, first in a paper given to the theology professor, then orally in an open session.[12]

The professor of arts taught physical science and mathematics three hours a week. These subjects were necessary, Calvin believed, because nature is God's vesture; in nature God continually reveals Himself to all men everywhere. This professor also taught advanced rhetoric, using Aristotle as his text and Cicero as his example.[13] The professor of Hebrew lectured from Aristotle, Plato, Plutarch, Christian philosophers, and Greek poets, orators, and historians, leaving the New Testament to the theology professor. Calvin and Beza lectured on Monday, Tuesday, and Wednesday,

---

11. Ibid., pp. 24-26.
12. Reid, "The Founding of the Academy," pp. 32, 33.
13. L. Nixon, *John Calvin's Teaching on Human Reason*, trans. J. Allen (New York: Exposition, 1963), p. 131.

alternating weeks.[14] They engaged in Biblical exposition, and it was primarily from these lectures that Calvin's commentaries come.

His Educational Philosophy

The education offered at the academy was in many ways humanistic, emphasizing—in addition to Scripture and theology—rhetoric, classical languages, the arts, and elegance of expression. While Calvin considered the Scriptures the authoritative revelation of God, he constantly referred to pagan writers who were *the* authorities in matters of language and expression. He did, however, hold that the arts are "gifts of God, ... instruments, as it were, to assist men in the accomplishment of important purposes."[15] Elsewhere he said similarly:

> ... those arts ... that have nothing of superstition, but contain solid learning and are founded on just principles, ... no doubt ... have come forth from the Holy Spirit; and the advantage which is derived and experienced from them, ought to be ascribed exclusively to God.[16]

Knowledge and learning are not, according to Calvin, merely for one's enjoyment or to satisfy one's intellectual curiosity. One should learn in order to teach others. But to teach, one's thinking must be clear, direct, and untrammeled with conceit and mannerisms. Calvin's own preaching and writing were plain, direct, and unmistakable; "... of all the 16th century writers," wrote Reid, "Calvin is probably the easiest to read today."

Calvin believed that a true knowledge of God cannot be found in nature, the liberal arts, or science, but only in Scripture.

> To understand the Scriptures is man's ultimate objective. Such things as philosophy, science, and eloquence had as their ultimate purpose man's deepest comprehension of what God says through the scriptures.[17]

Fundamental to Calvin's educational philosophy, as to anyone's, was his view of human nature. He regarded it as totally depraved, incapable of any good act or thought. All elements of man, he

---

14. Ibid. There were three lectures in theology, eight in Hebrew and Old Testament, three in ethics, five in Greek orators and poets, three in physics and mathematics, and five in dialectics and rhetoric.

15. *Commentary on I Corinthians*, p. 73.

16. Ibid.

17. *Institutes of the Christian Religion*, 1:401.

thought, are evil and depraved—man's flesh, sensuous appetites, affection, will, and intellect.

> Original sin, therefore, appears to be an hereditary pravity and corruption of our nature, diffused through all parts of the soul.

> ... infants themselves, as they bring their condemnation into the world with them, are rendered obnoxious to punishment by their own sinfulness, not by the sinfulness of another.

> Everything in man, the understanding and will, the soul and body, is polluted.

> ... for man has not only been ensnared by inferior appetites, but abominable impiety has seized the very citadel of his mind.

Calvin saw man as a soul to be redeemed. There is no goodness or personhood to be unfolded from within; the pupil must be held in close discipline to escape the ravages of sin within his nature.

Because of his sinfulness, man cannot come to a true knowledge of God by any human means. Calvin insisted that man's only hope is "regeneration, whereby he could grasp the meaning of God's revelation in Scriptures."[18] Until God touches a man's heart, even "head" knowledge is rather useless. When God does act, however, man can by faith see all things *sub specie aeternitatis*. Because of this, Calvin insisted that all students in the university sign the Confession of Faith. Why teach unbelievers, who could never have true knowledge? True knowledge ultimately is the gift of God.[19]

The Old and New Testaments were the crown and rule of the academy. Calvin held that the Greek and Roman writers, through God's grace, had learned much concerning this world, but that this was no substitute for a true, saving knowledge of God, revealed in the Scriptures. Without them no man can gain eternal life. Calvin said,

> No man can have the least knowledge of truth and sound doctrine without having been a disciple of the Scripture.

Of the role of human reason in interpreting the Scriptures, Calvin said:

> ... the testimony of the Spirit is superior to all reason. For as God alone is sufficient witness of Himself in His own Word, so also, the

---

18. Calvin was referring to I Cor. 2:9ff. See *Commentary on I Corinthians*, p. 106. Also see *Institutes*, 1:85-92.

19. This is discussed fully in R. S. Wallace, *Calvin's Doctrine of Word and Sacrament* (Edinburgh: Oliver and Boyd, 1953), pp. 66ff.

Word will never gain credit to the hearts of men until it be confirmed by the eternal testimony of the Spirit.[20]

In Calvin's Geneva there was, according to Frederick Eby, a "complete system of surveillance, supervision, guidance, and instruction" of which the schools were "but one of the agencies."[21] The others were the home, church, and state. Geneva was a theocracy, the church and state organs of one organism, originating with and deriving their authority from the same source—God the Creator. The government's function, in part, was

> to cherish and support the external worship of God, to preserve the pure doctrine of religion, [and] to defend the constitution of the church....[22]

Education, then, was to be reinforced by both church and state. Calvin exhorted the elders

> to discover experimentally whether the believer follows conscientiously...the commandments of the Church, whether he attends preaching frequently, not merely on Sundays, whether he receives the sacraments regularly and reverently, teaches his children constantly as a Christian should do and sends them to school.[23]

Furthermore,

> ...the home of every citizen, the most prominent as well as the least stand open at all times for the members of the consistorium.... At least once a year...shall every residence in the city be visited, in order to gain information through questions, examinations and observations in regard to the religious training.[24]

Calvin's view of society, human nature, and Scripture were fundamental to his educational philosophy and shaped his educational efforts in Geneva.

Selected Bibliography

Beza, T. *The Life of John Calvin.* Translated by F. Francis. Philadelphia: Gibson, 1836.

Bourgeaud, C. *Histoire de l'Universite de Geneve.* 4 vols. Geneva: George and Cie, 1900-1934.

---

20. Ibid., p. 79.
21. F. Eby, ed., *Early Protestant Educators*, p. 242.
22. *Institutes*, 2:634.
23. Ibid., 2:635.
24. Ibid., 2:634.

Calvin, J. *Commentary on I Corinthians.* Translated by J. Pringle. 2 vols. Grand Rapids: Eerdmans, 1949.

——. *Institutes of the Christian Religion.* Translated by J. Allen. 2 vols. Grand Rapids: Eerdmans, 1949.

——. *Tracts and Treatises on the Doctrine and Worship of the Church.* Translated by H. Beveridge. *Tracts and Treatises,* vol. 2. Grand Rapids: Eerdmans, 1958.

Coetzee, J. *Calvin and the School.* Grand Rapids: Baker, 1959.

Eby, F., ed. *Early Protestant Educators.* New York: McGraw-Hill, 1931.

Niesel, W. *Calvin-Bibliographie 1901-1959.* Munich: Kaiser, 1961.

Nixon, L. *John Calvin's Teaching on Human Reason.* Translated by J. Allen. New York: Exposition, 1963.

Reid, W. S. "Calvin and the Founding of the Academy at Geneva." *The Westminster Journal of Theology* 18:1-33.

14

William Warren Filkin, Jr.

John Amos Comenius
(1592-1670)

John Amos Comenius, both honored and despised in his own day and almost forgotten for two hundred years after his death, was in a real sense a precursor of much contemporary educational theory and practice. The Moravian bishop, who has been described as "the first modern educator" and "the most comprehensive and systematic among the educators of the seventeenth century," was ahead of his time.[1] Because he was at least one of the first to treat pedagogy as a science and because he bequeathed to later ages the rudiments of that science, "the great library of pedagogy at Leipsig has been named in his honor 'Comenius Stiftung.' "[2] While Comenius's ideas do not completely parallel those of twentieth-century philosophers of education, working as he did against a seventeenth-century backdrop of educational sterility and rigidity, "none of the great educators is deservedly admired and so little criticized today as this erudite, wise, and benevolent bishop of an exterminated people. In the works of Comenius, one

---

1. J. S. Brubacher, *A History of the Problems of Education*, p. 202; R. Ulich, *History of Educational Thought* (New York: American, 1945), p. 168.
2. R. H. Quick, *Essays on Educational Reformers* (New York: Appleton, 1901), p. 119.

feels that a prophet is speaking; he was indeed a colossal figure, but only in recent years have his ideas received the respect they merit."[3] This respect was so long delayed for several reasons. For one, Comenius, with all his insight and wisdom, permitted himself to be duped by irresponsible, self-styled prophets; Comenius accepted their prophecies as divinely revealed and induced his fellow Moravians to do the same. Other reasons were his belief in universal education and the unpopularity of his sect.

His Life

Jan Amos Komensky was born in Nivnitz, a village in western Moravia. He later Latinized his name, as was the fashion, to Comenius. His forebears were followers of John Hus, whose interest in education had been outstanding. It was Hus's followers who had established the university at Prague, the earliest and most aggressive school in northern Europe; they had established elementary and secondary schools and taught catechism in their homes long before Luther. Both of his parents died when he was very young. Because of the carelessness of his guardians, Comenius received only a meager education in his early years. He did not begin to study Latin until he was sixteen, considered late in the educational pattern of the day. While studying Latin as part of his preparation for the Moravian ministry, he saw the unfortunate effect on his classmates, most of whom were at least ten years younger than he, of poor schooling methods.

He continued his studies in Germany, where he came under the influence of John Henry Alsted, a Calvinistic theologian interested in educational reform. Here he also was introduced to the principles advocated by Wolfgang Ratke and to the advanced system of education in the nearby provinces of the Dutch Republic. He therefore continued his study in Amsterdam, then the most enlightened and progressive center of culture in Europe. Eventually Comenius returned to Moravia, where he wrote books, taught school, and served as bishop of the Moravian Brethren, a group officially known as the *Unitas fratrum* and claiming doctrinal descent from John Hus. He sought to help his people who were suffering horrible persecution.

He married a well-to-do young lady and settled down in Fulnek in northern Moravia. Tensions between Roman Catholics and

---

3. F. Eby, *The Development of Modern Education*, p. 178.

Protestants appeared resolved, but in 1618 the Thirty Years' War broke out. Ministers of non-Roman churches were jailed and killed, "heretical" books were burned, and Catholicism was forced upon the whole population. Comenius's ministerial status forced him to flee for his life, leaving behind his pregnant wife and small son. He never saw them again; they and the newborn baby died of the plague brought to town by the soldiers. He lost all his possessions, including his library and most of his manuscripts.

In 1628 he, along with all Protestant ministers, was banished from his native land. He took refuge in Poland, and for several years was rector of the Moravian gymnasium at Leszna, or, as the Germans call it, Lissa. There he made his most important contribution to the theory and practice of education and wrote some valuable books on educational method.

He went to England in 1641 in the hope of starting his *pansophic* college, a center from which universal knowledge was to be dispensed. His hope that Parliament would help finance the project failed to materialize, and his stay in England was cut short by an Irish revolt. His London visit, however, was not without practical results of considerable value, wrote Matthew Spinka.[4] Comenius became widely known among English scholars, and through them his fame reached the colonies in New England. While Comenius was in London, he was apparently invited to become president of Harvard College: "When John Winthrop, Jr., traveled to Europe to invite some outstanding educator-theologian to become president of Harvard College, he visited Comenius (1642), and he may have asked Comenius to fill this office. New England clergymen were interested in Comenius' views on church discipline and on educating and converting American Indians."[5]

The Swedish government invited Comenius in 1642 to reform Sweden's schools and promote a national system of education. He remained in Sweden for six years, writing Latin textbooks, grammars, and lexicons. This was work he disliked, but these books were acclaimed throughout Europe. One of them was *Latest Method in Languages.*

In 1650 he accepted an invitation from the Prince of Transylvania to come to Saros Patak, Hungary, where there was a settlement of the banished Brethren. There he directed a school, seek-

---

4. *John Amos Comenius, That Incomparable Moravian*, p. 84.
5. J. C. Osgood, "Comenius, Johann Amos," in *Encyclopaedia Britannica* (Chicago: Encyclopaedia Britannica, 1963), 6:131.

ing to make it a *pansophic* school and a model for reformed education. But personality conflicts and disputes dissipated his energies and prevented broader adoption of his ideas. There he produced his most celebrated book, the famous *World in Pictures (Orbis sensualium pictus)* which was one of the first textbooks with pictures ever printed.

It was in Hungary that he came under the influence of Drabik, who claimed to have prophecies from God. Drabik persuaded Comenius to tell the Count of Hungary that the latter was destined to overthrow both the Hapsburgs and the pope. None of this helped either Comenius or the count. Almost the entire Moravian church, along with many other Protestants, had followed Comenius in accepting Drabik's prophecies. "Imagine the effect produced, when eight months after Comenius' death, Drabik, the prophet whom Comenius followed, formally retracted all the prophecies and went over to the Roman Catholic faith. The reaction was terrible."[6]

Once more Comenius returned to Lissa but was finally driven out by the Poles—apparently because he had publicly welcomed the Swedish king, Charles Gustavus, to the country. When Gustavus left in 1657, the Poles plundered the city. They marked Comenius's house for special violence and nothing was preserved. All his books and manuscripts were burned, including his valued work on *pansophia.* Comenius spent his remaining years in Amsterdam, writing and helping his Moravian people.

His Educational Philosophy

S. S. Laurie listed forty-two books concerning education written by Comenius. In all he wrote some two hundred works, several of which are available in English translation.

While in Lissa, Comenius never ceased to work on his comprehensive treatise, *The Great Didactic.* Writing in Czech, Comenius completed it probably in 1632, but it was not published until 1657 when a Latin translation appeared in Amsterdam. After the original manuscript was rediscovered in Lissa, it was published in Prague in 1848. Not until 1896 was it "translated into English and edited with biographical, historical and critical introductions by M. W. Keatinge, M.A., reader in education at the University of Oxford."

---

6. M. W. Keatinge, in *The Great Didactic,* part 1, pp. 98, 99.

This work is the single most fruitful source for Comenius's educational philosophy.

His patterns for teaching and learning on all age levels must be viewed in connection with his grandiose scheme for teaching everyone everything, a plan he named *pansophia*—that is, "universal wisdom." He hoped to publish an encyclopedia of universal knowledge to which all European scientists would contribute. He also hoped to establish a *pansophic* college, in which laboratories would encourage scientific research, and he sought a method of instruction which would enable every person, to the limit of his capacity, to avail himself of the benefits of knowledge of all sorts. All of these ideas grew out of his faith in the power of education to save mankind.

Looking upon knowledge as a panacea for all of man's ills, he believed that the knowledge of nature, of one's self, and of one's relations to others and to God would lead inevitably to morality and piety. Knowledge, virtue, and piety are the aim of education; the most basic of the three is knowledge. His firm belief in *pansophia* led him to reorganize completely all knowledge and to disseminate it through the schools.

He believed that if all knowledge is unified, it will be accessible to all; and that such accessibility to the masses will solve all economic, political, and social problems which stand in the way of human happiness.

Comenius was greatly influenced by Bacon's emphasis upon the inductive method, but that method, Comenius wrote, requires "generations of effort, and, besides, it is useless for the construction of Pansophia, since it deals only with natural phenomena, while Pansophia treats the whole universe."

Comenius presented eighteen aphorisms which, said Keatinge, constitute the philosophic basis of his *pansophia.*

1. Universal knowledge, so far as it can be obtained by man, has as its objects God, nature, and art.
2. A perfect knowledge of these three is to be sought.
3. The knowledge of things is perfect when it is full, true, and ordered.
4. Knowledge is true when things are apprehended as they exist in reality.
5. Things are apprehended in their essential nature when the manner in which they have come into existence is understood.
6. Each object comes into existence in accordance with its "idea," that is to say, in relation to a certain rational conception through which it can be what it is.

7. Therefore, all things that come into existence, whether they are the works of God, or nature, or man, do so in accordance with their "ideas."

8. Art borrows the "ideas" of its productions from nature, nature from God, and God from Himself.

9. In fashioning the world, therefore, God produced an image of Himself, so that every creature stands in a definite relation to its Creator.

10. As all things share in the "ideas" of the Divine mind, they are also mutually connected and stand in a definite relation to one another.

11. It follows that the rational concepts of things are identical, and only differ in the form of their manifestation, existing in God as an Archetype, in nature as an Ectype, and in art as an Antitype.

12. Therefore the basis of producing, as of apprehending, all things is harmony.

13. The first requisite of harmony is that there should be nothing dissonant.

14. The second is that there should be nothing that is not consonant.

15. The third is that the infinite variety of sounds and concords should spring from a few fundamental ones, and should come into being by definite and regular processes of differentiation.

16. Therefore, if we know the fundamental conceptions and modes of their differentiation, we shall know all things.

17. Such rational conceptions can be abstracted from phenomena by means of a certain method of induction, and must be posited as the norms of phenomenal existence.

18. These norms of truth must be abstracted from those objects whose nature is such that they cannot be otherwise, and which are at every one's disposal for the purpose of making experiments, that is to say, from natural phenomena.[7]

The extent to which Comenius's great work on *pansophia* improved on other encyclopedias will never be known because his manuscript was destroyed when Lisa was sacked and burned. "Had God only spared me the *Sylva Pansophiae*," he cried, "all else would have been easier to bear; but even this is destroyed."[8]

Comenius was accumulating, organizing, and unifying knowledge not for its own sake, but to advance human welfare and universal peace. In this sense Comenius had something of the purpose and burden of the reconstructionist in education. He wrote:

There is needed in this century an immediate remedy for the frenzy which has seized many men and is driving them in their madness to their mutual destruction. For we witness throughout the world disastrous and destructive flames of discords and wars devastating king-

7. Ibid., pp. 33, 34.
8. Ibid., p. 87.

doms and peoples with such persistence that all men seem to have conspired for their mutual ruin which will end only with the destruction of themselves and the universe. Nothing is, therefore, more necessary for the stability of the world, if it is not to perish completely, than some universal rededication of minds by universal peace and harmony, however, I mean not that external peace between rulers and peoples among themselves, but an internal peace of minds inspired by a system of ideas and feelings. If this could be attained, the human race has a possession of great promise.[9]

Comenius's ideal of undergirding world stability through education, John S. Brubacher commented, far outran the imagination of his day. His great confidence in the power of education to transform society he further stressed in chapter 6 of *The Great Didactic.* For example:

The seeds of knowledge, of virtue, and of piety are, as we have seen, naturally implanted in us; but the actual knowledge, virtue, and piety are not so given. These must be acquired by prayer, by education, and by action. He gave no bad definition who said that man was a "teachable animal." And indeed, it is only by a proper education that he can become a man. . . .

Let none believe therefore, that any can really be a man, unless he have learned to act like one, that is, have been trained in those elements which constitute a man. This is evident from the example of all things created, which, although destined for man, do not suit his uses until fitted for them by his hands. For example, stones been given to us as material with which to build houses, towers, walls, pillars, etc.; but they are of no use until they are cut and laid in their place by us. Pearls and precious stones destined to adorn man must be cut, ground, and polished. The meals which are of vital use in daily life, have to be dug out, melted, refined, and variously cast and hammered. Till this is done they are of less use to us than common earth. . . .

Education is indeed necessary for all, and this is evident if we consider the different degrees of ability. . . . What are the rich without wisdom but pigs stuffed with bran? What are the poor who have no understanding of affairs but asses laden with burdens? . . .

For those who are in any position of authority, for kings, princes, magistrates, pastors of churches, and doctors, it is as necessary to be imbued with wisdom as it is for a guide to have eyes, an interpreter to have speech, a trumpet to be filled with sound, or a sword to have an edge. Similarly, those in subordinate positions should be

9. Quoted in I. L. Kandel, "John Amos Comenius, Citizen of the World," *School and Society* 55 (1942): 404.

educated that they may know how to obey their superiors wisely and prudently, not under compulsion, with the obedience of an ass, but of their own free will and from love of order. . . . It follows that one man excels another in exact proportion as he has received more instruction.[10]

Comenius's view of education was grounded in his view that children are not born human but are capable of becoming human, given proper social training. In chapter 6 of *The Great Didactic* he cited examples of infants seized and raised by wild animals; not until they were enculturated by company with human beings did they act like humans.

Comenius's call for universal (male and female, rich and poor) free education, based on his beliefs that "man's natural craving for knowledge" must be satisfied and that without education man cannot be man, was historic. "Never before in the history of the world had a great statesman proposed" it, according to Mortimer J. Adler and Milton Mayer.

His Educational Methodology

From Comenius's point of view, all schools prior to his time had been failures, but he was convinced that "schools can be improved." In chapter 12 of *The Great Didactic* he wrote:

I promise a kind of school in which:
1. The whole youth is being educated (except those whom God has denied reason).
2. There should be taught all that can make men wise, honest and pious.
3. Education, which is preparation for life, should be finished before adulthood.
4. Education should be carried out not with beating, severity and any kind of coercion, but easily, pleasantly, and, so to speak, by its own momentum.
5. Not a semblance of education ought to be provided, but genuine education, not a superficial but thorough education; that means the rational animal should be led by his own rather than a foreign reason. He should get accustomed to penetrating to the roots of things and to take into himself their true meaning and usage, rather than read, perceive, memorize, and relate other people's opinions. The same ought to be the case with respect to morality and piety.
6. Education ought not to be painful but as easy as possible, everyday only four hours ought to be spent for public instruction, and

10. Part 2, pp. 52-56.

this in such a way that one teacher should suffice for the simultaneous instruction of a hundred pupils. And he should do that ten times more easily than is now done with one pupil.[11]

Modern educators would agree with much of this, but they would disagree, for instance, that one teacher can teach one hundred pupils. They also would disagree with Comenius's third point, although Comenius may have been saying only that the rudiments of education (e.g., "reading, writing, and arithmetic") should be mastered before one reaches adulthood. If this is what he meant, probably all would agree. Comenius's general principle that "education should be carried out not with beating, severity and any kind of coercion, but easily, pleasantly, and, so to speak, by its own momentum" is remarkably modern! In a day when education was distasteful, the idea that learning should be pleasant was revolutionary, and the idea that education should be conducted "by its own momentum" is close to the idea that the pupil must have within himself the desire and will to work and learn on his own. In his preface to *World in Pictures,* Comenius wrote:

> Let it be given to children into their hands to delight themselves withal as they please, with the sight of the pictures, and making them as familiar to themselves as may be, and that even at home before they be put into school.[12]

And this was written some three hundred years ago!

The teacher. Comenius laid down certain principles for the teacher. Instruction must follow "in the steps of nature."

1. It must begin early and before the mind is corrupted.
2. The minds must be made ready for it.
3. It must proceed from the general to the particular, and,
4. From the easier to the more difficult.
5. Progress must not be rushed.
6. The minds must not be forced to do anything but that to which they aspire according to their age and motivation.
7. Everything must be related through sense impression, if possible.
8. Everything must be applied immediately.
9. Everything must be taught consistently according to one and the same method.[13]

---

11. Quoted in Ulich, *Three Thousand Years of Educational Wisdom,* p. 346; cf. *The Great Didactic,* chap. 17, p. 127.

12. *Orbis pictus,* p. xviii.

13. Quoted in Ulich, *Educational Wisdom,* p. 346; cf. *The Great Didactic,* chap. 17, p. 127.

Point 5 appears to emphasize the importance of adequate motivation, and point 8 may bear on Comenius's point that education is "preparation for life."

The task of the teacher is explained in *The Great Didactic:*

> The task of the pupil will be made easier, if the master, when he teaches him anything, shows him at the same time its practical application in every-day life. This rule must be carefully observed in teaching languages, dialectic, arithmetic, geometry, physics, etc. If it be neglected, the things that you are explaining will seem to be monsters from the new world, and the attitude of the pupil, who is indifferent whether they exist or no, will be one of belief rather than of knowledge. When things are brought under his notice and their use is explained to him, they should be put into his hands that he may assure himself of his knowledge and may derive enjoyment from its application. Therefore, those things only should be taught whose application can be easily demonstrated.[14]

Organization and curriculum. Comenius's emphasis upon graded instruction is well known. He divided the school into five levels:

First was the "mother school," or the "school of the mother's knee," for children under six. Comenius's *School of Infancy* described the "mother school," which may be considered an anticipation of the present-day kindergarten. "The educational significance of the period of early childhood," wrote Adolph E. Meyer, "was first called to our attention by Comenius."[15]

Second was the vernacular school for children six to twelve. It was to be divided into six classes, and it was to give to all, both boys and girls, the fundamentals which would prepare them for life. As its name suggests, instruction was to be given in the mother tongue.

Third was the Latin school for youths aged twelve to eighteen and preparing either for service in the church or state or for university studies. In this school the mother tongue, Latin, Greek, and Hebrew were to be divided into six classes: grammar, physics, mathematics, ethics, dialectic, and rhetoric.

Fourth was the university for youths from eighteen to twenty-four. It was to give more advanced instruction in every subject taught in the Latin school.

---

14. P. 140.
15. *The Development of Education in the Twentieth Century*, 2nd ed. (New York: Prentice-Hall, 1949), p. 384.

Fifth was the College of Light, corresponding to Bacon's House of Solomon. It was to

> spread the light of wisdom throughout the human race with greater success than has hitherto been attained and benefit humanity by new and useful inventions.[16]

Comenius's concept of curriculum must ever be associated with his idea of *pansophy*. He wanted everything known to be taught to everyone. Keatinge was not as generous at this point: "Against Comenius, as against his predecessors and contemporaries, the accusation may be brought that, in spite of professions of a desire to widen the school curriculum and shake off the more binding traditions of the past, he still retained Latin as the concentration-point of his system, and allowed it to usurp more than its fair share of attention." Keatinge did add, however, that "a brief consideration of the circumstances will suffice to show that the blame lies less with Comenius than with the strength, born of tradition, that enabled the Latin language to blockade every avenue that led to polite learning or scientific pursuits."[17]

Teaching methods and textbooks. Comenius, along with Rousseau, insisted on direct observation rather than mere verbal learning. He anticipated the emphasis upon creative work. He saw the significance of family life for the educational experience. He insisted upon the right of the child to express his nature freely. He was, in fact, "one of the first Renaissance educators ... to systematize the teaching process."[18]

Comenius's methodology made its greatest impact in his own day largely through his textbooks, which were used throughout Europe. His first attempt at simplifying the teaching of Latin was his *Precepts of Easier Grammar (Grammaticae facilioris praecepta)*. Following a few years later was the better-known *Gate of Languages Unlocked (Janua linguarum reserata)*, which Comenius intended as an introduction to Latin vocabulary. But when this proved too difficult a text, Comenius prepared the *Vestibule (Vestibulum)*, which contained but a small part of the words in the *Gate* and was to serve as an introduction to it. Comenius also wrote gram-

---

16. *The Great Didactic,* chaps. 27-32, pp. 255-94.
17. In *The Great Didactic,* part 1, p. 103.
18. T. Brameld, *Patterns of Educational Philosophy: A Democratic Interpretation* (Yonkers-on-Hudson, N.Y.: World, 1950), p. 242.

mars, lexicons, and treatises to accompany the *Gate* and the *Vestibule.*

A few years later Comenius published a more advanced reader, *Entrance Hall (Artrium)*, sometimes referred to as the *Sapientiae palatium.* It was on the same plane as the *Gate,* and it too dealt with the "real" things of life. Later Comenius began a fourth work, the *Thesaurus,* which was to contain selections from certain Latin writers but which was never completed.

The most popular work in the series was his *World in Pictures.* It carried Comenius's principle of sense appeal to its logical conclusion by illustrating the text with pictures. Published in 1657, it was a simplified edition of the *Gate.* Each chapter was headed by a rather complicated picture, in which were numbers referring to corresponding lines in the text. It includes such items as "Barbering," "Making Bread," "Ravenous Birds," "Brewing," "Temperance," and "Humanity."[19]

His Significance

One is inclined to agree with Frederick Eby's evaluation that Comenius's greatest weakness was his shallow and inaccurate knowledge of the mental life. He held to what is called today "faculty psychology." In chapter 7 of *The Great Didactic,* he wrote:

> And if someone is to advance toward wisdom he must be opened up for it in the first years of his life when his industriousness is still burning, his mind is malleable, and his memory still strong.

Comenius did reflect his times, believing in the faculty of imagination, and in the training of the memory and other formal disciplines. But he also was ahead of his time. He recognized the great importance of children's emotions in the educational process. He acknowledged individual differences and provided for them in the structure of the schools and in teaching methods. And he emphasized "learning by doing."

> What has to be done must be learned by practice. Artisans do not detain their apprentices with theories, but set them to do practical work at an early stage; thus they learn to forge by forging, to carve by carving, to paint by painting, and to dance by dancing. In schools,

---

19. E. Dale, *Audio-Visual Methods in Teaching,* pp. 59, 60.

therefore, let the students learn to write by writing, to talk by talking, to sing by singing, and to reason by reasoning.[20]

Comenius should be extended the courtesy of being considered in the light of the general insights into education of his day. Viewed in this light, his suggestion that the teacher must grasp "the right occasion in order [for the student] to learn more effectively" sounds much like E. L. Thorndike's familiar "law of readiness" and today's "teachable moment."

As a one-man revolution against meaningless words and ideas, he was practical and realistic. In his insistence upon firsthand experience, he was careful to say that schools should provide experiences not readily available to students in their homes.

"That incomparable Moravian," despised, hunted, persecuted, was actually a precursor of much contemporary educational theory and practice: for example, that learning must begin long before formal schooling; learning must follow an "order of nature" in the child's growth; learning should be pleasurable; learning should have present meaning to the student by being applied to his life and work; the pupil must be "ready" to learn what is being taught; the pupil must be interested and motivated from within; the pupil must be involved in the learning process, especially through firsthand sense experience; the teacher should refrain from using fear, physical force, and punishment; and education is for all who are able to learn—boys and girls.

This is not to suggest, of course, that there is a historical connection between these emphases in Comenius's work and their prominence in contemporary educational theory and practice. Had Comenius belonged to a more popular religious sect and had he not been duped by Drabik and other "prophets," he might have made a greater contribution during his own day. Insofar as his philosophy of teaching and learning is sound, he should be recognized, studied, and remembered.

Selected Bibliography

Brubacher, J. S. *A History of the Problems of Education.* New York: McGraw-Hill, 1947.
Comenius, J. A. *The Great Didactic.* Translated and edited by M. W. Keatinge. New York: Russell, 1967.

---

20. *The Great Didactic,* part 2, pp. 194, 195.

———. *Orbis pictus.* Translated and edited by C. W. Bardeen. Syracuse, N.Y.: Bardeen, 1887.

Dale, E.. *Audio-Visual Methods in Teaching.* Rev. ed. New York: Dryden, 1954.

Eby, F. *The Development of Modern Education.* 2nd ed. New York: Prentice-Hall, 1955.

Keatinge, M. W. *Comenius.* New York: McGraw-Hill, 1931.

Laurie, S. S. *John Amos Comenius, Bishop of the Moravians: His Life and Educational Works.* Syracuse, N.Y.: Bardeen, 1892.

Spinka, M. *John Amos Comenius, That Incomparable Moravian.* Chicago: University of Chicago, 1943.

Ulich, R. *Three Thousand Years of Educational Wisdom.* Cambridge: Harvard University, 1948.

15

Kenneth O. Gangel

August Hermann Francke
(1663-1727)

The Thirty Years' War left the German people exhausted. This was the last of Europe's great struggles over religion, and by the time it culminated in the Peace of Westphalia in 1648, the protagonists had largely forgotten the significant issues which initiated it. During the war "lawless armies plundered and devastated northern Europe, and 10 million of Germany's 16 million people were killed. Whole cities were destroyed, and almost none were left unscathed; orphaned children roamed the woods like packs of wild animals."[1] Controversy raged among Protestant church leaders, and many of the clergy were ruled by secular civil authorities. Religious education centered on intellectual development and orthodox doctrine rather than personal purity and holy living. The clergy themselves were poor examples of Biblical teaching. Church services tended toward a formal rigidity which repudiated the dynamic vitality of the New Testament.

Into this sterile setting came Philip Spener, a young graduate student of theology at the University of Geneva. In 1663 he became professor of theology at the University of Strasbourg, and just

---

1. C. Manschreck, *A History of Christianity*, vol. 2 (Englewood Cliffs, N.J.: Prentice-Hall, 1964), p. 264.

three years later he was called to pastor a Lutheran church in Frankfurt. During his pastorate Spener developed what came to be known as pietism. Deeply concerned to improve moral and religious conditions in his parish and in the city at large, he emphasized a return to devotional living, personal Christianity, and a serious and practical study of the Scriptures. In the year that Spener had joined the Strasbourg faculty, August Hermann Francke was born in Lubeck.

His Life

The first influences on Francke were pietistic. His parents impressed upon him early the importance of a devoted Christian life, and while still a boy, he determined to devote his years to the gospel ministry. There is no question about the brilliance of young Francke. Albert Henry Newman suggested that "as a student his life was exemplary, but was possibly more ascetical than was wholesome."[2] After some years of private instruction Francke entered the gymnasium at Gotha and there was influenced by the philosophy of Comenius. His unusual intellectual capacities enabled him to enter the University of Erfurt at the age of fourteen. There he met several students of Spener and participated in Bible study clubs. From Erfurt Francke went to Kiel, and from there to Leipzig, where he earned his degree in 1685. Young Francke had studied philosophy, theology, history, church history, rhetoric, and other subjects, but his primary interest had very quickly become Biblical languages. After finishing at Leipzig, Francke spent two years (1685-1687) on the faculty of that university. There he had direct contact with Spener, and Francke became a "convert" to pietism. During these years Francke helped found the *Collegium philobiblicum,* a club which was devoted to the exegetical and devotional study of the Scriptures and which exerted strong influence not only at the university but throughout that part of Germany.

Then Francke divorced himself from academic life for two years, studying privately and clarifying his personal philosophy of life and education. When he returned to the Leipzig faculty in February 1689, he was an articulate spokesman for pietism. Opposition was great, however, and just one year later he accepted a call to

---

2. *A Manual of Church History,* vol. 2 (Chicago: The American Baptist Publication Society, 1902), p. 528.

the chief pastorate in Erfurt. But students who had followed him from Leipzig stirred up opposition at the University of Erfurt, and he left his parish under pressure in September 1691. Through Spener's influence Francke was invited to be a pastor in Glaucha and an unsalaried teacher (first of oriental languages, then of theology) at the new University of Halle. There he served until his death in 1727.

The extent of Francke's educational ministry at Halle is almost unbelievable, prompting Frederick Eby to describe him as "the noblest example of the practical educator of Germany."[3] Among Francke's notable achievements were the opening of: an alms-supported elementary school for the poor in 1692; an alms-supported orphan school in 1695; a school for teachers *(Seminarium praeceptorium)* in 1705; a private boarding school for students preparing for college; a publishing house of Biblical literature; and a free boarding house for students. Newman assessed these institutions: "At his [Francke's] death twenty-two hundred children were receiving training in this institute; one hundred and thirty-four [orphans], under one hundred and sixty-seven male and female teachers, and two hundred and fifty university students were supplied with their dinners there. The pedagogical work was organized under eight inspectors, and this children's school was a valuable object-lesson for the Christian world."[4] Lars Qualben noted that the University of Halle became under Francke "the great Pietist center which supplied Europe with teachers, pastors, foreign missionaries, and influential laymen."[5]

His Theology

The aim of education, Francke wrote in his *Brief and Simple Treatise on Christian Education,* is to honor God. Good instruction must combine godliness and wisdom, conveying a knowledge of Christ through piety, prayer, Bible study, and evangelism. All good students, regardless of their wealth and status, can acquire this knowledge and discipline.

> All learning and knowledge is folly if it doesn't have as its foundation true and pure love toward God and man.

---

3. *The Development of Modern Education* (Englewood Cliffs, N.J.: Prentice-Hall, 1952), p. 247.
4. *A Manual of Church History,* 2:529.
5. *A History of the Christian Church* (New York: Nelson, 1942), p. 365.

Pietism did not emerge from a vacuum; it was a reaction against the scholastic form of Lutheranism, described by Williston Walker as "external and dogmatic." Pietism, on the other hand, is "an assertion of the primacy of the feeling in Christian experience, a vindication for the laity of an active share in the upbuilding of the Christian life, and the assertion of a strict ascetic attitude toward the world."[6] Pietism may have overreacted to scholastic Lutheranism's emphasis on orthodoxy and systematic theology, but its commitment to a high view of Scripture and to its study was one of the movement's major contributions. The Halle pietists have been condemned for their "unproductiveness in the field of strict scholarship," for their failure to perceive either "that the new foundation of theology upon conversion and the edifying study of Scripture needed to be harmonized with orthodox theology, or that the entire body of systematic theology must be reconstructed. . . ."[7] Robert Ulich argued, however, that pietists did not neglect true theology: "Theology, rather than being mere erudition and contemplation, should aim at discipline of the will and the affections with the purpose to improve men, not merely to teach them."[8]

Francke and the pietists remained in the Lutheran church, forming an *ecclesiolae in ecclesia*. They emphasized dramatic conversion, claiming that regeneration took place then rather than at baptism. And they separated themselves from worldly activities such as "dances, cards, and the theater," as well as from state educational institutions. Issues of church and state "could be offensive or irrelevant to Pietists," noted Martin Marty.

His Educational Philosophy and Methodology

The link between theology and educational philosophy was so obvious to Francke that he spent very little time delineating a formal relationship, proceeding rather to build his educational system on theological premises, stated or unstated.

Francke developed his educational programs around the concept that information about God's truth could bring his students to the

---

6. *A History of the Christian Church* (New York: Scribner, 1918), p. 146.

7. C. Mirbt, "Pietism," in *The New Schaff-Herzog Encyclopedia of Religious Knowledge,* ed. S. M. Jackson, vol. 9 (New York: Funk and Wagnalls, 1911), p. 58.

8. *A History of Religious Education* (New York: New York University, 1968), p. 138.

point of regeneration and then build them up in the faith. In *Pietas hallensis* he wrote:

> The *End* we aim at, and the Means we make use of for obtaining the same, are all of a Piece. The Word of God is instilled into the Children from their Youth up. Unfeigned *Faith* in our *Lord Jesus Christ* is laid for a Foundation, and a real Sense of *Godliness*, attended with a conscientious Behavior, are the most material Points, to the obtaining whereof, our earnest endeavours are constantly directed.[9]

Francke's programs reached a wide segment of the German people, but his particular concern seems to have been the poor. He maintained that the mark of a godly nation is the care for the needy within its ranks, and he vowed to do all he could to meet the physical needs of peasant children as well as their educational needs.

> The Prayers of poor Fatherless Children, and of all such as enjoy the Benefit of Hospitals, are the strongest Wall and Fortress to defend a City and Land from the Invasions of any Adversary; as on the contrary, the Tears or Sighs of poor distressed People, who commonly express their Grievances in that manner, when they lie neglected under extreme Necessity, draw down the dreadful Displeasure of Almighty God, against that unhappy Nation wherein such Cruelty is practiced.[10]

Head, heart, and hands are inseparable in Francke's educational programs. Children are taught by example to live as Christ directed and thus to honor God. This must be taught to all, rich or poor, in the home and school. Francke's approach to Christian education is very home-centered. He frequently attributed the degeneration and unhappiness he saw all around him to the tragic neglect of Christian training in the home.

The teacher. The teacher was an integral part of Francke's educational system, and no aspect of the teacher's role was more important than that of being a good example.

> Especially must a teacher be careful that his pupils should not notice anything wicked in him. For children notice everything, whether good or bad.... children who see their teachers or fathers drunk, angry, or unchaste and hear them swear and slander and observe through their example the vanity of the world and the pleasures of

---

9. *Abstract of the Marvelous Footsteps of Divine Providence* (London: J. Downing, 1707), pp. 35, 36.
10. Ibid., p. 40.

the flesh and luxurious life will thereafter not easily be brought to fundamental hatred for these vices.[11]

It is extremely important that the teacher show love. Discipline is important, but the instructional process is never to be interrupted by harsh or angry outbursts.

Profane words and ridicule are absolutely not to be used with children, since they are more hurt than helped thereby. A teacher may not call them, out of impatience, oxen, asses, pigs, dogs, beasts, fools, scoundrels, swineherds, and so on, and still less children of the devil.

Physical punishment may on occasion be necessary, but it must always be suited to the individual child and administered with the greatest care and discretion, "for more children can be won with words than with blows." Francke embraced the doctrine of *in loco parentis,* which is generally rejected in higher education today.

Although Francke retained the traditional lecture method of teaching, he believed that each child needs to be trained to observe, concentrate, reason, and think for himself.

Francke's concern for quality teaching was most obvious in his influential Teachers' Seminary. Starting as a special table in the university dining room, the institution grew until requirements for graduation included two years of study and three of practice teaching. Graduates of the school were generally considered the best prepared of any in Germany. The *Seminarium praeceptorum* trained elementary teachers; the *Seminarium inselectum,* secondary teachers. Standards were rigid: moderate dress, temperate use of alcohol and tobacco, a serious commitment to teaching, and an affection for and patience with children. Qualben complained that the pietists' code "bordered on Pharisaism" and that theirs was a "gloomy, austere, and legalistic" Christianity. Whether or not that be true, Francke's interest in trained teachers was a positive innovation. Paul Beck noted that Francke took care "to appoint such teachers as would set a holy example" for the students.[12] In one address to his teachers Francke said:

Attend to my words, dear children! Attend to the word which is spoken to you from God! Now, before your hearts are seduced by the world, while you are in the morning of life, pray God to implant

---

11. In K. B. Cully, ed., *Basic Writings in Christian Education* (Philadelphia: Westminster, 1960), p. 225.

12. *Memoirs of Augustus Hermann Francke* (Philadelphia: American Sunday School Union, 1831), p. 149.

His love within you, and to make you humble, and obedient, and holy. Ask him so to impress his fear upon your minds, that you may be enabled to keep his commandments all your days. Remember that it often brings a fearful curse upon men, to neglect God in their youth, and to follow after the desires of the flesh, and give themselves up to the pleasures of the world. You may now think it would be happiness itself, to live in the indulgence of all your wishes; but a time will come, when you will think very differently, and when you will know what misery he must suffer who disobeys God. See to it then, dear children, that you repent from the heart, and believe in Jesus Christ. Then will your happiness be secure.[13]

The curriculum. The Holy Scriptures were the core of Francke's curriculum at all levels. Beck pointed out that Francke "made the Scriptures, in some form or other, the subject of most of his lectures, not merely giving a cold and formal explanation of its truths, but applying them to the hearts and consciences of his pupils, and teaching them how they should apply the same truths to others." The dominance of Scripture at the elementary level is obvious in the daily schedule advised by Francke (see table 1).[14] His involvement with the schools was strictly supervisory except in the department of religious instruction: "This he made the grand object of attention; the cultivation of the moral feelings of the pupils was esteemed of paramount importance." To this end he would catechize them, and he would lecture them on various subjects, not confining himself to any fixed plan. All of his lectures were "eminently practical. He addressed his young hearers, as a father would his children, giving them directions as to their habits, studies, conversation, devotions. . . ."[15]

Francke recognized the importance of books to education, but he also equipped his *paedagogium* with a botanical garden, a cabinet of natural history, a laboratory for the study of chemistry and anatomy, and a workshop for glass-cutting, copper-engraving, and wood-carving.

While he was developing the curriculum in his children's schools and teachers' colleges, Francke also was reforming the theological curriculum of the University of Halle. There he emphasized the study of Biblical languages, the application of that study in the art of preaching, and the techniques of pastoral theology. Students,

---

13. In *Memoirs*, pp. 149, 150.
14. Cully, *Basic Writings in Christian Education,* p. 228.
15. Beck, *Memoirs,* p. 84.

Table 1

Time	Weekdays	Sundays
7-8	Song, prayer, Bible reading, catechism	Church service
8-9	One-half hour Bible reading, one-half hour catechism for older children	
9-10	One-half hour explaining quotations and Proverbs to younger children; one-half hour study of Psalms and New Testament by older children	
10-11	Writing	
2-3	Prayer and Bible reading Reading, music, and reading for younger children on different days	Church service
3-4	One-half hour reading by younger children; one-half hour study of quotations and sayings by older children; one-half hour of older children reciting quotations, sayings for younger	
4-5	Catechism	
5-6	Evening prayers at church	

who received free board and lodging for from four to six years, "were required to read the Old and the New Testaments in the *Grundsprachen,* to write commentaries on all of the books of the Bible and to learn to use *die orientalischen Hilfssprachen* for a more thorough understanding of the Sacred Scriptures."

His Significance

Francke, wrote C. B. Eavey, "advocated no narrow, impractical education but an enlarged, enlightened work conducted on Christian principles. Physical, mental, and spiritual development were all regarded as necessary; in the courses of study he outlined and emphasized the spiritual, the useful and the realistic. Everything was to contribute to the honor of God and the good of fellowmen. The intellect and the reason received much care and attention; the purpose was to train them in the view of the occupation the pupil would enter in after life. The spiritual was central in every course of study; secular subjects were secondary, deemed to have value only as they could contribute to spiritual life. Every means was employed to keep children from developing evil tendencies and to nurture good ones."[16]

Francke's strong emphasis on individual Christian living did not prevent him from being too idealistic regarding the power of education to change society. In *Pietas hallensis* he mused that through education

> the country will be cleared by degrees of suborn beggars, thieves, murderers, highwaymen, footpads, and the whole pack of loose and debauched people, who (as we may find if we search into the true reasons of such overflowing wickedness) commonly let loose the reins to disorder and impiety, because they never imbibed as much as the least Tincture of a good education.[17]

Francke's emphasis on practicing what is learned in the classroom gave birth to the Danish-Halle missionary project, a vast achievement which falls beyond the bounds of this chapter. Suffice it to say that without Francke's influence and support, the missionary effort in India would have collapsed shortly after its birth. Soon after that effort began, Francke began selecting the missionaries, commissioning ten before his death; all had been his students and co-workers at Halle.

Among Francke's more famous debtors were John Wesley and the early Methodists, Nikolaus Zinzendorf and the Moravians, and American Lutheran leaders H. M. Mühlenberg and J. C. Kunze. Indeed Francke's influence on Christian education even up to the present is virtually immeasurable.

Selected Bibliography

Beyreuther, E. *August Hermann Francke*. Marburg: Francke, 1956.

Brown, D. W. "The Problem of Subjectivism in Pietism: A Redefinition by Special Reference to the Theology of Philipp Jakob Spener and August Hermann Francke." Ph.D. dissertation, Northwestern University, 1962.

Guerlike, H. E. F. *The Life of August Hermann Francke*. Translated by S. Jackson. London: Seeley and Burnside, 1837.

Kramer, D. G. *August Hermann Francke: Ein Lebensbild*. Halle: Waisenhaus, 1880-1882.

———. *August Hermann Francke's Padagogische Schriften*. Langensalza: Beyer, 1885.

Otto, A. *August Hermann Francke*. 2 vols. Halle: Waisenhause, 1902-1904.

---

16. *History of Christian Education* (Chicago: Moody, 1964), p. 183.
17. *Abstract of the Marvelous Footsteps*, p. 38.

Pinson, K. S. *Pietism as a Factor in the Rise of German Nationalism.* New York: Columbia University, 1934.

Ritschl, A. *Geschichte des Pietism.* Bonn: Marcus, 1880.

Schroeder, P. J. "August Hermann Francke, 1663-1963." *Concordia Theological Monthly* 34:664-68.

16

T. F. Kinloch

Nikolaus Ludwig Zinzendorf (1700-1760)

Until the 1930s Zinzendorf had not received the attention which, as a reformer of religious education, he deserved. There were two reasons for this. First, in his lifetime his many eccentricities prejudiced people against anything he said or did. In particular some of his two thousand hymns contained expressions which all regret and none can justify. And second, until a certain scholar had ransacked the Moravian archives, Zinzendorf's views on education were unknown and inaccessible.

The son of a noble who occupied a prominent position at the Saxon court, Zinzendorf lost his father almost in infancy and was brought up under strong religious influence by his maternal grandmother, a noble specimen of the pietist aristocrat. When he was ten, he was sent to Halle and remained in Francke's *Paedagogium* for six years. He already instinctively felt (in later years it became a firm conviction) that every child is born to be happy and that in education play is no less essential than work. At Halle he had to work eleven hours a day (5 to 12 and 2 to 6), and there were no games. In later years he described this as "slavery." An ardent believer in liberty, he thought it better for children to learn less and enjoy freedom than to be compelled to fill their heads with knowledge that was for the most part useless in later life.

His family wished him to follow in his father's footsteps and serve the state. With this end in view he studied law, traveled, and obtained an appointment at court, but his heart was not in law. At the earliest possible moment he bought an estate near Dresden and settled down, determined, with three other friends as a "Union of Four Brethren," to imitate Francke (i.e., to found an orphanage, to write and publish devotional literature, and to work for foreign missions). Something happened, however, which changed the whole course of his life.

At the time Luther began his work of reformation, the "Bohemian Brethren" numbered 200,000. But through the Counter-Reformation, the Brethren, insofar as they formed a visible church in Bohemia and Moravia, were almost utterly destroyed. For many years, however, they continued to exist in Hungary and Poland. Even in Moravia itself a "hidden seed" preserved something of the beliefs and practices of their fathers. Two families of this "Hidden Seed" escaped from Moravia in 1722, and, at Zinzendorf's invitation, settled on his estate. During the seven years which followed, some three hundred refugees made their way from Bohemia and Moravia to Berthelsdorf, and there they built a town called Herrnhut. The number of settlers was increased by the advent of other refugees from various quarters (some of whom cherished strange beliefs). Out of these mixed materials the *Unitas fratrum* (Unity of the Brethren), as the Moravian Church is more correctly called, was formed, or rather, shall we say, re-formed. At first Zinzendorf found his refugees a difficult body to handle. He was a rather eccentric aristocrat; for the most part they were eccentric artisans. Zinzendorf knew little of them; they knew little of him. At times, despite his unbounded kindness, some of the refugees described him as "the Man of Sin." But one evening, it is said, something like a miracle took place at a communion service. A change came over the turbulent refugees, which in later days they could only explain by saying, "We learnt to love." Henceforward the *Gemeine*, as they called themselves (the Congregation, the Brotherhood), formed a happy band of Christians. Years afterwards a visitor described it as an earthly paradise. Zinzendorf eventually became the group's devoted leader.

The Materials of Education

The catechism. When he was twenty-two, Zinzendorf published a catechism which he called *Pure Milk.* It consisted of seventy-eight questions and answers, and was intended to help mothers in the training of young children.

Anyone who reads this catechism will at once recognize its revolutionary character. Instead of asking how the sum and substance of doctrine can be presented in such a way that children can easily learn it by heart, Zinzendorf asked himself the question, "How best can I lead a child to love and serve God as He is presented in Christ?" He began with the child's body and showed that it is the frail, perishable dwelling place of the soul. As over against the body which is born to perish, the soul is made for heaven, the home of God. In the Bible He has given us a book which tells us how to live on earth. The fall is treated in the most literal way, for Eden was a real place to Zinzendorf. There man ate the forbidden fruit, and sickness and distress came into the world. But Jesus came as a physician to heal the sick, and He does so still, for He is not dead. We obey His commandments because we love Him. Happiness lies in friendship with Jesus, in loving the heavenly Father and in showing our love by seeking to do His will.

Here at the very outset Zinzendorf revealed certain views which he held through life. He did not invite the child to come up on a platform where grown-up people sit; he did not ask him to learn to speak as grown-up people do. He stepped down from the platform and stood beside the child. He looked at the world through the child's eyes. To him, from first to last, the childlike was the divine. Zinzendorf did not ask children to speak like adults, to think like adults, to feel like adults. There is a time for all things, as the Preacher said (Eccles. 3:1). God meant children to be *children,* not adults in miniature. Zinzendorf was convinced that children are born to be happy; so long as they are children they cannot but be happy. To ask them to forego their birthright, to seek to make them hurry through childhood, as some would do, is altogether wrong.

A little later Zinzendorf produced a catechism for older people. It is not a dogmatic treatise. Though very long, it is very simple. Most of the answers, indeed, consist of short passages of Scripture.

The older he grew the less Zinzendorf cared for formal catechetical teaching of the old-fashioned sort. "Through it," he said, "the child learns to chatter about hundreds of things which he can neither believe nor understand." To *make* a child learn his catechism, to punish him if he fails to learn it or learns it amiss, as was the custom in those days, was to Zinzendorf little short of infamy. "To introduce children," he once said, "at one and the same time to the cudgel, the rod, and the wounds of Jesus, to punish them for not knowing the details of the Passion, is altogether wrong."

These, then, are the first two great characteristics of Zinzendorf's theory of religious education: the head must never be allowed to outrun the heart; and outward compulsion can *never* produce religion.

The hymnal. "It is an established and well-known fact," said Zinzendorf in the year before he died, "that our hymns provide the best method for inculcating religious truths and for conserving those in the heart." "According to our way of singing," said a Moravian writer, "the materials of instruction are both presented and reviewed through song: hence we do not sing through entire hymns of ten to twenty verses, but rather separate stanzas or half-stanzas from as many hymns as the sequence of thought of the subject matter requires."

The young Moravian had two textbooks: the Bible and his hymn-book. His religious teaching largely consisted of a simple exposition of some portion of Scripture, interspersed with antiphons and responses taken from hymns. This, to use Zinzendorf's favorite phrase, was the "liturgical method" of religious education. The hymns sung at Herrnhut were almost entirely Christocentric, or expressions of feelings which love of Christ awakens in the heart. There were a great many festival services (Zinzendorf believed that monotony is bad for the adult and fatal for the child), and many services at which there was nothing but hymn singing of this antiphonal kind. The Moravians have made more use of the hymn as a means of instruction than any other body of Christians, and this is entirely due to Zinzendorf.

The Bible. Two further points are worth attention. Zinzendorf believed that many passages in the Bible refer almost exclusively to Jews and are, therefore, of little interest or concern to Christian children. In view of this he shortened the Bible. What is more, over a hundred years before the Moffatts and the Weizsäckers began to turn the Bible into "modern speech," Zinzendorf had done the same thing. It is true that he did not finish his task; nonetheless he saw clearly that there is a place in religious education for a shortened Bible, a Bible translated into the idiom of contemporary speech.

Each year Zinzendorf carefully selected 365 verses from Scripture (these were sometimes printed as a booklet). Each day one of these verses was chosen by lot. This was the motto for the day, the theme, the center round which revolved the reading, talking, and singing of that particular day.

The Philosophy of Education

We must now turn our attention to that in Zinzendorf's teaching which is at once most characteristic, and at the same time difficult to explain.

When he opened his orphanage, he at first followed the Halle method of dividing the children in his dormitories into three classes—the dead, the awakened, and the converted—doing his utmost to see the children "converted"; he preached to them, prayed with them, talked with them one by one about their soul's salvation. In course of time, however, he ceased to believe in the permanent value of these very youthful "conversions." He ceased to desire them and adopted an entirely different method based on a completely different point of view. Zinzendorf came to believe that there is no need for a child born in a Christian home to wander into the "far country,"[1] or to experience that sense of misery and contrition which was demanded by Francke and other pietists from all who passed from death unto life. Of the unknown God, said Zinzendorf, we can know nothing. All that we can know of Him is that which is revealed in the God-Man, Jesus Christ. The whole purpose therefore of Zinzendorf's teaching is to make the child see Christ "as clearly as he can see a house," to dwell in His presence continually, to live with Him and for Him at every moment of his life. This "walking with Christ" is the very heart and soul of religious education. It is not something purely "otherworldly"; it is a way of life which may be lived in the most concrete possible form. It embraces every conceivable activity and is suffused throughout with joy.

Thus Zinzendorf became the champion of freedom—the first

---

1. Zinzendorf laid great stress on I Cor. 7:14.

great champion of freedom in the realm of religious education. The old have no right, he insisted, to impose their own particular opinions upon the young; parents have no right to demand that their particular form of religious experience shall be repeated in identical form in their children (this is where he broke with Francke). So long as the child "walks with Christ" he may safely be left to himself, for he is being taught at every moment of his life by the best of all teachers, Christ's Holy Spirit.

The function of the teacher, therefore, is to suggest rather than to inform in a purely dogmatic way, for the central point in teaching is not dogma but the child himself. We have to pray to be made like children; they have no need to become like us. They emerge from the baptismal font as "anointed princes" and are to be treated as such. Even in questions of purely secular education, the child must be given the utmost freedom. The syllabus and the timetable are to be made for him; he is not to be fitted into them.

Zinzendorf, then, is in all educational matters an apostle of freedom, a convinced believer in individualism. Self-activity, directed by the Holy Spirit in a religious environment, is the best form of religious education. That which is inherent in the child, which develops from the child with the help of Christ, is the basis of all true religious education, rather than something imparted to the child in dogmatic form by older people.

The danger of this emphasis on individual development is that it may end in egoism, but Zinzendorf felt that he had overcome this difficulty. In the very nature of things, he maintained, fellowship with Christ involves service to one's neighbor. It is impossible to be a Christian and an egoist at the same time. Those who love Christ know that they are not their own; they exist to carry out their Father's will.

Community-wide Education

We must now consider that which Zinzendorf regarded as the most characteristic and important feature in his system of religious education. He divided the whole community into groups according to age, sex, and "condition" (marital status). For the whole community, education was a process that never ceased. By this method he sought to give each individual that particular kind of education required to meet the varied needs of his age and circumstances. Each "choir" had its own ideal, its own regular meetings, its own litanies, and its own special festivals, days of covenanting, and so forth.

Parents, for instance, were organized into one group *(Ehe-Chor)* and received instruction in such matters as concerned them. They heard addresses on the Christian ideal of marriage, the duties and privileges of parents, the proper method of conducting a Christian home, and the right way of training children. Zinzendorf himself had been peculiarly fortunate in having been brought up by a woman who, while believing in allowing the utmost freedom, gave no sign of weak indulgence. "Parents," he said, "who become the slaves of their children's whims turn them into little devils." He himself was most happily married and, a hundred years before the English father, had abandoned the Roman attitude *(patriapotestas)* and made himself the friend and confidant of his own children, allowing them the widest liberty.

As against the older type of Moravian, who was often suspicious of married love and was prone to look upon sexual attraction as a moral evil, Zinzendorf expressly taught that "children are begotten and born only unto the Lord, as in his Presence." Few men have had a nobler view of married life and the sanctity of the home than Zinzendorf.

There were ten other choirs: one for infants in arms (Zinzendorf had wonderful skill in handling babies); one for little children; one for boys and another for girls; one for older boys and another for older girls; one for young men and another for young women; and one for widowers and another for widows. It is impossible to deal with each of these choirs in detail. Two important facts, however, deserve attention.

Zinzendorf presented the boy Jesus to the child as his ideal. All the teaching given in the junior choirs was concentrated on this. Jesus was once a child, and the happiness of all children (they are born to be happy) lay in thinking about Jesus, in constantly communing with Jesus, in asking themselves how, had Jesus been a boy in Herrnhut instead of Galilee, He would have behaved. On this all the teaching, all the litanies, all the hymns, were based. As the child grows up, he is to think of Christ at a corresponding age, to think of Him, for instance, as the boy who worked in a carpenter's shop. Throughout their early life, children were trained to devote their whole attention to the earthly life of the boy Jesus. They were taught to regard Him as at once their ideal and their invisible Friend and Companion. All that savored of legalism was rigidly excluded. The utmost care was taken to preserve each child against every approach of evil. Otherwise, in almost complete freedom, their characters were allowed to develop through constant thought of Jesus, through constant intercourse with their loving Friend.

The four things that impressed and delighted Zinzendorf when he looked at children were their natural happiness, their frankness, their freedom from care, and what, for lack of a better word, we may call their sociability. Yet none knew better than he that this earthly paradise could not last forever. The child had to become an adult.

Until modern psychology appeared, it is safe to say that no man had paid more attention to the problems of adolescence than Zinzendorf. He saw the naiveté, the frankness of childhood give place to self-consciousness and a sense of shame. He watched the melancholy, the desire for solitude, the awkwardness, the ever-changing moods. He saw that the natural happiness of childhood was giving place to mysterious longing which the youth was utterly unable to explain. This, said Zinzendorf, is the most dangerous period in the life of man. It is the time of crisis, the time when the youth definitely chooses the right or wrong course in life.

How did he deal with this problem? First of all, by tactful suggestion that such a situation must sooner or later arise, so that the youth was not taken utterly unawares. Second, by urging the child in all cases of difficulty or distress to consult the *Kinder-Vater*. At the head of each choir was a carefully chosen leader whose business it was to win the love and confidence of each child. The ideal *Kinder-Vater* was so very hard to find that Zinzendorf felt it was far easier to come by the ideal bishop. Finally the child was reminded that Christ had once been an adolescent and had experienced the same misgivings, the same unhappiness. He had been exposed to the very same temptations, and He had vanquished them. Christ knew from personal experience what suffering meant—had He not died upon the cross? Those who put their trust in Him would find that their faithful friend would not fail them. At this period of life, we may add, the ideal presented to the adolescent was the Christian knight, *sans peur et sans reproche*.

It has been said that the contradictions in Luther's character are due to the fact that his mind was a battlefield on which two epochs fought with one another. It has been suggested that the same is true of Zinzendorf. He stood between two eras, between the old "authoritarian teaching" and the "naturalism" which we associate with Rousseau (whose *Emile* appeared a year after Zinzendorf died). Shortly before his death he expressed the conviction that the religious education given at Herrnhut was superior to any other; "a great leap forward" had been made and the methods which had obtained for 150 years were left behind. Not through speculation, but through personal experience in dealing with children he had found a better way.

It may be that Zinzendorf's method in other hands—the same holds good of Thomas Arnold—will not yield equally satisfactory results, that a form of education well suited to the needs of a small, exceptionally devout community is not applicable to the varied schools of a pluralistic society. Zinzendorf's theory and his method may be equally defective, yet no teacher of religion can fail to profit by being brought into contact with one who, despite his many weaknesses, has much to teach. He reverenced children; he loved them as few have done. He was one of them; they knew it and they loved him. Few men—*none* known to this writer—have equaled him in the art of addressing children, in making the Bible live for children, in touching the hearts of children. Nor has any rivaled him in the yet more difficult task of dealing with the adolescent.

Selected Bibliography

Greenfield, J. *When the Spirit Came*. Minneapolis: Bethany, 1967.

Langton, E. *History of the Moravian Church*. London: Allen and Unwin, 1956.

Lewis, A. *Zinzendorf the Ecumenical Pioneer*. Philadelphia: Westminster, 1962.

Meyer, H. *Child Nature and Nurture According to Nicolaus Ludwig von Zinzendorf*. Chicago: Abingdon, 1928.

Weinlick, J. *Count Zinzendorf*. Nashville: Abingdon, 1956.

Part Four

A.D. 1750-1900

Important religious educators appeared in Great Britain, on the Continent, and in the United States during the final 150 years with which this volume is concerned. These years witnessed the dominance of Deism and romanticism, both of which were at odds with historic Christian orthodoxy, in the last half of the eighteenth century; the resurgence of Christianity in nineteenth-century Europe and the spread of the gospel to all the continents by various evangelical societies; and the flowering of theological liberalism, with its roots in German rationalistic philosophy, in the late 1800s.

During the late eighteenth century England was the scene for the Methodist revival and the rise of the Sunday-school movement; and during the first half of the nineteenth century, for the reformation of the public schools and the activity of the Tractarians. Representatives of these four forces played crucial roles in the development of Christian education.

John Wesley (1703-1791) was at once the founder of the Methodist revival and a pioneer of popular education. He not only preached and wrote voluminously, he criticized public schools and began his own. He encouraged intellectual and moral discipline as well as self-respect. He did much to spread knowledge and culture, especially among the poorer classes, breaking down barriers of privilege and creed and making learning accessible to all.

Wesley also encouraged the development of Sunday schools, and while some contend that one of the early schools he organized was the first Sunday school, the school begun by **Robert Raikes** (1735-1811) in Gloucester in 1780 was more likely the first. Raikes brought children off the streets on Sundays to instruct them in religion as well as traditional subjects. He emphasized direct study of the Bible rather than memorizing catechism, and his schools had a great impact on the morals of their students.

The transformation of England's public schools from places of lawlessness, moral laxity, and minimal learning to places which produced men of both principle and scholarship must be credited to **Thomas Arnold** (1795-1842) as much as to anyone. The schoolmaster of Rugby advocted an education which permeates public life with the ethics of the gospel; the educated man is always a Christian gentleman and often a public servant.

Tractarian **John Henry Newman** (1801-1890) was concerned with education only on the university level. His ideal was an institution which harmonizes university education with Christian faith. Since religion is part of the universal experience and since the university should prepare students for life in general, not just for their vocations, university education must include religion.

The Continental educators whose influence on religious education was the greatest were Switzerland's **Johann H. Pestalozzi** (1747-1827), Germany's **Johann Friedrich Herbart** (1776-1841), and the more evangelical **Abraham Kuyper** (1837-1920) of the Netherlands.

Pestalozzi's most significant contributions were his sociological inquiry into education and his concern for the education of disadvantaged children. His natural theory of education was a way of cooperating with the natural development of the student's God-given powers.

Herbart, who successfully combined the talents of a philosopher and educator, considered the fundamental goal of education to be moral men. To achieve this goal all branches of knowledge are integrated into a system, and religion, rather than being taught separately, is drawn from the other subjects.

Kuyper was a Christian minister, not an educator. But he became the leader of a political party which devoted much attention to education, and he established the Free University of Amsterdam. All of learning must be in the context of Christian education, contended Kuyper; no subject can be clearly understood apart from Christianity.

The American educators whose ideas have been most seminal for modern religious education are **Horace Bushnell** (1802-1876), **William James** (1842-1910), and **John Dewey** (1859-1952). Bushnell, critical of the revival approach to ministering to children in the church, emphasized instead their natural Christian growth in an environment of love. He was optimistic about education's power to reform society.

James, probably America's leading psychologist-philosopher in his day, saw the usefulness of religion and philosophy in properly organizing the individual's life. Education requires an individual to determine his relation to the ultimates of the universe, insisted James. He pointed to the crisis that an individual experiences in discovering a meaningful religion.

Although Dewey was not a religious educator, his influence on modern religious (as well as secular) education has probably been greater than that of anyone else. With him are associated the concepts of pragmatic education, experimental thinking in education, activity-centered education (learning by doing), and life-oriented religion. For him experience was more vital than knowledge, including Biblical knowledge. He changed the school from a place where children prepare for life to a place where they live. It is to be an embryonic community, busy with occupations that reflect those in the larger society and permeated with the spirit of art, history, and science.

17

Elmer L. Towns

John Wesley
(1703-1791)

John Wesley was a pioneer of popular education. He conducted educational enterprises continuously for over fifty years, and some experts contend that he was the only leader of importance in eighteenth-century England who had a real and practical interest in educating children of all classes. The movement for popular education which Wesley helped inaugurate grew so rapidly that by the middle of the nineteenth century, a stigma was associated with illiteracy.[1]

The schools of Wesley's day admitted only the children of the upper classes, and these institutions fell far below his standards. Wesley's indictment of the educational system of his day was fivefold.

First, most of the schools were located in the great towns of England where the children's peers discouraged study.

Second, the schools admitted all sorts of children indiscriminately, with the worse ones tending to corrupt the better. (Wesley practiced expulsion in his schools, reporting in his *Journal* that when "one of the boys studiously labored to corrupt the rest,"

---

1. J. O. Gross, *John Wesley: Christian Educator*, p. 14.

Wesley "would not suffer him to stay any longer under the roof, but sent him home that very hour.")

Third, instruction in religion was extremely defective, provoking Wesley to charge that schoolmasters uninstructed in the elements of religion corrupted the faith of the young children.

Fourth, writing and arithmetic were neglected in favor of the classics and classical languages, including classics which are destructive to religion.

And fifth, the classics were taught in a random order, without grading them according to the difficulty of their subject matter or syntax.

The essence of Wesley's indictment was that religion and education should go hand in hand. The righteous prosper mentally as the green bay tree, while the unrighteous sow the wind of ungodliness and reap a whirlwind of perpetual ignorance.

Wesley called the boarding schools "nurserys of all manners of wickedness."[2]

> Boys should not be sent to them. Girls should not be [either]..., for there they will be taught by other girls [everything that a Christian woman ought not learn] and will be unable to continue in fear of God and save their souls.

Later Wesley warned Methodist parents that if they "would send your girls headlong to hell, send them to a fashionable boarding school!"

Early Methodists, including the first itinerant preachers, came largely from the underprivileged class which was deprived of an opportunity for education. Wesley knew that helping these people involved educating them. He sincerely believed that although Methodists were poor, they need not be ignorant, and he realized that the results of his revival would be permanent only if the revival was united with education. Wesley wanted his preachers to have a broad, general knowledge, insisting that they spend five hours daily in hard study. In 1745 he published a list of books covering such areas as practical and doctrinal divinity, philosophy, astronomy, poetry, and history to guide the preachers in their self-education. He went so far as to say that their success in preaching would be in proportion to their appeal to the hearers' minds.

In Alfred H. Body's judgment, "Credit must be given to Wesley for supplying a course of higher education. Wesley may be re-

---

2. *Works*, 3:34.

garded as the true successor to Erasmus by providing great provincial universities in his day, spreading knowledge and culture throughout the land, breaking down the barriers of privilege and creed, and making learning accessible to all."[3]

Influences on Wesley

Recognizing his enormous educational contributions, let us examine those individuals who influenced the formation of Wesley's educational philosophy.

Susanna Wesley. One of the chief sources of Wesley's detailed program of training children was his mother. Ten of the nineteen children born to the Epworth rector's wife survived infancy, and Susanna Wesley was almost exclusively responsible for their training. She refused to send them to the local schoolmaster, John Hollan, because she felt he was notoriously incompetent and wicked. She looked upon all her children as talents entrusted to her by God, and she desired to impart to them useful knowledge and, even more basic, to save their souls.

She made it her habit to converse one evening a week with each child separately. Thursday evenings were devoted to John, and so deeply was the boy impressed that at the age of eight his father judged him fit to receive Holy Communion.

Because Susanna found no textbooks that met her severe requirements, she prepared her own, suiting them to her children's needs. Three of them were *An Exposition of the Apostles' Creed, An Exposition of the Ten Commandments,* and *Religious Conference Written for the Use of My Children.*

Susanna wrote to her son John in later years: "I insist upon conquering the will of children betimes because this is the only strong and rational foundation of a religious education, without which both precept and example will be ineffectual."[4] But she did not believe in conquering their wills only by severe punishment. In another letter to John, Susanna articulated her principles of child rearing, the main points of which can be summarized as follows: (1) Because cowardice and fear of punishment often encourage a child to lie, anyone charged with a fault who would confess it and promise to amend, would not be beaten.

---

3. *John Wesley and Education,* p. 142.
4. Quoted in J. Wesley, *Journal,* 3:34.

(2) No sinful action such as lying, pilfering, playing at church, playing on the Lord's Day, disobedience, or quarreling ever went unpunished. (3) No child was beaten twice for the same fault. (4) Every signal act of obedience was commended and rewarded. (5) Anything done out of obedience or an intent to please, but not done well, should be accepted with kindness, and the child patiently shown how to do better in the future. (6) Personal property was inviolable and no one was permitted to invade the property of another to the smallest extent. (7) Promises were observed strictly. Once a gift was bestowed, the giver relinquished all rights to the gift. (8) No girl was taught to work until she could read well, and then she was taught to work with the same application and for the same time that she was held to reading.[5]

John Amos Comenius. Wesley visited Jena and Herrnhut and saw the Moravian schools in action. It is possible that at Herrnhut he discovered the practical application of the principles of John Amos Comenius (see chapter 14), for whom education was not merely a means to eradicate natural sin but a way to build moral control. One of Comenius's principles was that no subject is to be left until the students thoroughly understand it,[6] and Wesley echoed this:

> Above all, let them not read or say one line without understanding what they say. Try them over and over; stop them short almost at every sentence and ask them what do you mean by that; read it again. So that, if it be possible they must pass nothing until it has taken hold upon them.[7]

Another of Comenius's principles was that the child's will is to be completely surrendered to the teacher's, and Wesley agreed completely.

> A wise parent should begin to break ... [his child's] will the first moment it appears. In the whole act of Christian education ... there is nothing more important than this.... the will of the parent is to a little child in the place of the will of God. But in order to carry this point, you will need incredible firmness and resolution; for after you have once begun, you must never give way.[8]

The influence of Comenius's principles on Wesley is impossible

5. Ibid., 3:34-39.
6. Body, *John Wesley and Education*, pp. 49-51.
7. Quoted in Body, *John Wesley and Education*, pp. 49, 50.
8. Ibid.

to measure because so many of them were part of Susanna Wesley's independently formulated philosophy, but Comenius's principles certainly reinforced what Wesley had learned from his mother.

John Locke. Wesley, then, combined sound religious training with perfect control of the children. Concerning the latter he found much with which to agree in the works of John Locke, and he did not hesitate to adopt it. A number of passages from Wesley's works show not only a striking similarity in thought to Locke's *Some Thoughts Concerning Education,* but also a marked similarity in expression (see table 1). Locke, for example, wrote that most children are born with "some bias in their natural temper, which it is the business of education to take off or counter balance." Wesley wrote that "the bias of nature is set the wrong way: education is designed to set it right." Wesley's use of the term *bias* in this context is hardly natural, and the whole sentence is, according to Body, a typical Wesleyan abridgment. Body concluded that "in spite of the manifest differences between the schemes of education proposed by each man," such parallel passages as this leave one with the "strong feeling that Wesley was really indebted to Locke for much of his educational theory."[9]

9. Ibid., p. 59.

Table 1

Locke	Wesley
This ought to be observed as an inviolable Maxim, that whatever once is deny'd them [i.e., children], they are certainly not to obtain by crying or Importunity, unless one has a mind to teach them to be impatient and troublesome by rewarding them for it when they are so.	Let him have nothing he cries for; absolutely nothing, great or small: else you undo your own work.
Most Children's Constitutions are either spoiled or at least harmed by Cockering and tenderness. . . . Let his bed be hard, and rather Quilts than Feathers. Hard lodging strengthens the Parts; whereas being bury'd every night in Feathers melts and dissolves the Body.	All their beds have mattresses upon them, not featherbeds, both because they are most healthy, and because we would keep them at the utmost distance from softness and effeminacy.

His Educational Philosophy

To ascertain the relationship between Wesley's educational philosophy and his theology, one must turn primarily to "A Treatise on Baptism," "On the Education of Children," "On Family Religion," and "On Obedience to Parents." Also of help are several articles and tracts: "A Thought on the Manner of Educating Children" (originally published in 1783 in *The Arminian Magazine*), "A Short Account of the School Near Bristol," "A Plain Account of the Kingswood School," "Remarks on the State of Kingswood School," and "Serious Thoughts Concerning Godfathers and Godmothers."

Wesley believed that the entire human race, including its youngest members, is depraved; that both young and old are by nature entirely lacking in God's natural and moral image, and thus are entirely alienated from God. Salvation from sin is the main purpose of life, and conversion begins in repentance, which is the knowledge and conviction of man's despicable condition. When converted, man is born again and regenerated; when justified, man's relationship to God is changed. The outward consequences in the individual are holiness, or piety, which is communion with God and which increases as one uses the means of grace.

The first step in the redemption of a child, according to Wesley, is baptism. Adults must first repent and believe the gospel before being baptized, but children need not meet this condition because they cannot. Infants are in a state of original sin, and ordinarily this must be washed away by baptism for them to be saved. They are included in the covenant with God and are capable of being solemnly consecrated to Him. They can be consecrated only by baptism. They have the right to come to Christ, to be ingrafted into Him. Baptism regenerates, justifies, and gives the infant all the privileges of Christian religion. The baptism of children is not only proper, it is a sacred duty.

Wesley taught that through baptism "a principle of grace is infused" into children and that

> the work accomplished is so far effectual, that if they die before they commit actual sin, they will be eternally safe.[10]

The only way to conserve a child's innocence is to guard him completely against contamination during his helpless years and

---

10. *Works*, 6:14.

to build his character. As a result he may resist evil by his own strength when he comes of age. This task of guarding and character-building is the task of education.[11]

The grand end of education is to cure the diseases of human nature.[12]

The bias of nature is the wrong way; education is designed to set it right. This, by the grace of God, is to turn the bias from self-will, pride, anger, revenge and the love of the world, to resignation, lowliness, meekness and the love of God.

The work begun by parents is to be continued in the schools by instructors, and this is the reason Wesley felt that the parents' choice of schools is so important.

Granted Wesley's views on the salvation of children, why did he employ revival methods in working with them? He held, as was noted, that if a child dies before committing actual sin, he is eternally safe. But Wesley also held that it is natural for the child who survives to commit sin because the principle of nature is still working in him. And anyone who sins after his baptism has denied that rite and therefore must be born again if he is to be saved.

... any willful sin, such as lying, profaning the Lord's day or the Lord's name is a denial of baptism as much as sinful affections, and necessitates a new birth.

We conclude, then, that Wesley considered conversion universally necessary for children as well as for adults. In J. W. Prince's words, "Wesley did not hold that religious education makes conversion unnecessary, but that religious education and conversion supplement each other." Wesley's position in "On the Education of Children" was, in fact, that religious education should both cure the diseases of nature and train the child in religion. Prince wrote further that "the goal of all work with children at home, in the schools, in the Methodist society is to make them pious, to lead to personal religion, and to insure salvation. It is not merely to bring them up so that they do no harm and abstain from outward sin, nor to get them accustomed to use of grace, saying their prayers, reading their books, and the like, nor is it to train them in right opinions. The purpose of religious education is to instill

11. J. W. Prince, *Wesley on Religious Education*, p. 95.
12. *Works*, 2:310.

in children true religion, holiness and the love of God and mankind and to train them in the image of God."[13]

Wesley's educational philosophy can be summarized in several principles.

The child is a unit for salvation. John O. Gross wrote that Wesley "never considered a child as a child, but rather as a unit for salvation, bred in sin, apt to evil, and altogether as a 'brand to be plucked out of the burning.' "[14]

The child is capable of genuine religious life. It is difficult to say at what age Wesley expected to see holiness manifest in children. He frequently failed to record the ages of children to whom he referred in his *Journal* as having undergone religious experiences, but there are some exceptions.

On 8 April 1755 Wesley described a girl who died at 2½.

> Such a child ... is scarce heard of in a century.... If the brother or sister spoke angrily to each other, or behaved triflingly, she either sharply reproved or tenderly entreated them to give over. If she had spoken too sharply to anyone, she would humble herself to them and not rest till they had forgiven her. After her health declined, she was particularly pleased when that hymn was sung, "Abba Father," and would frequently sing that line herself: "Abba Father, hear my cry"![15]

On 28 June 1746 Wesley wrote of a three-year-old who refused to be comforted when she thought she had displeased God. She held daily prayers and was teaching other children the rudiments of Christianity.

And on 16 September 1744 Wesley described the deathbed conversion of a four-year-old who went "to God in the full assurance of faith."

Such excerpts from Wesley's *Journal* show that he "believed it was possible for very young children to be religious, and they also give some idea of the nature of the religion which, though striking him as unusual in children so young, he would cultivate as early as possible."[16] Wesley's view that children so young are capable of mature religious consciousness was grounded in his doctrine of grace. When the Spirit is the Teacher, there is no delay of learning.

---

13. *Wesley on Religious Education*, p. 96.
14. *John Wesley: Christian Educator*, p. 9.
15. 4:110, 111.
16. Prince, *Wesley on Religious Education*, p. 85.

If you say, nay, but they cannot understand you when they are so young, I answer, No; nor when they are fifty years old, unless God opens their understanding. And can He not do this at any age?

Wesley's Kingswood school was swept by recurring revivals, and most of the students saved were between the ages of six and fourteen. Wesley believed that he himself had been ripe for spiritual change approximately at age ten, for this was when he thought he had sinned away the "washing of the Holy Ghost" he had received at baptism.

The child must receive religious instruction as soon as he can reason. Conscious religious instruction should begin with the dawn of reason.

Scripture, reason, and experience jointly testify as that, inasmuch as the corruption of nature is earlier than our instruction can be, we should take all pains and care to counteract this corruption as early as possible.[17]

The child must be cured of the disease of sin through education. To praise children for other than religious worth teaches them to value what is unworthy.

They who teach children to love praise, train them up for the devil.

Children should be commended exceedingly sparingly and then only if with it they [are taught] that God alone is praiseworthy and the source of all that His children possess for which they are commended.

To strike at the root of their pride, teach your children as soon as possible that they are fallen spirits; that they are fallen short of that glorious image of God wherein they were first created; that they are not now as they once were, incorrupt pictures of the God of glory; bearing the express likeness of the . . . Holy Father's Spirit, but more ignorant, more foolish, and more wicked than they can possibly conceive. Show them that, in pride, passion, and revenge, they are now like the devil. And that in foolish desires and groveling appetites they are like beasts of the field.[18]

This practical application of Wesley's doctrine of original sin may seem severe, but it was basic to his concept of Christian education.

The child's will must be broken. Wesley's view of discipline was harsh, but his reason for breaking a child's will was to save his soul. Even before the child can speak, his parents should

make him do as he is bid, if you whip him ten times running to

---

17. *Works,* 7:459.
18. Ibid.

effect it. Let none persuade you it is cruelty to do this; it is cruel not to do it. Break his will now and his soul will live and he will probably bless you through all eternity.[19]

But Wesley balanced admonitions such as these with others that urged discipline "by mildness, softness and gentleness . . . by advice, persuasion and reproof." He even warned that if teachers exercise needless severity, "it will not be strange if religion stinks in the nostrils" of their students.[20]

His Educational Methodology

At times Wesley instructed his followers concerning the methods which a teacher should use and the characteristics of a good teacher.

The pedagogical methods which he advocated can be summarized in several principles.

Secure the students' attention before teaching. Wesley recognized that "to draw and fix the attention of the children is one of the greatest difficulties in speaking to them."

Use words that the children understand, words which they use themselves. Carefully observe the few ideas the children already have and graft into them what is being taught.

To speak of God and use the words of the assembly's Catchism, that "the chief end of man is to glorify God and enjoy Him forever," is to employ terms beyond any capacity of little children.

Use illustrations from everyday life.

In speaking of God, interest children first in the sun, in its warmth, its work in causing flowers and grass to grow. Then point to God as the power behind the sun, causing it to shine, giving it its warmth. From that, it is easy to speak of His power and love, even to the smallest things such as a child.

Establish a relationship of love. The teacher can then say to the student:

God loves you. He loves to do you good. He loves to make you happy. Would you then not love Him? You love me, because I love you and do you good. But it is God that makes me love you. Therefore, you should love Him. He will teach you how to love Him.[21]

---

19. Quoted in Body, *John Wesley and Education,* p. 49.
20. *Works,* 2:303.
21. Ibid., pp. 304, 305.

Be patient, and repeat yourself many times. ". . . if teaching is to bear any fruit," wrote Wesley, one must "teach patiently."

> You must tell them the same thing ten times over or you do nothing.[22]

> Some children are inconceivably dull, others so giddy and perverse that if the teacher follows his own inclination he will give up in despair. I remember to have heard my father asking my mother, "How could you have the patience to tell that blockhead the same thing twenty times over?" She answered, "Why if I had told him but nineteen times I should have lost all my labors." What patience indeed, what love, what knowledge.[23]

The good teacher, then, must be patient. He must also be capable of governing students. In "A Thought on the Manner of Educating Children," an article published in 1783, Wesley wrote:

> Even religious masters may not have the spirit of government to which some even good men are stranger. They may habitually lean to this or that extreme, of remissness or of severity. And if they give children too much of their own will, or needlessly and churlishly restrain them; if they either use no punishment at all, or more than is necessary, the leaning either to one extreme or the other, may frustrate all their endeavors.[24]

The teacher must also have within him the spirit of true religion. As for those pretenders among the ranks of religious instructors, Wesley held that they, thinking they have religion when they have none at all, add pride to their vices.

Wesley considered good teachers so crucial to the success of religious training that he did not hesitate to change teachers in the Kingswood school when things were not going well there. After dismissing Mr. Simpson and deciding to replace him with Thomas McGeary, a young man of twenty-two, Wesley wrote to McGeary:

> You seem to be the man I want. As to salary, you'll have 30 pounds a year; board, etc., will be 30 more. But do not come *for money.* (1) Do not come at all unless purely to raise a Christian school. (2) Anybody behaving ill, I will turn away immediately. (3) I expect you to be in the school eight hours a day. (4) In all things, I expect you should be circumspect. But you will judge better by considering the printed rules. The sooner you come, the better.[25]

---

22. Ibid., 7:91.
23. Ibid., 1:68.
24. Ibid., 7:459.
25. *Methodist Magazine* (1876), p. 324.

Twelve months later the school experienced a gracious outpouring of God's Spirit. In 1786 Wesley visited the school and found it in excellent order.

> It is now one of the pleasantest spots in England. I found all things just according to my desire; the rules being well observed and the whole behavior of the children showing that they were now managed with the wisdom that cometh from above.

On 11 September 1789 he wrote:

> I went over to Kingswood: sweet recess! where everything now is just as I wish. . . . I spent some time with the children; all of whom behaved well: several are much awakened, and a few are rejoicing in the favor of God.[26]

Thus Wesley's belief in the importance of the teacher was confirmed.

His Educational Accomplishments

Having studied the influences on the formation of Wesley's educational philosophy and the chief principles of the latter, it remains to see the practical outworking of those principles.

The Kingswood and charity schools. Wesley did more than condemn the schools of his day; he set up and ran his own. He also endorsed several private mistresses in schools of the right sort for Methodist people. The schools which Wesley established for the higher education of Methodist boys reflected his belief in the primacy of religious education.

The school at Kingswood was to be a model Christian institution as well as an educational center superior in many respects to any other school which Wesley had seen, at home or abroad. He outlined the curriculum and prepared textbooks in English grammar, French, Greek, and Hebrew. These textbooks total 1,729 printed pages, indicating the immense labor involved in Wesley's quest for excellence. His famous rule forbidding Kingswood students to play has haunted Methodists from time to time since Wesley's day:

> The student shall be indulged with nothing which the world calls play. Let this rule be observed with strictest niceity, for those who play when they are young, will play when they are old.

---

26. *Journal,* 8:10.

This prohibition may stem from Wesley's memories of childhood when, as an undersized youth, Wesley was often bullied and beaten for sport by his fellow students at Charterhouse. But more likely the rule reflects the practice of the Herrnhut Moravians.

Children's sermons and hymns. Wesley preached to children on many occasions, writing in his *Journal* on 13 June 1790, for example, that he had "preached to the children of our Sunday school, six or seven hundred of whom were present." In 1790 he published *Forty-Four Hymns for Children,* many hymns from which were later included in his brother Charles's *Hymns for Children and Others of Ripe Years.* John introduced his *Forty-Four Hymns* with these words:

> There are two ways of writing or speaking to children; the one is to let ourselves down to them; the other, to lift them up to us. Dr. Watts has wrote in the former way and has succeeded admirable well speaking to children and leaving them as he found them. The following hymns are written on the other plain. They contain strong and manly sense, yet expressed in such plain and easy language a child may understand. But when they do, they will be children no longer, only in years and stature.

This hymnal was one of Wesley's last publications, showing that even in his old age his concern for children did not decrease.

Methodist "bands." Wesley was also concerned for the education of adult Methodists, and he did not leave it entirely to the preachers whom he helped train. During Wesley's days at Oxford he, as well as Charles Wesley and George Whitefield, was part of the Holy Club, a small group organized for study, prayer, self-examination, and good works—including the visitation of prisoners and the sick. Later, recognizing the value of small groups, he divided the Methodists into "bands,"

> ... putting the married and single men, and the married or single women, together. The chief rules of the bands (that is, little companies; so that old English word signifies) run thus: in order to confess our faults one to another, and pray one for another that we may be healed, we intend, (1) To meet once a week, at the least. (2) To come punctually at the hour appointed. (3) To begin with singing or prayer. (4) To speak each of us in order, freely and plainly, the true state of our soul, with the faults we have committed in thought, word or deed, and the temptations we have felt since our last meeting. (5) To desire some person among us (thence called a leader) to speak his own state first, and then to ask the rest, in

order, as many and searching questions as may be, concerning their state, sins, and temptations.[27]

Some Methodists did not want to join a band, however, and toward the end of his ministry Wesley began to deemphasize bands and emphasize the Sunday school. One might infer that the latter even replaced the former, but it is only an inference. At any rate, the bands, encouraging as they did reciprocal honesty, confession, and self-support, were similar to what is being promoted by the contemporary group-dynamics movement.

Although Wesley did much to form popular opinion and advance the intellectual condition of the English people (he wrote 371 books on an enormous range of subjects), he was not an educational innovator; he was a product of the eighteenth century and shared its blindness to the meaning of childhood. Nevertheless, his recognition of the crucial role that education must play in the Methodist revival and his educational achievements made Wesley a significant Christian educator of his century.

Selected Bibliography

Body, A. H. *John Wesley and Education*. London: Epworth, 1936.

Gross, J. O. *John Wesley: Christian Educator*. Nashville: Methodist Board of Education, 1954.

Kelly, C. H. *Wesley: The Man, His Teaching and His Work*. London: Free Church College, 1891.

Prince, J. W. *Wesley on Religious Education*. New York: Methodist Book Concern, 1926.

Tyerman, L. *The Life and Times of the Rev. John Wesley, M.A.* New York: Harper, 1872.

Wesley, J. *Journal*. Edited by N. Curnock. 9 vols. London: Epworth, 1938.

———. *Works*. Edited by J. Emory. 7 vols. New York: Hunt and Eaton, 1831.

---

27. Quoted in M. Piette, *John Wesley in the Evolution of Protestantism* (London: Sheed and Ward, 1936), p. 457.

18

Elmer L. Towns

Robert Raikes
(1735-1811)

Histories of religious education generally date the beginning of the modern Sunday-school movement in 1780 when Robert Raikes began his school in Gloucester, England. That Raikes's was the first Sunday school, however, has been challenged.[1]

Earlier "Sunday Schools"

The claim is widespread that the school begun in 1737 by John Wesley while serving the Christ Church Parish in Savannah, Georgia, was the first Sunday school. Wesley described the school's "general method": ". . . a young gentleman, who came with me, teaches "between thirty and forty children to read, write and coste accounts. Before school in the morning and after school in the afternoon, he catechizes the lowest class, and endeavours to fix something of what was said in their understanding as well as in their memories. In the evening he instructs the larger children. On Saturday, in the afternoon he catechizes them all. The same I

---

1. More than twenty counterclaims are listed in C. Trumbull, *Yale Lecturer on the Sunday School: Its Origin, Mission, Methods and Auxiliaries* (Philadelphia: Wattles, 1888), p. 112.

do on Sunday before the evening service. And in the church, immediately after the Second Lesson, a select number of them having repeated the Catechism and been examined in some part of it, I endavor to explain at large, and enforce that part, both on them and the congregation."[2] But this school did not meet only on Sunday, and Wesley seemed both pleased and surprised when he encountered a Sunday school almost fifty years later in 1783: "Who knows but that some of these schools may become nurseries for Christians?"[3]

Another early school, one which seems to have been overlooked by authors dealing with the origins of the Sunday school, was begun by Hannah Bell in 1769 in High Wycombe, England. She described it to Wesley in a letter written in 1770: "The children meet twice a week, every Sunday and Monday. They are a wild company, but seem willing to be instructed. I labor among them, especially desiring to promote the interest of the Church of Christ."[4]

Dr. Joseph Bellamy, a pastor in Bethlehem, Connecticut, was credited by historian Joel Hauser with having begun a Sunday school in 1740. Bellamy, wrote Hauser, "was accustomed to meet the youth of his congregation on the Sabbath, not merely for a catechetical exercise, but for a recitation from the Bible, accompanied with familiar instructions suited to the capacities of the young."[5]

In 1744, according to the records of the First Moravian Church of Philadelphia, the wife of Pastor James Greeming "organized a Sunday school of thirty-three children, who were gathered from the neighborhood, to keep them from running the streets, and to receive religious instruction."[6]

Still another school was begun in 1739 in Ephrata, Pennsylvania, by a group which had separated from the Dunkards (German Baptists). The group's records, as quoted by historian Edwin Rice, indicate that the school was organized "to give instruction to the indigent children who were kept from regular school by em-

---

2. *Works*, ed. J. Emory, vol. 7 (New York: Hunt and Eaton, 1831), p. 322.
3. Quoted in L. Tyerman, *The Life and Times of the Rev. John Wesley, M.A.* (New York: Harper, 1872), p. 506.
4. Quoted in Wesley, *Journal*, ed. N. Curnock, vol. 5 (London: Epworth, 1938), p. 104.
5. Quoted in E. Rice, *The Sunday-School Movement and the American Sunday-School Union*, p. 426.
6. Quoted in J. T. Farris, *Old Churches and Meeting Houses In and Around Philadelphia* (Philadelphia: Lippincott, 1926), p. 115.

ployment which their necessities obliged them to be engaged at during the week, as well as to give religious instruction."[7]

These five schools, however, lack four characteristics that set apart Raikes's school and merit for it the claim of being the first modern Sunday school.

First, general education was the cornerstone of Raikes's school while the earlier schools were primarily for religious indoctrination. As the Sunday school developed, general education was soon dropped in favor of Christian teaching, but Sunday school still served as a broadening experience for many common people with little formal education.

Second, Raikes's Sunday school received popular acceptance and continued to grow; the earlier schools received only limited acceptance and eventuallly ceased to exist.

Third, Raikes's students studied the Bible directly rather than only being catechized.

And fourth, Raikes's school was evangelistic. It was not evangelistic in the same way that contemporary "Child Evangelism" classes are; no records preserve "decisions" or "professions of faith" such as occurred in Wesley's or Whitefield's preaching services. But Raikes's school was known for its impact on the students' morals, for the transformation of their lives, and this is evidence of its evangelistic thrust.

Raikes's First Sunday School

Raikes was born in 1735 to the printer and crusading editor of *The Gloucester Journal,* a Tory newspaper. Robert's father was the first to report the proceedings of Parliament, for which he was reprimanded at the bar of the House of Lords in the days of George I. Robert, who would succeed his father as publisher of the *Journal,* received a liberal education at home.

As an adult Raikes was a "fair, well-looking man, about medium height and comfortably stout, buckish and stylish in appearance with his dark blue coat and white fancy waist coat, with silver-gilt buttons, cambric frills and ruffs, nankeen breeches, white stockings, and buckles on his shoes." He carried a stick in his hand when not occupied with his gold snuff box, and he wore a three-cornered hat over a brown wig. His "gay and joyous tempera-

---

7. Quoted in Rice, *The Sunday-School Movement,* p. 427. Rice wrote, "The ancient records were freely and fully shown to us."

ment" made him an affectionate husband and father and a transparent and outgoing individual. He was "a good businessman, steady, methodical and very tenacious of purpose, kindly and benevolent, and not without a touch of the vanity that often marks self-made men."[8]

Religiously, Raikes was described by George L. Merrill as an "evangelical with a leaning toward mysticism,"[9] and by John McClintock as "a truly devout man" who "carried his Christianity into every-day life" and who was "not only scrupulous about his church attendance on the Sabbath, but made it the rule to frequent early morning prayers on week-days at the Gloucester cathedral."[10]

Raikes had a long-standing interest in the lowly and degraded classes of his day, visiting prisons and going through the streets seeking to do whatever good he could. He used his newspaper to influence public opinion in favor of the suffering lower class, and he was largely responsible for the improvement of prison conditions in England at the close of the century. In a famous letter to Colonel Townley of Lancaster, published in the *Gentleman's Magazine,* Raikes described an incident which had much to do with his beginning a Sunday school.

> The beginning of the scheme was entirely owing to accident. Some business leading me one morning to the suburbs of the city, where the lowest of the people (who are principally employed in the pin factory) chiefly reside, I was struck with concern after seeing a group of children wretchedly ragged, at play in the streets. I asked an inhabitant whether those children belonged to that part of town, and admitted their misery and idleness. "Ah, sir," said the woman to whom I was speaking, "Could you take the view of this part of town on Sunday, you would be shocked indeed; for then the street is filled with multitudes of those wretches who come on release of the day of employment, spend their time in noise and riot, playing at "chuck" and cursing and swearing in a manner so horrid as to convey to any serious minded, an idea of hell rather than any other place.[11]

In *The Gloucester Journal* Raikes reported similar conditions in surrounding towns and villages.

---

8. G. L. Merrill, *The Development of the Sunday School, 1780-1905,* p. 1.
9. Ibid.
10. "Raikes, Robert," in *Cyclopaedia of Biblical, Theological, and Ecclesiastical Literature,* 8:883.
11. 303 (1784).

Farmers and other inhabitants of the towns and villages, complained that they received more injury to their property on the Sabbath than on all of the week besides; this, in a great measure, received from the lawless state of the younger class, who are allowed to run wild on that day, free from every restraint.[12]

The actual organization of the Sunday school was described by Thomas Stork, rector of St. John the Baptist in Gloucester, in his journal. He reported that he and Raikes talked one day of "the deplorable state of the lower classes of mankind," and particularly of the lamentable situation "of the poorer children." They resolved to do something about it and "immediately proceeded to the business." They procured "the names of about ninety children, [and] placed them under the care of four persons for a stated number of hours on Sunday. As minister of the parish I took upon me the superintendence of the schools and one-third of the expense." Stork attributed the progress of the schools "to the constant representation which Mr. Raikes made in his own paper, *The Gloucester Journal,* of the benefits which he perceived would arise from it."[13] Rice reported that Raikes had in view the reformation of the country, and because he considered it useless to appeal to the parents, "began directly with the children, in the belief that ignorance is the first cause of idleness and vice."[14]

Raikes's Methodology

Students and discipline. The pupils of Raikes's Sunday school included both sexes, not just boys as Merrill contended; Raikes wrote in a letter in 1787 that it was his practice that "the sexes [be] kept separate."[15] Raikes himself took a personal interest in the well-being of the students, whom he described as "evil-smelling outcasts":

I give some little token of my regard, as a pair of shoes, if they are barefooted, and some who are very bare of apparel, I clothe.[16]

Popular treatments of Raikes generally report that he marched unwilling children to his school "with clogs and logs of wood tied to their feet and legs, just as cattle were hobbled when graz-

---

12. Quoted in Rice, *The Sunday-School Movement,* p. 421.
13. Quoted in W. R. Stephens, *A History of the English Church,* 7:300, 301.
14. *The Sunday-School Movement,* p. 14.
15. Quoted in Rice, *The Sunday-School Movement,* p. 438.
16. Ibid.

ing on the town commons in that day."[17] But this cannot be documented. William Brick, a product of Raikes's first Sunday school, in a testimonial at Raikes's funeral reported that the parents, not Raikes, "hobbled" the children: "Some terrible bad chaps went to school when I first went. They were always bad 'uns, coming in. I know the parents of one or two of them used to walk them to school with 14-pound weights tied to their legs... sometimes boys would be sent to school with logs of wood tied to their ankles, just as though they were wild jackasses, which I suppose they were, only worse."[18] However the children were brought to the school, Raikes believed in discipline once they were there. As Brick told it: "When a boy was very bad, he [Raikes] would take him out of the school, and march him home and get his parents to 'wallop' him. He'd stop and see it done and then bring the urchin back, rubbing his eyes and other places. Mr. Raikes was a terror to all evil doers and a praise to them that did well. Everyone in the city loved and feared him."[19]

Curriculum and textbooks. The curriculum of the earliest Sunday school included reading and writing, and the chief textbook was the Bible. The purpose of the school, wrote Raikes, was "to furnish opportunities of instruction to the children of the poorer part of the parish without interfering with any industry of the weekdays." Raikes was quoted by W. H. Groser as saying that the object of Sunday school was "to teach children and others to read, and to instruct them in the knowledge of their duty as rational and accountable beings."[20]

Raikes's use of the Bible as the primary text distinguished his Sunday school from the parochial schools of the day, which used primarily catechisms, creeds, and confessions. Raikes did employ supplementary texts, however. Merrill referred to one titled *Redinmadesy* ("reading made easy"), a children's introduction to reading. Rice listed an entirely different set of texts prepared by Raikes. *Sunday School Scholars* was in use in 1783, although the only edition now available is dated 1794. It passed through many editions, the last being issued in 1824. *A Copious School Book and*

17. Ibid., pp. 14, 15.
18. Quoted in J. H. Harris, *Robert Raikes: The Man and His Work*, pp. 37, 38.
19. Ibid.
20. *An Humble Attempt To Make the Path of the Sunday School Teacher Straight and Plain* (Philadelphia: American Sunday School Union, 1861), p. 24.

a Comprehensive Sentimental Book contained, according to Rice, "the alphabet, spelling, moral and religious lessons, and stories and prayers adapted to the growing powers of children."[21] The 1794 edition of the *Scholars Companion* consisted of 120 pages and was divided into four parts. Part 1 had the alphabet and twenty-five simple lessons (simple, Biblical sentences like "God is one," "God is love," "The Lord is good to all," and "The Lord of Hosts is His name").[22] The rest of the book was devoted to Old and New Testament passages stating man's duty to God and neighbor, and to the history of man's redemption.

Sunday school began at 10 A.M. At noon it was dismissed, resuming at 1 P.M. with another lesson. Then the students attended church, after which they were catechized. At 5 they were sent home and exhorted not to play in the streets.

Workers and organization. Raikes's school met first in Mrs. Meredith's kitchen and then, after the children drove Mrs. Meredith to despair, in Mrs. Brandon's kitchen. Both were paid for superintending as well as for the use of their kitchens. Raikes wrote:

> The master or mistress [of the school] was only the tenant in whose kitchen the school was held, and was paid partly for services rendered and partly for rent....[23]

Raikes added that "when the school grew and assistants were needed, they were also paid. This was the rule."[24] From the very beginning, however, some workers were unpaid, and within four years the paid teacher was beginning to pass from the scene. As Rice explained it: "If monitors, visitors, and others could be found to give their time, why might not persons competent for oversight as well, and thus all the instruction be secured without pay?"[25] Paying mistresses and masters alone even made the schools expensive and tended to limit their usefulness. Raikes himself described the progress from paid to voluntary workers:

> The paid teacher, at first, was made responsible for the good behavior, cleanliness and ability of children to read and repeat their

---

21. *The Sunday-School Movement.*
22. Ibid., p. 19.
23. Quoted in Rice, *The Sunday-School Movement,* p. 422.
24. Ibid.
25. Ibid., p. 17.

lessons; then the work of the Sunday School as a religious agency passed into other hands whose work was purely voluntary.[26]

Raikes indicated that the transition from paid to voluntary workers coincided with the school's transition from a secular to a religious agency.

As the Sunday-school movement grew, Raikes created a Sunday-school "board," or committee, which supervised the school and managed it according to rules prepared by Raikes.

> Behind the master, mistress and asssistants, there was the patron or committee ... to give directions to the master or mistress and personally superintend the religious instruction given to children.[27]

Not all of the teaching was done by adults. In the boys' classes, which usually were limited to five students, the advanced pupils "monitored" the younger ones. Raikes described this practice in a letter:

> The children who show any superiority in attainment are placed as leaders of the several classes and are employed in teaching the others their letters, or in hearing them read in a low whisper, which may be done without interrupting the master or mistress in their business.[28]

As for teaching methods, Raikes liked the use of illustrations, believing that he invented their use in teaching.

> I was showing my scholars, a little time ago, how possible it is for one invisible power to exist in bodies which will act upon other bodies without our being able to perceive in what manner they act. This I proved to them by the power of the magnet. They see the magnet draw the needle without touching it. Thus, I tell them, I wish to draw them to the paths of duty and thus lead them to heaven and happiness; and as they saw one needle, when it touched the magnet, then capable of drawing another needle, thus, when they became good they would be made instruments in the hand of God, very probably, of making other boys good.[29]

Raikes's methodology was based on several philosophical principles which Rice, who had access to a vast array of original sources, summarized: first, "vice in the child is an imitation of familiar sights and sounds"; second, "there is a time in the child's life when he is innocent" and his "faculties are active and receptive";

---

26. Ibid., p. 422.
27. Ibid.
28. Ibid.
29. Quoted in Rice, *The Sunday-School Movement*, but undocumented.

"good seeds cannot be planted too early"; and "the child takes pleasure in being good when goodness is made attractive."[30]

The Sunday School's Spread

Raikes intended the Sunday school to be "the instrument under God of awakening spiritual life in the children" and to "form the basis of national education."[31] This plan, which seems over-simplified to us, had to wait until 1780 to come to fruition proba-bly because not until 1779 were dissenters from the Church of England allowed by the "Enabling Act" to keep public or private schools, or even to tutor. Before this act was passed, then, the Sunday school was unavailable to Methodists, Baptists, and other dissenters as an instrument for religious instruction.

Not until three years after beginning his Sunday school did Raikes publicize it, first in an article in his own newspaper (3 November 1773) and then in a letter in the *Gentleman's Maga-zine* (25 November). Raikes waited this long, according to Mer-rill's quotation of him, "to see whether these degraded children, when disciplined and instructed would show the same evidence of human feelings and instincts as those more favorably situated."[32]

Wesley read Raikes's accounts and was very impressed with the Sunday school's possibilities. Before preaching at Bingley Church on 18 July 1774, Wesley "stepped into the Sunday school, which contains 240 children, taught every Sunday by several masters, and superintended by the curate. So many children, in one parish, are restrained from open sin, and taught a little good manners, at least, as well as to read the Bible. I find these schools spring-ing up wherever I go."[33] In *The Arminian Magazine,* which Wesley edited, he published his "Account of the Christian Charity Schools, Lately Begun in Various Parts of England." Later that year Wesley arrived in Leeds, where he was to preach, and found twenty-six Sunday schools with two thousand scholars and forty-five masters.[34]

According to Raikes, the Sunday-school movement spread in four years' time "so rapidly as now to include 250,000 children;

---

30. Ibid., p. 16.
31. Ibid.
32. *The Development of the Sunday School.*
33. *Journal,* 8:552, 553.
34. By 1883 the enrollment in Leeds Sunday school classes reached two thousand. J. Stoughton, *History of Religion in England* (London: Hodder and Stoughton, 1881), p. 433.

it is increasing more and more."[35] On 7 September 1785 "The Society for the Support and Encouragement of Sunday Schools in the Different Countries of England" was established. More commonly known as "The Sunday-School Society," it was one of the main reasons for the rapid growth of the movement. Its method, wrote Rice, "was to lease rooms in buildings in villages or localities where the poor needed instruction, hire teachers, and maintain schools under rules adopted by the Society, provide Bibles, testaments and other needed books gratuitously for the pupils, and have each school inspected by competent visitors; making all proceedings subject to the approval of a general committee composed of 24 persons, one half of whom were of the Church of England and one half from dissenting denominations."[36]

The Sunday-school movement expanded so rapidly that, when Lord Shaftsbury unveiled a statue of Raikes in 1831, it was claimed that Sunday schools in Great Britain then enrolled approximately 1,250,000 children.

Selected Bibliography

Harris, J. H. *Robert Raikes: The Man and His Work*. Bristol: Arrowsmith, 1899.

Merrill, G. L. *The Development of the Sunday School, 1780-1905*. International Sunday-School Convention, 1905.

"Raikes, Robert." *Cyclopaedia of Biblical, Theological, and Ecclesiastical Literature*, 8:883, 884. Edited by J. McClintock and J. Strong. New York: Harper, 1891.

Rice, E. *The Sunday-School Movement (1780-1917) and the American Sunday-School Union (1817-1917)*. Philadelphia: American Sunday-School Union, 1917.

Stephens, W. R. *A History of the English Church*. Vol. 7. New York: Macmillan, 1906.

---

35. Quoted in Rice, *The Sunday-School Movement*, p. 422.
36. Ibid., p. 22.

19

Gerald Lee Gutek

Johann H. Pestalozzi
(1747-1827)

Historians of education have usually referred to the well-known Swiss educator Johann Heinrich Pestalozzi as a pedagogical reformer, a sense realist, a naturalist, the originator of object lessons, and a disciple of Rousseau.[1] While all descriptions are accurate, the current revival of interest in Pestalozzianism stems from his educational philosophy, his ground-breaking sociological inquiry into education, and his early interest in the education of disadvantaged children.

Some may argue that Pestalozzi, having been a disciple of Rousseau, was no religious educator, that he was an irreligious naturalist or Deist. But Pestalozzi's religion, although influenced by Rousseau, was a form of Christian pietism which stressed the brother-

---

1. For treatments of Pestalozzi as an educational reformer and as a disciple of Rousseau, see E. E. Bayles and B. L. Hood, *Growth of American Educational Thought and Practice* (New York: Harper, 1966), pp. 97-113; H. G. Good and J. D. Teller, *A History of Western Education* (Toronto: Macmillan, 1960), pp. 240-67; and P. Monroe, *A Brief Course in the History of Education* (New York: Macmillan, 1934), pp. 303-19. K. Silber examined thoroughly the philosophical and sociological aspects of Pestalozzian theory in *Pestalozzi: The Man and His Work;* and H. S. Black treated the implications of Pestalozzianism for the education of disadvantaged children in "Education of the Disadvantaged."

hood of men and the fatherhood of God. Although Pestalozzi has not been known as a religious educator, his writings contain references to religious values and religious education. His condemnation of the rote memorization of the catechism and of sectarianism as part of the child's religious development make Pestalozzi a precursor of much modern religious education, as does his stress on man's emotions and capacity for love rather than on theological nuances. His "religion of the heart," with its pervasive themes of love and concern, should find a receptive audience among those concerned with the place of religious values in the education of man.

His Educational Career

Pestalozzi was born in Zurich, the child of middle-class Protestants of Italian descent. His parents were Johann Baptiste Pestalozzi, a physician and surgeon, and Susanna Hotz. With the death of his father in 1751, Pestalozzi's family was forced to live on a lower economic level. Young Johann Heinrich, growing up in a household ruled by women (his mother and a trusted family servant, Barbara Schmid) was a sensitive child isolated from "rough and tumble" boyhood experiences. He later complained that his childhood made him shy, socially inept, and an impractical visionary. It also made him highly introspective. But Pestalozzi did admit that his childhood had fostered a benevolent attitude that enabled him to sympathize with the oppressed and destitute.

He spent occasional short vacations with his grandfather, Andreas Pestalozzi, a pastor in the rural village of Hongg who also had charge of a small school. Young Heinrich accompanied his grandfather on visits to peasant households and came to sympathize with the poor farmers exploited by absentee landlords and city bureaucrats.

Pestalozzi received the education of an average middle-class Swiss child. He learned reading, writing, arithmetic, and the catechism in a vernacular elementary school and studied Latin and classics in a secondary school. After completing the two-year pre-professional course in the *Collegium humanitatis,* studying Latin, Greek, Hebrew, rhetoric, logic, and catechetics,[2] Pestalozzi studied philology and philosophy at the *Collegium carolinum.* During his col-

---

2. M. R. Walch, *Pestalozzi and the Pestalozzian Theory of Education: A Critical Study,* pp. 3-7.

lege years he joined the Helvetian Society, an activist group of professors and students who sought to reform Swiss life.

As he neared the completion of his education, Pestalozzi was still undecided as to a career. Initially, he had prepared for the ministry. He had turned from that to law, but his association with the Helvetians precluded a legal career. Discouraged, he abandoned further study.

Pestalozzi criticized his own formal education as irrelevant to social problems and practical life. Although wanting to help his fellow men, he did not know how.

> Our only wish was to live for freedom, beneficence, sacrifice and patriotism; but the means of developing the practical power to attain these were lacking. We despised all external appearances such as riches, honour, and consideration; and we were taught to believe that by economizing and reducing our wants we could dispense with all the advantages of citizen life.[3]

Influenced by Rousseau's plea for a return to nature, Pestalozzi theorized that the condition of the Swiss peasantry could be improved by combining agriculture, handicraft production, and education. Although he knew little about farming, Pestalozzi purchased sixty acres in the canton of Berne in 1769. That same year he married Anna Schulthess, and they took up residence on the farm. Their only child, Jean Jacques (named after Rousseau), was born the following year.

In 1774, Pestalozzi founded a school for poor children on his farm. Although his pedagogical theory was then rather primitive, he sought to combine the child's natural self-activity with practical work. He wanted his school to be like a home in which the students live, work, and learn together as a family. The children did agricultural and handicraft work and were taught arithmetic, religion, and morality. The school drained Pestalozzi's limited financial resources, and he had to close it in 1779.

From 1780 to 1797 he supported his family by writing—refining, clarifying, and publicizing his educational thinking, particularly his "natural philosophy of education." His *How Father Pestalozzi Instructed His Three and a Half Year Old Son* (1774) was an account of the education of Jean Jacques according to Rousseauean principles. He also wrote *Essays on the Education of the Children of the Poor* and *The Evening Hours of a Hermit*. His most successful work was *Leonard and Gertrude* (1781) an educational

---

3. Quoted in R. de Guimps, *Pestalozzi: His Aim and Work*, pp. 6, 7.

novel written to demonstrate the possibility of personal and social regeneration through education. *Christopher and Elizabeth* (1782) was a series of educational dialogues. *On Legislation and Infanticide* (1783) was an early work in educational sociology which examined the relationships between education, tradition, and morality. *Illustrations for My ABC Book* (1787) consisted of short illustrative epilogues on education and morality. *Researches into the Course of Nature in the Development of the Human Race* (1797) argued that education should be based on natural patterns of development.

After his return to active educational work, Pestalozzi produced several additional books. *How Gertrude Teaches Her Children* (1801) was a philosophical development of man's moral, intellectual, and physical powers. *Epochs* (1803) called for human regeneration by education. *Swansong* (1826), Pestalozzi's last work, defended his educational theory.

In 1797 Pestalozzi was appointed director of the orphanage in the war-ravaged village of Stans. Pestalozzi wrote of his experience there:

> Alone, destitute of all means of instruction, and . . . assistance, I united in my person the offices of superintendent, paymaster, steward, and sometimes chambermaid, in a half-ruined house. I was surrounded with ignorance, disease, and with every kind of novelty. The number of children rose . . . to eighty: all of different ages. . . .[4]

But this provided the opportunity to implement and test his theory of natural education. As a father who cared for his children, Pestalozzi worked to create a climate of emotional love and security. Then he instructed the children in drawing, writing, and physical activities. He encouraged them to share their work and learning as members of a family. The school showed some signs of success, but the massing of opposing Austrian and French armies in the vicinity forced it to close on 8 June 1799.

With the support of the Helvetian government and some friends, Pestalozzi then established a school in Burgdorf. One of his assistants was Joseph Neef, who later introduced Pestalozzian methods in the United States.[5] In 1804 Pestalozzi moved his insti-

---

4. "Pestalozzi's Account of His Own Educational Experience," in H. Barnard, ed., *Pestalozzi and Pestalozzianism*, p. 674.

5. The views of Pestalozzi and Neef on ethical education are compared in G. L. Gutek, "An Examination of Joseph Neef's Theory of Ethical Education," *History of Education Quarterly* 9 (1969): 187-201.

tute to Yverdon, where it remained until 1825. As the most successful of his schools, Yverdon attracted a steady stream of visitors, among whom were Johann Fichte, Friedrich Froebel, Andrew Bell, Johann Herbart, Robert Owen, and William Maclure.

His Educational Philosophy

Pestalozzi drew on several sources in formulating his educational philosophy, and since these sources were often contradictory, his ideas were sometimes inconsistent and often unclear. He was heavily influenced by the romantic naturalism of Rousseau's *Emile,* but he also shared in the intellectual climate of post-Enlightenment Europe, conceiving of nature as a universal mechanism the intrinsic patterns of which govern external phenomena and human nature. The latter follows certain patterns of natural development. Men, as well as plants and animals, grow according to their own inherent structural design. Like Comenius and Rousseau, Pestalozzi conceived of this growth as a continuous and gradual process.

Religiously, Pestalozzi was a humanitarian Christian pietist who did not conform to any particular sect's doctrine or ritual. In his view the worshiper, by means of spontaneous expression of emotion, experiences God through nature. Before man is capable of loving God, he must love his fellow man. The feelings of love, trust, gratitude, and obedience must first be developed in relationships with other people before they can be applied to God. The child learns to love his family first, then friends, then all members of the human family, and finally the most abstract Being, God. Through the inner workings of love, a person acquires genuine moral and religious values.

Pestalozzi rejected the doctrine of original sin. Since God is good, His handiwork—nature—must also be good. All natural phenomena, including man, share in this goodness. At birth the child is inherently good, endowed with a propensity to benevolence. Moral corruption results from the social, not the natural, environment. In an environment of love and care, the child's propensity to benevolence is nourished; in a loveless, emotionally insecure environment, the child's power to love becomes latent and he will be a selfish, disintegrated, unloving adult. What Pestalozzi called a "natural education," however, may enable man to overcome corruptive social influences and extend his powers of goodness to regenerate himself and society.

In addition to man's moral power to love are his intellectual power to think and his physical power to act. These three essential powers of "heart, head, and hand" enable man to engage in "self-activity." Natural education is to cooperate with self-activity in developing these innate powers.

Human growth, and thus education, begins with the infant's emotional relationship with his mother, whose love for him stimulates his own propensity for benevolence. The child responds to his mother's love by loving, obeying, and being grateful to her. Gradually he extends his trust of her to the rest of his family, his neighbors, and finally to the entire human race.

> The germs of love, trust, and gratitude soon grow. The child knows his mother's step; he smiles at her shadow. He loves those who are like her; a creature like his mother is a good creature to him. He smiles at his mother's face, at all human faces....[6]

Man's moral feelings are an outgrowth of the child's relationship with his mother. His values originate in the immediate, concrete, and particular situation before becoming generalized or abstract. Genuine morality comes from actual experience rather than verbal prescriptions. Each man reaches self-perfection through the mutual perfecting of his brothers. The truly complete human being is a humanitarian who practices brotherly love. Moral values, then, develop prior to intellectual and physical values, and guide both thought and action.

The growth of religious values is closely related to the genesis of moral values. Both are interpenetrating, and both arise from the individual's propensity to benevolence. Indeed, the various familial and social extensions of the child's loving relationship with his mother are forms of religious experience. As the child matures and becomes increasingly independent and self-reliant, his mother deliberately broadens the context of moral experience to include religious values, as Pestalozzi illustrated in *How Gertrude Teaches:*

> Mother: Child, there is a God whom thou needest, who taketh thee in His arms when thou needest me no longer, when I can shelter thee no more. There is a God who prepares joy and happiness for thee when I can no more give them thee....
>
> Child: I am a child of God; I believed in my mother, her heart showed me God. God is the God of my mother, of my heart and

---

6. *How Gertrude Teaches Her Children,* p. 183.

her heart. I know no other God. The God of my brain is a chimaera. I know no other God but the God of my heart. By faith in the God of my heart only I feel a man. The God of my brain is an idol. I ruin myself by worshipping him. The God of my heart is my God. I perfect myself in His love.[7]

The child develops intellectually by interacting with the objects and persons which are present in his environment, not by exposure to abstract, highly verbal ideas.

His Educational Methodology

As an educational reformer, Pestalozzi felt that the traditional school's stress on verbalism, rote, and corporal punishment produce an artificial learning environment that cripples the child's mind and distorts his natural development. Students on the elementary level primarily memorized texts, psalms, and the catechism. When they became bored and restless, the teacher, usually unprepared and untrained, resorted to corporal punishment. To Pestalozzi the humanitarian, this pedagogical despotism and barbarism brutalizes the children, repressing their natural spontaneity and self-activity. He wrote that children were penned up "like sheep, whole flocks huddled together, in stinking rooms" to contemplate "unattractive and monotonous letters."[8] Traditional schools, in Pestalozzi's opinion, shattered the unity of knowledge by compartmentalizing it into pieces of unrelated information; they separated theory from action; and they stifled children's creative powers by overemphasizing memorization. He criticized the so-called "learned classes," the products of these schools, for their use of contrived logic and their ignorance of both practical matters and nature.

> The great part of those fellows who have stories out of the Bible, or the newspapers, and new and old pamphlets, constantly in their hands and mouths, are little better than mere idlers. If one wants to talk with them about house-keeping, bringing up children, profit, or business, when they should give one advice how to set about this or that, which is of real use, they stand there like blockheads, and know nothing, and can tell nothing.[9]

Natural education. Finding few redeeming qualities in tradi-

---

7. Ibid., pp. 185, 195.
8. Ibid., p. 23.
9. *Leonard and Gertrude,* in Barnard, ed., *Pestalozzi and Pestalozzianism,* pp. 592, 593.

tional schools, Pestalozzi developed a "natural method of education" which embraces both a general and special phase.

The general phase requires the teacher to create an emotional climate of love and security. Since the child is naturally good, his impulses are good and to be cultivated. Pestalozzi encouraged a classroom permissiveness, allowing the student to act on his natural inclinations. The school is to be a specially-prepared environment of love. For Pestalozzi love is the dynamic force in human nature that makes self-perfection possible. Love stimulates and regulates all the powers in a naturally developed human being. The school is to extend the loving family relationship outward to the larger world of persons and objects.

The special phase consists of instruction, but it does not begin with the conventional school skills of reading and writing. Pestalozzi held that elementary education should begin with measuring (recognizing the form of objects familiar to children), counting (numbering the objects), and speaking (defining the objects). His educational method was based on two fundamental principles: sense impression is the foundation of all knowledge; and all instruction is properly reduced to the three elements of form, number, and language. Only after mastering these basic elements does the teacher provide instruction in reading, writing, arithmetic, geography, music, drawing, and nature studies.

Pestalozzi, a sense realist, considered sensory experience the surest means of knowing and dealing with reality. Natural phenomena manifest themselves to man as a bewildering sea of objects. For man to form clear concepts about reality, his senses must be educated. Pestalozzi also was concerned to cultivate all three of man's powers simultaneously and harmoniously, rather than emphasizing the intellectual and neglecting the moral and physical, as traditional schools had done. So he developed a set of graded exercises, experiences, and materials to educate the senses and develop all three powers. He referred to instruction as

the Art of helping Nature to develop in her own way; and this Art rests essentially on the relation and harmony between the impressions received by the child and the exact degree of his developed powers. . . . in all matters of instruction, it is necessary to determine, with the greatest accuracy, which of these constituents is fit for each age of the child, in order . . . not to lead him and confuse him with anything for which he is not quite ready.[10]

---

10. *How Gertrude Teaches Her Children,* p. 26.

Pestalozzi was convinced that a single, unitary process is the source of all human cognition. He referred to this process as *Anschauung*, and he defined it variously as intuition, conceptualization, sensation, observation, contemplation, perception, and apperception.[11] Through *Anschauung* the mind receives sensory data from objects, isolates the form underlying the diffuse sensations, and constructs precise concepts. Pestalozzi's educational method, then, stressed object lessons and the derivation of concepts through the process of sensation. The child is exposed to objects with the same essential characteristics and is to recognize their form, count them, and name them.

All instruction is to begin with the "near" and move to the "far." By beginning with the child's immediate experience and environment, his experience will be an unbroken series of interactions with the environment. Traditional verbal and literary instruction interfere with the ongoing flow of the child's experience. Textbook descriptions of reality, being indirect and not based on the child's experience, are memorized rather than genuinely understood. This continuity of experience requires that the movement from the child's home environment to that of the larger world be very gradual and steady. Pestalozzi referred to this continuity as the "widening circles of mankind."

Instruction also is to move from the "simple" to the "complex" and from the "particular" to the "general." Measuring, counting, and speaking are simpler and more particular than the skills for which they are necessary foundations. For example, the child begins with simple sounds, then proceeds to words, then to phrases, and finally to more complex sentences. In terms of geography, the child studies his home, school, and community before the more remote oceans and continents.

The teacher, being in Pestalozzi's framework a substitute for the loving parent, must be capable of giving and receiving love. But the teacher also must have mastered the method of natural education, which was designed to lighten the teacher's burden and help the student learn more efficiently. The good teacher, in Pestalozzi's description,

> should, at least, be an open-hearted, cheerful, affectionate, and kind man, who would be as a father to the children; a man made ... to

---

11. S. J. Curtis and M. E. A. Boultwood, *A Short History of Educational Ideas* (London: University Tutorial, 1953), pp. 340, 341.

open children's hearts, and their mouths, and to draw forth their understandings ... from the hindermost corner.[12]

He contrasted this with the more common schoolmaster whose purpose seemed to be

> to shut up children's mouths and hearts, and to bury their good understandings ever so deep under ground. That is the reason why healthy and cheerful children, whose hearts are full of joy and gladness, hardly ever like school.[13]

The model teacher, proposed Pestalozzi, is Christ, who by example taught men to live naturally and harmoniously. His instruction was not remote from His disciples' everyday lives, and his simple parables showed them how to develop their God-given powers.

In Pestalozzi's schools learning was to be motivated by the student's love for the teacher rather than by his fear, and the student was motivated to love the teacher by the teacher's love for him. The teacher was to dissociate punishment from learning so that the student would not associate the two and come to dislike learning. If children were disorderly, their conduct was blamed by Pestalozzi on their improper upbringing or an emotionally disadvantaged home. He even blamed many discipline problems on the teacher's inability to recognize and use the child's natural interests and abilities. In those rare cases when punishment was needed, it was to be applied calmly and with a parent's concern for the child's well-being.

Religious education. Pestalozzi included religious education in natural education, and his methods were very different from traditional ones which emphasized the catechism, creeds, ritual, and formal religious institutions.

In theory the catechism contains religious principles and truths which, when memorized by the child, he internalizes. But Pestalozzi distrusted the use of abstract and overgeneralized ideas which are foreign to a child's experience. Catechizing the child leads to parrot-like repetition without genuine understanding, to an appearance of comprehension without any internalization. Pestalozzi also opposed the use of catechisms because they are based on a defense-of-the-faith mentality by which the immature members of the denomination become committed to its particular dogma.

---

12. *Christopher and Elizabeth,* in Barnard, ed., *Pestalozzi and Pestalozzianism,* p. 667.
13. Ibid.

Rather than producing humanitarianism and Christlike love, traditional religious education fostered contention. Pestalozzi shared Rousseau's conviction that artificial social distinctions and institutions impede the externalization of man's natural goodness, and he regarded formal religious institutions as artificial. They become centers of power, and they subordinate the natural expression of religious experience to prescribed rituals. These, along with creeds, usually result in theological disputations and then in the division of Christians.

Pestalozzi wanted churches to concentrate instead on the humanization of man. They should return to the person of Christ as a figure who loved each man for his own sake and who in turn was loved by all. The pure function of the church is to promote a higher, more noble, and more natural life for men on earth by boldly portraying the human condition in terms of a reciprocal love relationship which embraces both man and God. A truly religious education seeks to perfect man's inherent moral, intellectual, and physical powers. Pastors are to cooperate with the teacher in naturally educating the children. Together the pastor and teacher are to develop the child's industrious habits and train him to live peacefully and productively, to do good toward his fellow men and worship God silently. Pestalozzi wrote that the pastor should base "his instructions in religion upon the doings and omissions of the children, their circumstances, and duties in life" so that when he talks with them of God and eternity he will seem "to be speaking of father and mother, of house and home—of things closely connected with this world."[14]

His Educational Goals

On an individual level Pestalozzi hoped to produce men with integrated personalities, whose human powers all had been harmoniously developed. Pestalozzi wanted to avoid one-sided specialists, hoping instead to achieve an integrated orchestration of the moral, intellectual, and physical powers that will carefully blend feeling, thinking, and acting into an inner unity. By developing his capacity to love and care for others, man is made aware of his moral responsibilities to himself and to his fellow men.

Pestalozzi stressed the role of the home in education but real-

---

14. *Leonard and Gertrude,* in Barnard, ed., *Pestalozzi and Pestalozzianism,* p. 660.

ized that industrialism was weakening the family structure by taking family members from the home and putting them in shops and factories. He believed that the school, as a social agency, had to take on the added responsibilities of providing the love and security which were absent in many families.

Through the proper education of individuals, Pestalozzi hoped to reform society into one which was founded on a humanitarian respect for the natural rights of every individual. Thus every man, including the poor and disadvantaged, has the right to receive a natural education and develop his natural powers. Traditional verbal education, Pestalozzi argued, is especially detrimental to deprived children; memorization of bodies of literature does not contribute to harmonious personality integration, and the neglect of vocational training does not produce efficient workers. The lack of loving families and teachers make these children emotionally insecure. Pestalozzi believed that each man is born into a particular socio-economic class, and because he is likely to remain in that class, he should receive training relevant to his station. This, Pestalozzi thought, will reduce poverty and rehabilitate the victims of unemployment. He hoped that education would eventually eradicate socio-economic class rivalries based on social artificialities. If men are made aware of their common human nature and mutual responsibilities, they will come to see that the welfare of all classes is interrelated.

Pestalozzi was an educator who made a place for religious values and experiences within the framework of his general philosophy of education. He applied the same principles to religious education that he did to natural education. For him nature and man are both good. The source of poverty, injustice, and immorality is a distorted and artificial social environment. Each individual possesses natural moral, intellectual, and physical powers and is capable of reforming himself. Pestalozzi's theory of natural education was a method of cooperating in the development of man's natural, God-given powers. Pestalozzi's childlike reverence for nature, man, and God is worthy of consideration by twentieth-century educators caught up in the traumas of a complex, technological age.

Selected Bibliography

Barnard, H., ed. *Pestalozzi and Pestalozzianism.* New York: Brownell, 1862.

Black, H. S. "Education of the Disadvantaged." *Educational Forum* 33: 510-21.

De Giumps, R. *Pestalozzi: His Aim and Work.* Syracuse, N.Y.: Bardeen, 1889.

Gutek, G. L. *Pestalozzi and Education.* New York: Random, 1968.

Pestalozzi, J. H. *How Gertrude Teaches Her Children.* Translated by L. E. Holland and F. C. Turner. Syracuse, N.Y.: Bardeen, 1894.

Silber, K. *Pestalozzi: The Man and His Work.* London: Paul, 1960.

Walch, M. R. *Pestalozzi and the Pestalozzian Theory of Education: A Critical Study.* Washington, D.C.: Catholic University, 1952.

20

Abraham Friesen

Johann Friedrich Herbart
(1776-1841)

The relationship between philosophy and pedagogy is necessarily close, for questions concerning epistemology and the nature of man are central to both. Yet few great philosophers have been outstanding pedagogues, and not many notable pedagogues have been profound philosophers. The reason for this may well be that philosophers tend to deal with man in the abstract, whereas teachers must confront him in the flesh. In Johann Friedrich Herbart, however, the educator and the philosopher became one. Herein lies at once the source of his importance and the cause of his obscurity. Although he integrated the various aspects of his thought into a system, Herbart assumed too much with regard to his theories of education and therefore failed to be sufficiently explicit.[1]

His Life

Herbart was the only son of a judicial and administrative counselor in Oldenburg, Germany, and of his young and strong-willed wife. The marriage proved to be singularly unhappy for Herbart's

---

1. Cf. also H. B. Dunkel, *Herbart and Herbartianism: An Educational Ghost Story*. I have drawn heavily from Dunkel.

mother and finally ended in divorce. Disappointed in marriage, she devoted herself to her son to such an extent that she became overprotective. She subjected the lad to a Spartan regimen and had him tutored at home until he was eleven. She supervised his education very closely, sitting in on his classes and even learning Greek along with him. Her overprotectiveness lasted well into Herbart's adult life; she even lived in Jena while he was a student there.

Herbart's tutor, Hermann Uelzen, who had been trained in the philosophy of Christian von Wolff as well as in Protestant theology, early succeeded in awakening Herbart's interest in ethics, psychology, and metaphysics. At the same time, Herbart studied the violin, cello, harp, and piano simultaneously, displaying a keen interest in and aptitude for music. In 1788 he entered the Oldenburg Latin school, where he was deeply impressed by Kant's philosophy and logic, particularly by his *Metaphysics of Morals*.

Although Herbart's parents wanted him to study jurisprudence at Jena in order to insure himself a decent living, he spent the next three years studying philosophy under Fichte and became his outstanding pupil. By 1796, however, Herbart was already divorcing himself from the teachings of Fichte and the current Idealism. In that year he wrote:

> However many happy thoughts may be scattered about in Fichte's deductions regarding natural right and morality, I consider the fundamental points, i.e., his theory of the recognition of a reasoning being as such, and his doctrine of freedom, as false.

Here is emerging the struggle between the philosopher and the educator; Herbart wanted to reconcile the philosophical concept of unlimited freedom with the limitations educators know exist.

> I am modest in my demands on human freedom. Leaving that to Schelling and to Fichte, I seek to determine a human being by the laws of his reason and nature, and to give him that which will enable him to make something of himself.[2]

Herbart's interest in education was leading him away from Idealism to what he considered a more realistic appraisal of man and his potential.[3]

---

2. Quoted in H. and E. Felkin, "Introduction," in J. F. Herbart, *The Science of Education*, p. 4.

3. That Herbart had some experience in teaching is apparent from his first letter to Friedrich von Steiger, in which he wrote: "*Schon ehemals nahm ich an dem Unterrichte einiger Kinder teil.*" Quoted in W. Asmus, *Johann Friedrich Herbart: Eine pädagogische Biographie*, p. 109.

In 1797 he became tutor in the home of Friedrich von Steiger in Switzerland. Here he first formulated those theories of education which were to shape all his subsequent pedagogical activities. In his application to von Steiger, Herbart had outlined his program of education for the three oldest sons. Every two months Herbart sent to the father extensive progress reports, only five of which have been preserved but which contain in embryo, if not in detail, most of Herbart's later ideas on education.

During his two years in Switzerland, Herbart visited Pestalozzi's school at Burgdorf several times. The impact of Pestalozzi's ideas on Herbart bore fruit in several treatises which Herbart wrote during a two-year stay in Bremen. He was particularly struck by Pestalozzi's attempt to ground his instruction in the child's "elementary sense perceptions" early in life. In an attempt to work out his own scheme, he wrote *A B C of Sense Perception.* Also written during this Bremen interlude were *General Thoughts for a Pedagogical Plan of Instruction for Higher Studies* (1801), and *On Pestalozzi's Latest Writing: "How Gertrude Teaches Her Children"* (1802). In the former Herbart enunciated what was to become a fundamental axiom for him: the current practice of teaching Latin before Greek was wrong since the Latin language and literature do not mirror the natural development of the human spirit as does the Greek. He added that instruction in all fields must be integrated into what he called "the circle of thought."

In May of 1802 Herbart went to the University of Göttingen. He completed his doctorate in philosophy and immediately began lecturing there as a *Privatdozent.* To avoid conflict with other lecturers in philosophy, Herbart lectured first on pedagogy. The next semester, however, he moved on to ethics, and after that to logic and metaphysics. During this time he was formulating a comprehensive system and publishing his results. *General Pedagogy, Chief Points of Metaphysics,* and *Chief Points of Logic* all appeared in 1806, *General Practical Philosophy* in 1807. His treatise on psychology did not appear until 1816 *(Textbook of Psychology);* it appeared in a more comprehensive form in 1824-25 *(Psychology as a Science).*

In 1808 Herbart accepted the prestigious chair in philosophy at the University of Königsberg, the same chair which Kant had once occupied. Herbart's literary productivity declined somewhat while there, but he did write and publish several volumes: *Textbook for the Introduction to Philosophy* (1812), *General Meta-*

physics (1828-29), *Letters on the Application of Psychology to Education* (1831), and *Encyclopaedia of Philosophy* (1831). When Herbart failed to be appointed Hegel's successor in the chair of philosophy at Berlin, he returned to Göttingen in 1833. His *Outlines of Pedagogical Lectures* was published in 1835, and his *Psychological Investigations* appeared just shortly before his death on 11 August 1841.

His Educational Goals

Morality. "The one and the whole work of education may be summed up in the concept—morality."[4] Herbart's primary goal in education was not merely to impart knowledge or even to make men better, but to make them "morally good." He conceded that education certainly has other goals, but if it fails to achieve this fundamental goal, there will be significant loss in the other areas as well. To achieve this goal Herbart sought to base his pedagogy on scientific principles. Unlike Kant who turned to logic, Herbart turned to aesthetics for this base.

To produce a morally good man, the teacher must create in the student a "good will—the steady resolution of a man to consider himself as an individual under the law which is universally binding." This good will manifests itself in the harmonious functioning of man's volition with his aesthetic judgment, for only that will is good which submits itself to this judgment. It was of the greatest importance to Herbart that this aesthetic judgment be nurtured in the child as early as possible. Herbart discussed this in "On the Aesthetic Revelation of the World as the Chief Work of Education." The aesthetic sense, for which music serves as a model,

> speaks in purely absolute judgments entirely without proof, without, in a word, enforcing its claims. It takes absolutely no consideration of the inclinations, neither favoring nor opposing them. It arises on the clear presentation of its object. There are precisely as many primary judgments as there are varied objects, which judgments are not related to each other in any way so as to be logically deducible from one another.[5]

These aesthetic judgments are involuntary and elicit feelings in

---

4. This was Herbart's opening sentence in "On the Aesthetic Revelation of the World as the Chief Work of Education." *The Science of Education*, p. 57.
5. Ibid., p. 64.

the same way that musical harmony brings forth pleasure and discord produces displeasure. No act of the will is involved. At the same time, as in the example drawn from music, these judgments do not concern single elements but the various combinations of the elements. The fundamental aesthetic relationships are simple, and it is only when these relationships become complex, as in a symphony or work of art, that conflicting opinions of the aesthetic value of a given "artistic" production are possible.

Whether a man achieves that inner freedom or not, and to what extent, depends

> on the psychological accident whether he is absorbed *first* in the calculations of egoism, or in the aesthetic comprehension of the world surrounding him. This accident *ought* not to remain one. The teacher *ought* to have the courage to assume that he can, if he begins rightly, determine that comprehension so easily and strongly through the *aesthetic revelation of the world,* that the free attitude of the mind will receive its law, not from worldly wisdom, but from pure practical [moral] considerations. Such a revelation of the world—the *whole* known world, and every known age—obliterating if necessary the bad impressions of undesirable environment, may with justice be called the chief work of education, for which that discipline, which awakens and controls desire, is nothing but the necessary preparation.[6]

This aesthetic revelation of the world begins in the home. It is therefore of the utmost importance that the home environment be conducive to shaping the right first judgments. The child "judges only what he observes, because what he sees is to him the only thing possible, and the pattern for imitation." If the parents do not provide this kind of environment, a good teacher may make up the deficiency if he gets the pupil soon enough. After the child has formed these basic judgments, the teacher simultaneously leads him upward into the "supersensuous world" and outward into the "actual world," for the two balance each other. The "deepening shadows" of the actual must be set off by the stronger light of the supersensuous. For

> God, the true centre of all practical [moral] ideas and of their illimitable workings, the Father of men and Lord of the world—He must fill the background of memory as the oldest and the first to whom all reflections of the mind, turning from the confused tangle of life, must always revert, that it may repose as in its true self in the rest of belief.[7]

---

6. Ibid., pp. 69, 70.
7. Ibid., p. 72.

Although Herbart expected a great deal from a moral education, he recognized that even this has its limitations.

> ... any teachings on property, duty and virtue needs to be supplemented with another because no teaching in the world is in the position to guard a man against inner suffering, transgressions and inner corruption. The need for religion is therefore obvious: man cannot help himself; he needs help from above![8]

Religion, therefore, supplements education, especially moral education, in that it performs a number of functions which nothing else can. First, religion opposes the eternal to the temporal, the ideal or complete to the transient and fallible, the perfect to the imperfect, and this is wholesome. Were the perfect not there to offset man's imperfections, man might well imagine that he has accomplished something. The eternal and the ideal put the deeds of men in perspective and constantly point the erring back to perfection. Second, religion consoles by pointing man to a providential God who accomplishes His ends in spite of man's shortcomings. It consoles the suffering man and diverts him from his daily cares, offering him a refuge in an immovable God who is the embodiment of love. But religion must offer man even more than this:

> A new world must open up to him for his world is ruined; the letters of accusation against him must be destroyed for he cannot pay the debt he has incurred; he must begin anew since he is incapable of continuing in the old.[9]

Religion, therefore, must also set standards, correct the erring, and give him power to begin again.

Morality is not the sum and substance of religion; the two must complement one another.

> It is necessary then, that moral culture which constantly impels to right self-determination in everyday life, should be combined with religious culture, that it may humble any imaginary belief that something has been accomplished. Conversely, moral is necessary to religious culture; for danger of mock holiness is imminent, when morality has not already a secure basis in self-observation, made with a view to self-improvement by means of self-blame.[10]

In many ways religion supports morality, but religion does more: it frees man from his burdens, and encourages him through the

---

8. *Sämtliche Werke,* 2:57. The translation is mine.
9. Ibid.
10. *Letters and Lectures on Education,* p. 108.

"good news" of the Bible. In the final analysis religion does not ask man for good works or morality but offers him unconditional grace.

Although Herbart believed that morality is the primary aim of education and religion a necessary supplement to it, he did not postulate either an intrinsically good or intrinsically evil human being.[11] He also rejected those philosophies the main principles of which are either fatalism or transcendental freedom. Herbart was more influenced in his view of man by the practical considerations of the educator. Thus he could argue that "the fundamental idea of education is the pupil's capacity for cultivation," a capacity which is by no means unlimited.

Knowledge and sympathy. In addition to the educational goal of morality, Herbart posited more immediate goals, such as the acquisition of knowledge, through which the higher aim is achieved. He argued that a "many-sidedness of interest should be cultivated in the student from the start.

> Every man must have a love for all activities, each must be a virtuoso in one. But the particular virtuosoship is a matter of choice; on the contrary, the manifold receptivity which can only grow out of the manifold beginnings of one's own individual efforts, is a matter of education. Therefore we call the first part of the educational aim— *many-sidedness of interest,* which must be distinguished from its exaggeration—dabbling in many things.[12]

This many-sidedness of interest must be balanced; each object of interest must be integrated into the student's broader circle of thought. At the same time, education should lead to the "harmonious cultivation" of the student's total potential. Therefore, although the teacher's aim is universalistic education, he is in fact limited by the student's capacity for cultivation, a capacity which is individualistic and must not be tampered with in any way.

Herbart stressed two aspects to this many-sidedness of interest: knowledge and sympathy. Knowledge results from a comprehension of objects, of their interdependence and their aesthetic relations. Whereas knowledge grows out of an interest in the objective, sympathy is interest in the subjective. The latter devotes itself in part to men as human beings, in part to society, and in part to the relation of both to the highest Being. Ideally, both should be

11. *The Science of Education,* pp. 135, 136.
12. Ibid., pp. 110, 111.

developed at the same time, yet the first is obviously necessary for the second since sympathy grows out of speculation about and taste for the first. Sympathy is more difficult to arouse since knowledge can easily become an end in itself.

The material in each course of study should be presented in a certain order. The first stage is the *descriptive* and is clearly limited to the earliest period of education. Here the aim is to stimulate the senses so strongly that the resulting mental presentations will be retained and readily recalled. The second stage is the *analytic*. The teacher breaks down the complex entities into their constituent elements and analyzes concepts and experiences which the students may have gathered both inside and outside the classroom. The emphasis on relationships between the various elements and experiences is important. The third and final stage is the *synthetic*. Beginning with simple elements, the teacher must show the student how to organize these into greater wholes.

Sympathy is to be gained largely from the study of history and religion, but both fields must be handled with extreme care so as not to misuse them.[13] By combining the early stages of historical instruction—the vivid presentation of true stories only—with an analysis and understanding of oneself, the student can begin to enter into historical events and sympathize with historical figures. The first historical figures to be studied should be somewhat idealized and exemplary if at all possible. Thus Herbart suggested that all students should begin their study of history by reading the *Odyssey*. Viewing history as an evolutionary process and man as an evolving being, Herbart further suggested that history be studied in chronological order, an order which mirrors the student's development.

Knowledge of oneself and sympathy with historical figures lead to an analysis of one's broader relationship to society, of the interrelationships and interdependence of society's members. Ethical ideals are developed which enable the student to judge not only his own actions but also those of historical personalities. Because it takes time to develop this moral sense, historical study must not at first dwell upon characters and events of questionable morality.

---

13. Cf., for example, the following remarks: "Everything bordering on religion needs great discretion" (*The Science of Education*, p. 161); and "I have often told you [Karl Steiger] I consider history to be in a certain sense a dangerous study" (*Letters and Lectures on Education*, p. 101).

If it does and the student errs in his judgment, the teacher must correct him.

Once the student understands something of man's dependence and limitations, he is ready for religious instruction. Religious interest must have been cultivated early in his life and impressed deeply upon him, so deeply that he will never doubt its basic assumptions and that in maturity he can find in it a haven in every adversity.

> Education must look upon religion not as objective, but as sub-jective. Religion befriends and protects, but nevertheless it must not be given the child too circumstantially. Its work must be directing rather than teaching. It must never exhaust susceptibility, and there-fore above all must not be prematurely made use of. It must not be given dogmatically to arouse doubt, but in union with knowl-edge of nature and the repression of egoism. It must ever point beyond, but never instruct beyond the bounds of knowledge, for then the paradox would follow, that instruction knows what it does not know; with the aid of the Bible it teaches historically and prepares the child for the Church.[14]

It must be emphasized that Herbart believed the teacher's duty to be not to teach dogmatic religious content but to nurture religious consciousness, a consciousness which is awakened in the home before any formal instruction begins. Herbart argued that even the souls of children "have a presentiment of an unseen power." For such a child

> who finds itself in close dependence on its parents and guardians, these visible persons certainly occupy the place which the feeling of dependence assigns to the unseen powers, and just for this reason, the earliest religious instruction is an exceedingly simple expansion of the relation of the parents to the children, as in the same way the first social ideas will be taken from the family.[15]

This subjective approach is to be taken well into the student's teens. All dogmatic preachments are eschewed, even to the extent of keeping the child out of church if necessary until this subjective assurance is firm. Religious questions naturally arise in the class-room when the student begins to reflect upon the various things he has learned, but the teacher must always "extract his meta-physics strictly from physics." Although he cannot go beyond this realm, he still must point beyond it, however.

---

14. *"Aphorismen zur Pädagogik,"* in *Johann Friedrich pädagogische Schriften,* ed. F. Bartholomai (Langensalza: Beyer, 1906), p. 420.
15. *The Science of Education,* p. 144.

Two aspects of religious instruction are especially the teacher's responsibility: the analytic and the synthetic. The first begins with the sympathy aroused in the student by the universal dependence of men. The student's attention is drawn to expressions of man's limitations made at various times in history. Arrogance and pride are decried, and worship is presented as the pure confession of humility. Reflection on this life leads, therefore, to a consideration of life's brevity, the transitory nature of pleasure, and the dubious worth of temporal wealth. At the same time frugality, contentment with one's lot, and the contemplation of nature are stressed. From the contemplation of nature the student is led "to a universal teleological search which however must remain in the sphere of Nature." The student is encouraged to keep the sabbath, to turn his mind to the solace of religion. Once the student has learned to "despise fantastic and mystic jugglery, as well as the affectations of mysticism, as being far beneath the dignity of religion," he is encouraged to attend church services.

Analytic religious instruction encourages the student to analyze his and his fellow man's need for religion; synthetic religious instruction creates and forms the idea of God in the student's mind. This must be done from his earliest youth in order for an idea of God to be founded in the depths of his heart and blend with everything else he encounters. The idea of God

> must always be placed anew at the end of Nature, as the *ultimate presupposition of every mechanism* which shall at some time develop to a given end.[16]

His Educational Psychology

Herbart based the science of education on two pillars: practical philosophy, which provides the goal (morality), and psychology, which determines the means of achieving this goal while pointing to the obstacles to its achievement. Psychology, therefore, provided Herbart with a scientific view of man which aids the teacher in shaping the morally good man. He intended his view of man to have no overt religious or philosophical overtones, but he conceived the human mind to be part of the soul and therefore made certain metaphysical assumptions.[17]

---

16. Ibid., p. 181.

17. Dunkel, *Herbart and Herbartianism*, pp. 101-21. To explain here these metaphysical assumptions would lead too far astray.

Herbart saw the soul not as "an aggregate of various capacities" but as "simple being [Wesen], not merely without parts but also without any multiplicity whatsoever in its quality." Harold B. Dunkel summarized Herbart's view of the soul: "As a real being it is not in time or space; it has no natural endowments or faculties, no forms, no categories, no anything except that single simple quality which it is."[18] This simple *what* of the soul must remain forever unknown. Nevertheless, insofar as it has feelings and desires, the soul is disposition. The mind, therefore—and this is important for Herbart's psychology—is built up out of the individual's experiences,

> particularly his social experience; and its structure is the specific organization arising out of the mutual relations of the single elements in a given mind at a particular time and place.

The real problem of the educator and psychologist, then, is to explain how the mind builds itself up.

Since the soul, of which the mind is a part, has only one inherent characteristic—that of self-preservation—the child's mind is largely a *tabula rasa* which absorbs and digests his experiences. Each experience results in a mental presentation, the simplest resulting from involuntary attention. This involuntary attention Herbart divided into primitive and apperceptive attention. The first, also called reflex attention, depends on the strength, uniqueness, and unexpectedness of sensuous stimuli. While primitive attention is the first to occur in the child, apperceptive is soon added. This is soon added. This occurs when the purely sensuous presentation calls to the child's consciousness previous similar experiences and arouses anticipation in him. Memory enters the picture because repeated presentations arouse related presentations in the mind. By controlling the child's environment, one can to a large extent determine his first mental presentations.

These first presentations form the basis of education. The teacher should begin instruction by presenting the simplest objects and repeating this until they are firmly fixed in the mind. Then he must vary the objects enough so that there are points of contrast as well as contact. By associating all new materials with what has gone before, the teacher gradually builds that "circle of thought" through which everything that is being taught is related to and integrated with that which has already been learned.

---

18. Ibid., p. 123.

Involuntary attention, however, may not always be sufficient. When it is not, the student must supplement it with an effort of his will.

Instruction is not the sum of the teacher's activity; the creation of moral character is. Here the will plays a crucial role. The formation of the good will that cooperates harmoniously with the aesthetic judgment is a complex process. Not only does the child enter the world free from original sin, it enters the world without any will at all "and is therefore incapable of any moral relation."

> ... there is only a wild impetuosity, impelling it [the child] hither and thither, a principle of disorder, disturbing the plans of the adults, and placing the future personality of the child itself in manifold dangers.[19]

To subdue this impetuosity force is sometimes necessary. This is not the long-range solution, however, for the "germs of this blind impulsiveness" remain in the child and even grow stronger with time. The long-range solution is to build the will and the aesthetic judgment to the extent that decisions can be made with "inner freedom." This is accomplished by carefully controlling the presentations that affect the will, and once it is, the restraints upon the youth can be removed. If the will is not formed by these controlled presentations or if the presentations are not controlled, the individual may fall prey to what Herbart called "worldly wisdom," which comes from following the selfish desires of one's own ego.

His Educational Methodology

Herbart argued that any plan of instruction must take into consideration the individual powers of the teacher and the pupil, and use these to the greatest advantage. The instructor should develop his own manner of instruction, one which is free from all affectation as well as all formalism. He should be flexible, utilizing every moment to the best advantage and allowing the subject matter to determine how it is presented.

The teacher should bear in mind several things. In the first stage of education, what is presented to the student should be presented as vividly as possible. According to Herbart, "this species of instruction has but one law—*to describe in such a way that the pupil believes he sees what is described.*" When the time is ripe—

---

19. *The Science of Education,* p. 95.

that is, when the student has accumulated enough knowledge—he is given leisure to reflect upon and analyze it. Therefore, presentations are soon interrupted with periods of analytical reflection. The timing of these periods is left to the teacher's instinct. The reflection must be guided by the teacher, and it is precisely at such times that the pupil's aesthetic sense and taste are nurtured. Similar periods of reflection are required for synthetic instruction during which feelings of sympathy are cultivated in the pupil. Thus, instruction cannot be continuous; it must allow for periods of physical activity when the student is totally diverted from academic pursuits.

Herbart particularly stressed six subjects: language, mathematics, history, natural science, geography, and composition. He distinguished between those which lead primarily to empirical knowledge (mathematics and the natural sciences), and those which engender sympathy for man and society (primarily history) and which form the moral judgment. The study of history should begin with the *Odyssey* because of its appeal to youths. Then they should study Herodotus's *Histories,* and then Plato's *Crito, Apology,* and portions of the *Republic.* All the while the student is encouraged to exercise his moral judgment.

The student can begin reading the *Odyssey* with a minimum of linguistic skill. Herbart recommended that languages, like composition, always be learned in conjunction with literature. A grammatical frame of reference can easily be postponed until the student has read Homer and Herodotus, for language skills are not an end in themselves but the means by which one gains access to the cultural treasures of the past. The student should begin with poetry, in which humanity is idealized; then advance to realistic Greek and Latin histories which portray man's foibles as well as his greatness; and finally proceed through the various historical epochs in chronological order.

Religion, the capstone of subjects which arouse sympathy in the student, unlike history is not to be taught separately, for both the analytic and the synthetic aspects of religious instruction must be drawn from other subjects: as Herbart remarked, metaphysics must be drawn from physics. Therefore, it is during the periods of analytic and synthetic reflection that the basic religious principles are formed.

Mathematics, which should initiate the other main branch of instruction, is obviously less important for the formation of moral judgment and sympathy, but it is necessary to the cultivation of that many-sidedness of interest which was to Herbart the mark of a well-educated man. Instruction in mathematics should begin early, and its utility or applicability, particularly to mechanics and astronomy, stressed. At least in its earlier stages, therefore, mathematics is not taught in isolation, although later specialization at the university may demand it.

The procedure for teaching mathematics is similar to that for the natural sciences. First is the presentation of a series of similar objects, a presentation which is repeated until the student is fully aware of their distinguishing characateristics. Then variations are introduced. For example, the teacher presents the general concept of a triangle. Once the student has this concept firmly in mind, the teacher introduces various kinds of triangles. In addition to analyzing the various kinds of triangles, the teacher also attempts to integrate this knowledge into a broader context. In this way knowledge is added to knowledge, analyzed, and then integrated into the student's ever-growing circle of thought.

Of greatest importance in forming this circle of thought and integrating into it the disparate educational elements is geography, the study of which should include all aspects of a given culture and should at least attempt to bring everything together.

Although Herbart held important university chairs in philosophy and wrote voluminously, he did not greatly impress the broader philosophical public of his day. This was probably because he was a realist in an idealistic age. His educational theories, however, have had a somewhat different fate. They were relatively obscure until 1864 when they suddenly became popular and "Herbartianism" became an international educational movement. Largely responsible for the revival was Tuiskon Zeller's *Foundation of the Doctrine of Educative Instruction,* which both popularized and modified Herbart's views. But Herbart's psychological views were dated, and by 1905 Herbartianism began to wane and its founder's educational theories returned to obscurity.[20]

Selected Bibliography

Asmus, W. *Johann Friedrich Herbart: Eine pädagogische Biographie.* Vol. 1. Heidelberg: Quelle and Meyer, 1968.

---

20. Dunkel, *Herbart and Herbartianism,* pp. 3-17.

Dunkel, H. B. *Herbart and Education.* New York: Random, 1969.

———. *Herbart and Herbartianism: An Educational Ghost Story.* Chicago: University of Chicago, 1970.

Herbart, J. F. *Letters and Lectures on Education.* Translated and edited by H. and E. Felkin. London: Sonnenchein, 1898.

———. *Sämtliche Werke.* Edited by G. Hartenstein. 12 vols. Leipzig: Voss, 1850.

———. *The Science of Education.* Translated by H. and E. Felkin. Boston: Heath, 1896.

Schwenk, G. *Das Herbart Verständnis der Herbartianer.* Weinheim: Beltz, 1963.

Seidenfaden, F. *Die Pädagogik des jungen Herbart.* Weinheim: Beltz, 1967.

21

William R. Feyerharm

Thomas Arnold
(1795-1842)

No book has done more to honor and publicize Thomas Arnold, the great nineteenth-century schoolmaster of Rugby School, than Thomas Hughes's *Tom Brown's Schooldays*. In that book Arnold's final observations to Tom on the duty of the Christian gentleman deftly capsulated the goals of the public school in mid-Victorian England.

> You talk of "working to get your living" and doing some real good in the world, in the same breath. Now you may be getting a very good living in a profession, and yet doing no good at all in the world, but quite the contrary, at the same time. Keep the latter before you as your one object, and you will be right, whether you make a living or not; but if you dwell on the other, you'll very likely drop into mere money-making, and let the world take care of itself for good or evil.[1]

A Rugby education exposed a boy to the classics, history, and the Scriptures; it was designed to produce both a scholar and a man of principle. It was an ideal significantly higher than that of most schools in the early nineteenth century. Unreformed schools bred academic lassitude and social chaos. Many conscientious parents

1. (London: Dent, 1949), p. 326.

employed tutors rather than expose their children to the brutality and moral laxity of a public school. By mid-century, however, the educational climate changed and the schools were respectable. Thomas Arnold was an important factor in this transformation.

His Life

Arnold was born in 1795, the son of a collector of customs and postmaster on the Isle of Wight. He attended school at Warminster and at the age of twelve was sent to the famous Winchester School. Four years later he went to Corpus Christi College at Oxford, where, after three years of the classics, he was awarded first class in *literae humaniores*. The next year he was elected a fellow of Oriel College and settled into a climate of scholarship and debate with some of the brightest minds in Oxford—including some of the early adherents of the Tractarian movement.

After four years of reading and tutoring, he was ordained and accepted the mastership of a school in Laleham, a small village just north of London on the Thames River. For almost ten years Arnold enjoyed the leisure of teaching in a small school and the industry of his inquiries into ancient history, which would culminate in several books on Roman history and in a translation of Thucydides. In 1828 he was appointed headmaster of Rugby and remained there until his death in 1842. In the course of fourteen years, he established himself as England's premier schoolmaster, becoming the foremost spoksman for a combination of Christian and classical education. In a way he was a latter-day John Colet, the early sixteenth-century reformer of St. Paul's School who combined the new interest in the classics with an emphasis on the ethical precepts of Christianity.[2]

His Theology

To fully understand Arnold's brand of Christianity and his reforming zeal at Rugby School one must understand the forces for reform in the first decades of the nineteenth century. The evangelical movement, a Wesley-like, low-church Anglican faction, countervailed the excesses of England's incipient industrial society while tending to justify England's wealth as a manifestation of its calling.

2. The two best biographies of Arnold are A. P. Stanley, *The Life and Correspondence of Thomas Arnold;* and A. Whitridge, *Dr. Arnold of Rugby.*

Prosperity, the evangelicals believed, was the fruit of industrious-
ness. They are noted more for their rejection of the slave trade,
child labor, and the slums of London, however, than for their
acceptance of England's role in the industrial revolution. They
helped erect a code of behavior which was at war with "habit and
indifference, vice and brutality." G. M. Young, the most skillful
essayist and historian of that age, remarked that by about 1830
the evangelicals' work was done. "They had driven the grosser
kinds of cruelty, extravagance, and profligacy underground. They
had established a certain level of behavior for all who wished to
stand well with their fellows. In moralizing society they had made
social disapproval a force which the boldest sinner might fear."[3]

Within the confines of these ambient evangelical principles and
the increasingly popular but radical Utilitarian principles, Arnold
charted his own philosophic course. It was distinct and not aligned
with sectarian thought, yet receptive to the general discourse
on Christian ethics. It was a lonely path. Arnold Whitridge, a
twentieth-century biographer, observed: "To his great sorrow Arnold discovered that he was drifting away from the traditional
Oxford point of view [the apostolic succession of the Church of
England] without approaching any nearer to radical or evangelical
principles."[4] He rebelled against the Tractarian claim of sacer-
dotalism, but neither could he accept the evangelicals' literal
interpretation of the Bible and their constant stream of tests,
phrased in Calvinistic legalisms, for salvation.[5]

Arnold's religious convictions excluded him from the ranks of
the Utilitarians, but he did agree with them that the Bible has
historical and scientific flaws. In his "Essay on the Right Interpretation and Understanding of the Scriptures" Arnold argued that
the Bible is an authentic record of revelation even if not inspired.
He rejected the contention that if all the Scriptures are not inspired and perfect, then Christianity cannot be "true." Thus, the
fundamental truth of the gospel is not contradicted by the Bible's
inconsistencies.[6] The Bible is a repository of moral truth, and it
was the great schoolmaster's desire to relate the gospel's ethical
meaning to everyday life.

Matters of doctrine and theological definition did not excite

3. *Portrait of an Age* (London: Oxford University, 1964), p. 4.
4. *Dr. Arnold of Rugby*, p. 157.
5. Stanley, *Life and Correspondence*, p. 73.
6. E. L. Williamson, *The Liberalism of Thomas Arnold*, pp. 79, 80.

Arnold. He envisioned a church which encompasses all sects. He would have been comfortable with an institution including both high churchmen and dissenters. He could not, however, abide the religious skepticism of the Utilitarians. For this reason he refused an appointment at University College, London, which was founded to divorce religious from secular studies. In his mind, religion is the very heart of education. Early in 1828 he wrote to a friend that his object at Rugby would be, "if possible, to form Christian men." He thus began his work at Rugby intending to Christianize, not merely civilize, the scholars, and he pursued this goal so intensely that he set a new course in the public schools.

His Reforms at Rugby

If Arnold set about to reform Rugby, it was not through the curriculum. The Renaissance, classical education remained essentially intact. By the end of his career a sixth former, or upperclassman, had worked his way through Vergil, Cicero, Sophocles, and Aeschylus. Young maintained that had it not been for Arnold and the abundance of classically trained teachers, "a modern alternative" to the classical curriculum might have developed in England, particularly among the new proprietory schools which served the growing middle class. In these schools science and technology were becoming popular subjects. Instead Arnold sought to teach traditional subjects in a rather nontraditional way. He introduced tutors, and he stressed Greek and Latin composition and translation, hoping to develop the schoolboy's sensitivity to the past and to great rhetoric, as well as develop his English composition. He did introduce into the curriculum modern languages, subjects foreign to Eton and Winchester, and a thorough study of history. But the classics were the core of the curriculum, and it was the diligent wrestling with Greek and Latin grammar and verse which not only introduced the liberal arts but also shaped character. The boy who disciplined himself to master Greek and Latin acquired, in the eyes of Arnold, habits of perseverance and industry.

When Arnold heard that he was being considered for the headmastership of Rugby, he reported to a fellow clergyman his concern for maintaining discipline.

> According to my notions of what large schools are, founded on all I know and all I have ever heard of them, expulsion should be prac-

ticed much oftener than it is. Now, I know trustees in general, are averse to this plan, because it has a tendency to lessen the numbers of the school, and they favored quantity rather than quality.... yet I could not consent to tolerate much that is tolerated generally, and, therefore, I should not like to enter on an office which I could not discharge according to my own views of what is right.[7]

Armed with the prerogative of the *ratio ultima,* he set about to discipline Rugby. He steered away from the conventional practice of masters ruling solely with an iron hand, which had been unsuccessful at Rugby. Rather he turned government over to the oldest boys in the sixth form ("my desire is to teach my boys to govern themselves") and met with them periodically.[8] Thus an old tradition, whereby the sixth formers enjoyed a substantial measure of independence from school regulations, was replaced with a new one, whereby they were responsible for establishing order in the community. Fagging, the use of younger boys to perform menial tasks, was retained, although some of the former abuses were corrected. Flogging also continued, but it ceased as the boys moved into the upper forms. As they approached the status of gentlemen, chastisement was deemed the more appropriate punishment.

If some of Arnold's disciplinary measures are unenlightened by our standards, nevertheless he apparently restrained the heavy hand of expulsion and flogging, preferring moral suasion as a means of setting his scholars onto the track of Christian gentlemanliness. There has been much discussion of his advocacy of athletics as a means of introducing manliness, *esprit,* and cooperation. Although he tolerated sports and occasionally watched the afternoon matches, it is inaccurate to associate him with the cult of "muscular Christianity" which later developed in England's public schools. Instead he used the pulpit on Sunday evenings or the informality of the sixth-form room to exhort and inspire his students concerning their Christian duty. His effectiveness stemmed from his energy, the force of his personality, and his sensitivity to the response that young men show to the voice of a leader and the call to battle. He gave Christian principles a dramatic quality. Tom Brown noted: "It was not the cold voice of one giving advice and warning from serene heights, to those who were struggling and sinning below, but the warm, living voice of one who was fighting for us and by our sides, and calling on us to help him

7. In Stanley, *Life and Correspondence,* p. 73.
8. A. Briggs, *Victorian People,* p. 155.

and ourselves and one another." Tom added that "it was this
thoroughness and undaunted courage which more than anything
else won his way into the hearts of the great mass of those on
whom he left his mark."[9]

Hughes noted in *Tom Brown's Schooldays* how Arnold often
lapsed into homiletics when he reminded future sixth formers of
their duty.

> Quit yourselves like men then, speak up, and strike out if necessary
> for whatsoever is true, and manly, and lovely ... but only to do your
> duty and help others to do theirs. ... it is the leading boys for the
> time being who give the tone to all the rest, and make the school
> either a noble institution for the training of Christian Englishmen,
> or a place where a young boy will get more evil than he would if he
> were turned out to make his way in London streets.[10]

Such advice evidently took hold; the boys, so imbued with a code
of duty and honor, would not tell a lie to Arnold because he
always believed them.[11] His insistence upon the truth was characteristic of the general reformation of mid-Victorian manners,
especially among the growing middle class.

His Legacy

Arnold's legacy was this transformation of manners which he
helped to effect. This transformation was part of the increasing
sensitivity to ethical principles in social intercourse, and he helped
to direct this moral consensus into education. His reforms were by
no means radical, but the intensity with which he shaped the
Christian gentleman was a new element in the nineteenth-century
public school. "The gospel at work," which was later popularized
by Samuel Smiles, was one expression of Arnold's educational
philosophy. "Mere intellectual acuteness" was esteemed less than
the slow cultivation of intellect and integrity through plodding
labor. In time, the code of industry and duty characterized public
school education, although it doubtless was more myth than fact
in many schools. Nevertheless this educational ideal saved England's public schools. As the British civil service expanded and
recruited through governmental examinations, a public school
education became essential. It bred a caste of leaders, ostensibly

9. Hughes, *Tom Brown's Schooldays*, pp. 128, 129.
10. Ibid., p. 151.
11. Briggs, *Victorian People*, p. 157.

men of respectability and duty, who would maintain a tradition of probity and service. In his early years of public school life a young boy came to accept rule by his superiors, and in his final years he learned to rule. Such indoctrination was indispensable to the civil service. Arnold's school would be honored for its essential contribution to the governing of England and its growing empire.

Selected Bibliography

Arnold, T. *Christian Life*. London: Fellowes, 1841.

——. *Introductory Lectures on Modern History*. Oxford: Parker, 1842.

——. *Miscellaneous Works*. London: Fellowes, 1845.

——. *Sermons Preached in the Chapel of Rugby School*. Rev. ed. London: Fellowes, 1945.

Bamford, T. W. *Thomas Arnold*. London: Cresset, 1960.

Briggs, A. *Victorian People*. Chicago: Phoenix, 1970.

Stanley, A. P. *The Life and Correspondence of Thomas Arnold*. 2 vols. London: Fellowes, 1844.

Whitridge, A. *Dr. Arnold of Rugby*. London: Constable, 1928.

Williamson, E. L. *The Liberalism of Thomas Arnold*. University: University of Alabama, 1964.

Wymer, N. G. *Dr. Arnold of Rugby*. London: Hale, 1953.

22

Bernard Ramm

John Henry Newman
(1801-1890)

Newman was born in London in 1801. He was educated at Oxford, receiving his degree in 1820 and continuing his studies as a fellow of Oriel College. He was ordained to the Anglican priesthood and served the churches of St. Clement and St. Mary in Oxford.

His Career

The state of the Anglican church in Newman's time was deplorable. A group of Oxford men (hence "the Oxford movement") set about to reform the church, and their first venture was to publish *Tracts for the Times* (hence "the Tractarian movement"). Originally pamphlets, some of the tracts eventually became books. Newman wrote the first and the last of the ninety tracts in 1833 and 1841. The latter contained Newman's claim that the Church of England's *Articles of Religion* were not really anti-Roman Catholic but correctives for the abuses of the times.

Newman came to the conclusion that Anglicanism is inconsistent Roman Catholicism. To harmonize his convictions and his affiliations he entered the Roman church in 1845, after which he left

Oxford and spent the major part of his life in an oratory. An oratory is a difficult institution for Protestants to grasp in that it is a church and yet it is not. Its functions are praying, preaching, teaching, and offering the sacraments. Newman carried on an academic life in the Roman church, writing, preaching, lecturing, and teaching virtually until his death in 1890.

Due to the low state of Roman Catholic education in Ireland, Newman was persuaded to become rector of a new university in Dublin which the church desired to create. Newman was reluctant because he did not consider himself adequately equipped, but he accepted, and it was in this connection that he gave his famous lectures on *The Idea of a University*. The difficulties of starting the university were too great (Newman claimed he crossed St. George's channel fifty-six times in the interests of the university),[1] the adventure failed, and he returned to the oratory. Late in life Newman received two impressive honors: Trinity College in Oxford made him an Honorary Fellow in 1877 and Leo XIII made him a cardinal in 1879. Although he left Oxford after his conversion, Newman was in heart, blood, and soul always an Oxonian.

His *Collected Works* number forty volumes, but his fame rests on just a few of them. *An Essay in Aid of a Grammar of Assent* is his religious epistemology, or theory of knowledge. *Apologia pro vita sua* defended his decision to become a Catholic, responding especially to Charles Kingsley's charge that the Roman church in general and Newman in particular did not consider truth for truth's sake a virtue. *An Essay on the Development of Doctrine* attempted to show that the elaborate Roman church of the nineteenth century was the logical flowering of the simple church of the Book of Acts.

Due to Newman's lack of a traditional Catholic scholastic education, many Catholic scholars of the day were suspicious of him. He has found such a ready reception by twentieth-century Catholics, however, that one can speak of a "Newman renaissance."[2]

---

1. *Autobiographical Writings*, p. 333.
2. The best biography and the best bibliography, especially of Newman's own writings, are still W. S. Lilly, "Newman, John Henry," in *Dictionary of National Biography*, ed. S. Lee, vol. 40 (London: Smith and Elder, 1894), pp. 340-51. Another very valuable select bibliography is in *On the Scope and Nature of University Education*, pp. xxiii, xxiv. An excellent bibliography on Newman's educational theory is F. De Hovre, *Catholicism in Education*, pp. 367-69.

In analyzing Newman as a Christian educator, one is confronted with serious limitations.

First, Newman was totally occupied with university education.[3] He had nothing significant to say about education below this level or about seminary education. His occasional remarks about the education of children are insignificant. Some of the oratories in France (e.g., the Oratory of St. Phillip Neri) were very progressive in children's education, but the author could find no evidence that this was due to Newman's career. Newman did warn against too much rationalism, too much formalism, too much passivity on the student's part, and too little mental discipline. Newman's ideal was that of Oxford—lecturing, reading, and conversing, particularly with the dons.

Second, his educational work consisted only of reading, preaching, lecturing, and some teaching at the oratory. His one effort at administration—the Irish university—was a failure. As he said:

Neither by my habits of life nor by vigour of age, am I fitted for the task of authority or rule or of initiation.[4]

And third, while Newman did contribute somewhat to the theory of learning in *An Essay in Aid of a Grammar of Assent,* that work is really a mixture of logic, philosophy, religion, and psychology. Scientifically controlled experiments concerning the theory of learning (which are relevant to Christian education) did not start until the early twentieth century.

It might appear strange, then, that Newman is counted a great Christian educator, but his *The Idea of a University* is a classic, and in it as well as in other writings he said some things about Christian education which are important even if they have no immediate "cash value," or application.

His Educational Views

Newman tried to work out a theory of religious knowledge, and he wrote *Grammar of Assent* to defend the epistemological integrity of the act of faith, which he discussed under the notion of assent. He explained in some detail the various logical, factual, and psychological conditions that enter into various truth-

---

3. I attempted to reconstruct Newman's idea of a Christian university in *The Christian College in the Twentieth Century,* pp. 52-71.
4. *University Education,* p. 207.

statements, or agreements that certain propositions are true. He showed that assent is one of the credible and justifiable ways of coming to the truth—the so-called "illative sense." Faith is "illative assent" and is therefore philosophically and logically respectable.

Newman also tried to harmonize university education with Christian faith. Speaking in musical terms, the "fundamental vibration" of a university education is not religious. Nevertheless, the "overtones," which follow out of necessity from the "fundamental," contain theological and Christian materials. Newman would not consider a Bible institute education adequate for a Christian. The Christian scholar must be a university man; but the university man is also a moral man (in harmony with the Greek and Latin tradition of education), a religious man (since theology is part of universal knowledge), and a gentleman.

The enormous expansion of scientific knowledge in the nineteenth century had tremendous impact on university education: many of the new universities omitted theology, religion, and Christianity from their curricula, and utility replaced the traditional classical goals of education. To Newman, however, education's goal is the creation of what he called the "philosophical mind," a mind that appreciates the great literature of the past, the education of one's sense of taste, the general moral elevation of personality, and the ability to see the structure or pattern of any body of learning or any proposed theory. Education does not concentrate on a narrow skill but hones, broadens, and equips the entire mind. Learning facts, details, and information is necessary, but they are not the end of education; they help to hone the total mind and to create the "philosophical mentality."

Training is not education, and to Newman science and utility are training; science and utility do not produce the philosophical mind. Newman was not opposed to science, but he believed very firmly that training and education are two different things. Further, if one wants to play the game of utility consistently, one must grant that the educated man is the man with the most utility. But the application of the philosophical mentality to every task enriches every facet of society, and what greater utility is there than this?

Newman challenged purely secular education, arguing, in harmony with classical ideals, that education must make a man moral. It inculcates virtues into his personality and produces a gentleman, a man with not only social graces, excellent tastes, and liberal knowledge, but also moral and religious fiber.

Because theology is one of the great subject matters of education and is not merely a topic peculiar to Christianity, education needs theology. A university which omits theology betrays its charter to teach universal knowledge.

Further, man as a sinner cannot keep sin out of the various parts of the university curricula. It is theology which can detect, expose, and correct the influence of sin upon the educative process.

Again, the university, being a human corporation, is weak and unsteady, and the church universal, armed with the learning and stability gained through its centuries of existence, can help the university compensate for its weakness and unsteadiness.[5]

His Contemporary Relevance

As archaic as a "Catholic Oxford" may have seemed a decade or so ago, some of Newman's basic insights are taking on new life and relevancy.

Education is for life. The concept of the university's function in modern society is being revolutionized. An entire library has been written since the 1960s on the new role of the university. For example, the journal *Daedalus* has published article after article on the subject; the Winter, 1970, edition, entitled "The Embattled University," was entirely devoted to it. The new generation is making the point that the traditional goals of the university are proper, but they do not go far enough. University education should be for life, not merely for vocation or specialized research. Further, universities should engage in the process of social, political, and economic transformation. This makes Newman's words ring with a new relevancy:

> ... a university training is the great ordinary means to a great but ordinary end; it aims at raising the intellectual tone of society, at cultivating the public mind, at purifying the national taste, at

---

5. This did create for Newman the problem of academic freedom in a very acute way. How can we reconcile the role of theology and the church in university education and yet retain the ideal of academic liberty? His solution was that *ordinary* education in the university be restricted to established, non-controversial matters which will not upset the student. Controversial and speculative matters are to be debated by scholars in their journals and societies. As Newman put it, scholars need elbow room. With the explosion of knowledge in the twentieth century and the enormous mushrooming of the paperback book, Newman's solution comes apart; it is now an impracticable and impossible solution.

supplying true principles to popular enthusiasm and fixed aims to popular aspirations, at giving enlargement and sobriety to the ideas of the age, at facilitating the exercise of political power, and refining the intercourse of private life.[6]

Of course, the Christian college will add the Christian dimension to "education for life."[7]

The concept of education for life goes counter to the communist's idea of a university, which makes it only the resource pool for the technologically educated people needed by the state. Anything beyond that is an "extra," or "fringe benefit," for the state.[8]

Faith is valid. In the *Grammar of Assent* Newman attempted to show that there is a way of knowing that is different from ordinary logical inference and factual verification, but that is equally valid and dependable. He called it the "illative sense," and faith is of this order. Faith need not take a back seat with respect to its philosophical credentials.

One of today's most popular writers among Christian scholars is Michael Polanyi. In *Personal Knowledge* and *The Tacit Dimension* he attempted to do for our generation what Newman did for his, as farfetched as the parallel may appear on the surface.[9] He tried to show that the process of knowing is not the simple, direct method suggested by the scientific experimenter, but a very complex process involving the total person, and this is as true in science as in other areas. Religious knowledge—which stresses the personal, the total person, the elements that cannot be reduced to explicit statements—is not so different from the so-called scientific way of knowing. Or, to put it oddly, knowing in science is far more a religious kind of knowing than the scientist is aware of or is willing

---

6. *University Education*, p. 152.

7. On the surface no two books seem so radically different as Newman's *On the Scope and Nature of University Education* and Jerry Rubin's *Do It!* (New York: Simon and Schuster, 1970). Boil away the pathology of Rubin's book and look beyond the incredibly erratic exposition, and there is a common thesis with Newman: university education is not to be primarily the work of technologists and research scholars in socially and politically isolated enclaves. Universities are to be places for the creation of productive and mature personalities, and the sources of correction and reform of society at large. Of course, there is a danger here. The push for relevancy and reform can itself be oppressive and deny certain kinds of research, and so in its own way destroy academic freedom. And without real academic freedom universities intellectually stagnate even if operated by the so-called "freedom-loving New Left."

8. Cf. G. S. Counts, *The Challenge of Soviet Education*.

9. New York: Harper, 1958; Garden City: Anchor, 1966.

to admit. Thus in different ways Newman and Polanyi came to almost identical conclusions.

Religion belongs in the colleges. Much of *The Idea of a University* is devoted to showing that a university without theology is both incomplete and unprotected. One of the amazing developments of the 1960s was the reintroduction in major American state universities of courses in religion, majors in religion, and even doctorates in religion. A group of university professors—not seminary professors—have banded together somewhat informally to get religion back on the campus, and each year they publish a huge volume called *The Religious Situation*.[10]

University education has thus come back to Newman. Although Newman thought narrowly of theology and Christianity, and of Catholicism in particular, the basic motivation and motif is the same: religion is a part of universal experience; it is a major factor in all cultures. Religion must be brought back to the university campus in order to do it justice.

Selected Bibliography

Counts, G. S. *The Challenge of Soviet Education.* New York: McGraw-Hill, 1957.

De Hovre, F. *Catholicism in Education.* New York: Benziger, 1934.

Harrold, C. F. *John Henry Newman.* New York: Green, 1945.

Newman, J. H. *An Essay in Aid of a Grammar of Assent.* Garden City: Image, 1955.

———. *Apologia pro vita sua.* New York: Dent, 1912.

———. *Autobiographical Writings.* Edited by H. Tristram. New York: Sheed and Ward, 1957.

———. *On the Scope and Nature of University Education.* New York: Dent, 1915.

Polanyi, M. *Personal Knowledge.* New York: Harper, 1958.

Ramm, B. *The Christian College in the Twentieth Century.* Grand Rapids: Eerdmans, 1963.

Walgrave, J.-H. *Newman the Theologian.* New York: Sheed and Ward, 1957.

---

10. Boston: Beacon. For the general religious stir in our universities, I have already mentioned the journal *Daedalus*. Other journals are *Zygon* (the relationship of religion to science); *The Christian Scholar;* and *Memo to the Faculty* (published periodically by the Center for Research on Learning and Teaching at the University of Michigan). Also of interest is R. Bender, *A Bibliography of Materials Related to the Re-examination of Faith in the Scholarly Community* (General Board of Education of the Methodist Church, 1964).

23

Elmer L. Towns

Horace Bushnell
(1802-1876)

Horace Bushnell is, as George Albert Coe wrote, one of the most important figures in the history of religious education in America: "If it were necessary to give a date to mark the transition to the modern conception of Christian training we could not do better than to name the year 1847, which saw the first issue of Horace Bushnell's *Christian Nurture*."[1] Of Bushnell's dictum that "the child is to grow up a Christian and never know himself as being otherwise," Paul H. Vieth wrote in 1947 that it "is now widely known and accepted."[2]

Busnell was opposed to the traditional practice of revivalism, a practice which he described in 1853 in his twentieth-anniversary sermon at North Congregational Church in Hartford, Connecticut:

> Things had come to such a pitch in our churches by the intensity of the revival system, that the permanent was sacrificed to the casual, the ordinary swallowed up and lost in the extraordinary, and Christian piety itself reduced to a kind of campaigning or stage-effect exercise.[3]

1. *The Religion of the Mature Mind* (Chicago: Revell, 1962), p. 305.
2. *The Church and Christian Education* (St. Louis: Bethany, 1947), p. 20.
3. In H. S. Smith, ed., *Horace Bushnell*, p. 43. Many of Bushnell's unpublished sermons, letters, and discourses are in this volume.

He was particularly opposed to the use of revivalism with the children of the church, believing that they are,

> in a sense, included in the faith of their parents, partakers with them in their covenant, and brought into a peculiar relationship to God, in virtue of it.... they are to grow up as Christians, or spiritually renewed persons. As to the precise time or manner in which they are to receive the germ of holy principle, nothing is affirmed.[4]

Thus Arthur Cushman McGiffert credited Bushnell's *Christian Nurture* with doing "more than any other single factor to break down the extreme individualism of the old puritanism."[5] And Sandford Fleming credited Bushnell with reversing the then-traditional practice of regarding children "in precisely the same manner as adults, with no recognition of any differences in their religious characteristics or in their normal religious experiences."[6]

Further evidence of Bushnell's importance is the name of one of America's most famous chairs of Christian education—Yale Divinity School's "Horace Bushnell Professorship of Christian Nurture."

His Life

Horace Bushnell was born on 14 April 1802 in Bantam, Connecticut. His father, a farmer and small-time manufacturer, had been raised a Methodist, and his mother, an Episcopalian, but both became members of the Congregational church of New Preston, Connecticut, the town to which the Bushnells moved when Horace was three. There Bushnell grew to young adulthood, professing Christian faith in 1821. In a manuscript dated 3 March 1822, Bushnell recorded an experience he had at about the time he had joined the church: he had been "led to Jesus" and had given evidence of deep conviction.[7]

Bushnell entered Yale College in 1823, and before graduating in 1827, he entertained serious intellectual doubts. He was strongly influenced by the English poet-philosopher Samuel Taylor Coleridge, who felt that Christianity is understandable primarily by intuition: Christianity appeals not so much to the intellect as to the ethical and spiritual feeling. Bushnell thus became convinced

---

4. "The Kingdom of God as a Grain of Mustard Seed," *New Englander* 2 (1844): 610. Also in *Horace Bushnell*, p. 375.

5. *The Rise of Modern Religious Ideas* (New York: Macmillan, 1915), p. 277.

6. *Children and Puritanism* (New Haven: Yale University, 1933), p. 185.

7. In M. A. Cheney, ed., *Life and Letters of Horace Bushnell*, p. 21.

that religion appeals primarily to the emotions for its compelling demonstration.[8]

After graduation he tried teaching (in Norwich, Connecticut) and journalism (in New York City), only to be convinced that neither was his vocation. Early in 1829 he returned to Yale to study law, and he soon became a tutor in the college. Two years later, in 1831, a great revival swept Yale; Bushnell's intellectual doubts disappeared and the course of his life changed. That same year he entered Yale Divinity School, and upon graduation in 1833 he was called by North Congregational in Hartford.

In 1849 Bushnell issued a work entitled *God in Christ* which, among other things, claimed that the incarnation and the trinity are truths of Christian experience. This constituted a radical departure from current New England theology. Although the Hartford Central Association, of which Bushnell was a member, did not proceed against him, the Fairfield West Association did. The case was considered by successive meetings of the General Association of Connecticut from 1849 to 1854, and despite the fact that few Connecticut ministers were sympathetic to his views, the association did not formally condemn Bushnell.

He relinquished all pastoral duties at North Congregational in 1859 and died in Hartford on 17 February 1876.

His Theology

The central idea of New England Calvinism in Bushnell's day was the transcendence of God. God's sovereignty was magnified almost to the point of obscuring His indwelling presence in men, which was what Bushnell emphasized. Because God is present in man's world, the child can be expected to grow up within the kingdom of God through participation in the organic life of the Christian family. Bushnell sought to modify a rigid supernaturalism, yet was afraid of the rising tide of naturalistic thought which threatened to undermine Christian faith.[9] He argued against a literal interpretation of Scriptural statements about God:

---

8. H. S. Smith, *Horace Bushnell*, p. 27. Smith traced the effect of Coleridge on teachers and pupils at Yale during Bushnell's time there as a student. Bushnell later claimed that when he had first read Coleridge he found it foggy, but subsequently it became "lucid and instructive." *Life and Letters*, p. 208.

9. H. Bushnell, *Nature and the Supernatural* (New York: Scribner, 1858), pp. 20-31.

...if God is to be Himself revealed, He has already thrown out symbols for it, filling the creation full of them, and these will all be played into metaphor.... And ... we can say nothing of Christ so comprehensively adequate as to call Him the metaphor of God: God's last metaphor! And when we have gotten all the metaphoric meanings of His life and death, all that is expressed and bodied in His person of God's saving help and new-creating, sin-forgiving, reconciling love, the sooner we dismiss all speculations on the literalities of His incarnate miracles, His derivation, the composition of His person, His suffering—plainly transcendent as regards our possible understanding—the wiser shall we be in our discipleship.[10]

This view of God was one of the reasons some of Bushnell's contemporaries considered him a heretic.

A man's view of salvation is usually at the center of his theology, and Bushnell wrote of Christ's work that it

terminates, not in the release of penalties by due compensation, but in the transformation of character, and the rescue in the matter, of guilty men from the retributive causation provoked by his sins.[11]

The death of Christ was not an atonement for man's sin but a moral example to man. To be restored to God, a man should cease to sin. Thus man's relationship to God is determined by man's character rather than by an act of God's Son.

What are the implications of this doctrine for personal religious faith? Bushnell did not believe it necessary to "embrace ... Christ as a sacrifice" or to see Christianity as a "vicarious religion." But he did affirm

that no one ever becomes a true Christian man, who does not rest himself in God, or give himself over to God, in objective faith and devotion, somehow.[12]

While Bushnell emphasized the subjective character of religious faith, he also recognized the need for an objective religion.

Therefore, we need, all alike, some objective religion; to come and hang ourselves upon the altar of sacrifice sprinkled by the blood of Jesus, to enter into the holiest set open by His death, to quiet our soul in His peace, clothe it in His righteousness, and trust Him as the Lamb of God that taketh away our sin. In these simple, unselfish, unreflective exercises, we shall make our closest approach to God.[13]

Thus Bushnell vacillated from subjective to objective faith. Per-

10. "Our Gospel a Gift to the Imagination," *Literary Varieties* 3 (1881): 249.
11. *Vicarious Sacrifice* (New York: Scribner, 1877), p. 449.
12. *God in Christ* (Hartford: Hamersby, 1867), p. 264.
13. Ibid., pp. 267, 268.

haps he was concerned about his critics and attempted to invest historic Christian terms and symbols with new meanings and significance.

His View of Christian Nurture

Bushnell had a unique doctrine of the family. He considered it a unity, a body, in that "a power over character is exerted therein, which can not properly be called influence." This power is exerted by parents over children "not only when they teach, encourage, persuade, and govern, but without any purposed control whatever."[14] Bushnell wrote further that the child

> sees the world through his parents' eyes. Their objects become his. Their life and spirit mold him. If they are carnal, coarse, passionate, profane, sensual, devilish, his little plastic nature takes the poison of course. . . . he lives and moves and has his being in them.[15]

The parents' power is absolute before the child learns to reason, and it affects the child throughout his life. Bushnell felt that a long line of godly fathers and mothers might effect a religious temperament in the child, producing a godly consciousness and stemming his tendency to compromise his integrity. Character development begins even in early infancy.

> Never is it too early for good to be communicated. Infancy and childhood are the ages most pliant to good.

Bushnell baptized infants primarily because of his belief in the unity of the family (illustrated in the New Testament by the

14. *Christian Nurture*, pp. 93, 94. Bushnell's work on Christian nurture apparently began when the Hartford Central Association invited him to address the question, "Do the right of infant baptism and the household covenant contemplate the fact that a child should grow up a Christian or a converted person?" On 4 August he did that, and no one seriously objected to his views. But after the Massachusetts Sabbath School Society published his address in 1847 under the title *Discourses on Christian Nurture*, Bennett Tyler, a leading Calvinist, accused Bushnell in an open letter of propagating "error of a very dangerous tendency" with regard to depravity and regeneration. Several other theologians followed Tyler's suit, and the Society quickly suspended publication of the *Discourses*. Bushnell responded with a forty-eight-page pamphlet attacking the Society and defending his doctrine. Later that year he published *Views of Christian Nurture and of Subjects Adjacent Thereto*, which combined his *Discourses*, the forty-eight-page pamphlet, and a sermon entitled "The Kingdom of God as a Grain of Mustard Seed." Twelve years later Bushnell added several essays to the volume and shortened the title to *Christian Nurture* (1861). The most recent reprinting is the one by Yale University in 1966.

15. Ibid., pp. 106, 107.

baptism of entire families), and he accepted them into church membership.

> The propriety of this membership does not lie in what those infants can or can not believe, or do or do not believe, at some given time, as, for example, on the day of their baptism; but it lies in the covenant of promise, which makes their parents, parents in the Lord; their nurture, a nurture of the Lord; and so constitutes a force of futurition by which they are to grow up, imperceptibly, into "faithfuls among faithfuls," in Christ Jesus.[16]

This led to Bushnell's view that the child born in a Christian home is to be nurtured, not converted.[17]

Bushnell explained his oft-repeated axiom that "the child is to grow up a Christian and never know himself as being otherwise."

> In other words, the aim, effort, and expectation should be, not, as is commonly assumed, that the child is to grow up in sin, to be converted after he comes to a mature age; but that he is to open on the world as one that is spiritually renewed, not remembering the time when he went through a technical experience, but seeming rather to have loved what is good from his earliest years. I do not affirm that every child may, in fact and without exception, be so trained that he certainly will grow up a Christian.[18]

Bushnell anticipated orthodox reaction to his view of Christian nurture in a sermon on regeneration. Crucial to his defense was his definition of a Christian.

> But my child is a sinner, you will say; and how can I expect him to begin a right life, until God gives him a new heart? This is the common way of speaking, and I state the objection in its own phraseology, that it may recognize itself. Who then has told you that a child can not have the new heart of which you speak? Whence do you learn that if you live the life of Christ, before him and with him, the law of the Spirit of Life may not be such as to include and quicken him also? And why should it be thought incredible that there should be some really good principle awakened in the mind of a child? For this is all that is implied in a Christian state. The Christian is one who has simply begun to love what is good for its own sake, and why should it be thought impossible for a child to have this love begotten in him?[19]

Bushnell implied that the child achieves right standing before God

---

16. Ibid., pp. 166, 167.
17. Bushnell, *Sermons for the New Life* (New York: Scribner, 1867), pp. 108, 109.
18. Ibid., p. 4.
19. Ibid., p. 9.

by living the "good life." But how can the young child do good when he has no will of his own, or believe when he has no power to comprehend or make rational choices? Bushnell believed that the parents' faith includes faith on the part of the child, and that the righteous nature of the parents is transmitted to the child. He argued that if evil can be imputed to children (as the Calvinists believed), righteousness can also be imputed to them. He discerned a natural flow of Christian life from the parent to the child, a flow that continues as the child grows and that finally diminishes as he matures.

> ... this is the very idea of Christian education, that it begins with nurture or cultivation. And the intention is that the Christian life and spirit of the parents, which are in and by the Spirit of God, shall flow into the mind of the child, to blend with his incipient and half-formed exercises; that they shall thus beget their own good within him—their thoughts, opinions, faith, and love, which are to become a little more, and yet a little his own separate exercise, but still the same in character.[20]

Bushnell also anticipated two more possible objections to his views. His was no liberal, humanistic concept of human nature.

> There are many who assume the radical goodness of human nature and the work of Christian education is, in their view, only to educate or educe the good that is in us. Let no one be disturbed by the suspicion of a coincidence between what I have here said and such a theory. The natural depravity of man is plainly asserted in the Scriptures. . . .[21]

Nor did he replace the work of the Holy Spirit in the regeneration of children with the work of parents.

> ... the strong language I have used concerning the organic connection of character between the parents and the child ... is not designed to assert [that there is] a power in the parent to renew the child, or that the child can be renewed by any agency of the Spirit less immediate than that which renews the parent himself.[22]

Bushnell distinguished between children of Christian parents and those of unbelievers; the former are to be nurtured, the latter converted.

Bushnell's view of Christian nurture was by no means rejected in all orthodox circles. Charles Hodge, a Princetonian Calvinist who was one of the best-known theologians of the day, summarized

---

20. Ibid., p. 21.
21. Ibid., p. 15.
22. Ibid., p. 22.

the central truth of *Christian Nurture:* "There is an intimate and divinely established connexion between the faith of parents and the salvation of their children; such a connexion as authorizes them to plead God's promises, and to expect with confidence, that through his blessing on their faithful efforts, their children will grow up the children of God." Hodge considered this "the great truth . . . that gives his [Bushnell's] book its chief value," although he thought the form in which this truth appeared in *Christian Nurture* to be "strange" and "distorted."[23]

And a reviewer in *The Methodist Quarterly Review,* while not "pledging ourselves to all Bushnell's views," contended that "the doctrines of his book, or similar ones, must be proclaimed from our housetops. No part of the world needs them as do the American churches, with whom baptized children seem to be regarded as little heathens—just as if they had not been baptized at all."[24]

His Educational Methods

Bushnell did not, as Coe pointed out, write "from the standpoint of general pedagogy,"[25] but he did develop some methods of education which parents could use in the home. He developed five principles in particular: (1) many things are to be taught "not formally or theologically, but implicitly, in a kind of child's version"; (2) the child's times of interest should be watched for, and religion should not be thrust upon him when it is unwelcome; (3) the child's questions should be carefully listened to and answered; (4) teaching should center about Jesus Christ, as Himself the truth incarnate, and the parent should so live as to make his own life an interpreter of Jesus' life; and (5) the parent should endeavor constantly "to make the subject of religion an open subject, and [to] keep it so. . . ."[26] In connection with the second principle, Bushnell advised parents to play with their child "when he wants to play, [and to] teach him when he wants to be taught."

Bushnell urged parents to make use of their child's "instinct of imitation."

We begin our mortal experience, not with acts grounded in judgment or reason, or with ideas received through language, but by simple

23. "Bushnell on Christian Nurture," *Biblical Repertory and Princeton Review* 19 (1847): 502ff.

24. 31 (1849): 156.

25. *The Religion of the Mature Mind*, p. 305.

26. *Christian Nurture*, pp. 376-80.

imitation, and, under the guidance of this, we lay our foundations. The child looks and listens, and whatsoever tone of feeling or manner of conduct is displayed around him, sinks into his plastic, passive soul, and becomes a mold of his being ever after.[27]

Parents were warned by Bushnell not to teach their children that: (1) they are "regenerated in their baptism"; (2) they are unregenerated and need to be converted as a heathen; (3) they need to be regenerated because of their faults or their love of play; (4) they are "too young to be good, or to be really Christian"; (5) they "can never pray, or do any thing acceptable to God, till after they are converted or regenerated"; and (6) they must do good works and build character for themselves ("Salvation by faith, is the only kind of religion that a child can support").[28]
Parents should be careful not to discourage true piety in their children by: (1) ill-temper, pettishness, and passion; (2) "too much of prohibition"; (3) "hard, unfeeling" government or "over-bearing absolutism"; (4) "an over-exacting manner" or "an extreme difficulty of being pleased"; (5) "holding displeasure too long, and yielding it with too great difficulty"; (6) "hasty and false accusations"; (7) anxiety and over-concern; (8) the application of "tests of character that are inappropriate to their age"; and (9) denying to them "an early recognition of their membership in the church, and an admission to the Lord's table."[29] The third point raises the matter of "family government," which Bushnell explained elsewhere is: (1) "to be government, using authority and maintaining laws and rules over the moral nature of the child"; (2) "to be regarded as a vicegerent of authority, set up by God and ruling in His place"; (3) "to bear rule for the same ends that God Himself pursues, in the religious order of the world"; and (4) "to secure ... a style of obedience in the child that amounts to a real piety."[30] The home, indwelled by "a domestic Spirit of grace," should be "the church of childhood, the table and hearth, a holy rite. ..." In it "Christ Himself, by that renewing Spirit who can sanctify from the womb, should be practically infused into the childish mind."[31]

---

27. A sermon reprinted in J. L. Hurlbut, ed., *Sunday Half Hours with Great Preachers* (Philadelphia: Winston, 1907), p. 363.

28. *Christian Nurture*, pp. 371-75.

29. Ibid., pp. 295-308.

30. *Sermons for the New Life*, p. xviii. These points, taken from the table of contents, are explained and analyzed in the text.

31. *Christian Nurture*, p. 12.

Bushnell's approach to education—exhibiting a greater interest in experiences and imitation than in the transmission of content or in indoctrination—was a forerunner of religious educational practice a century later. Coe wrote that Bushnell "put himself, perhaps unconsciously, into the central current of the great educational reform of the nineteenth century."[32]

His optimistic view of human nature burst like a rocket in the black night of what many have called "the pessimism of Calvinism" in New England. He reflected the growing American middle-class confidence in the reforming powers of good men—with the help of natural science and the industrial revolution—and its shift away from the dogmatic, creedal approach to Christianity to a more scientific one. Bushnell was a member of the growing American cult of education, believing that education can solve any problem, even the religious one.

Selected Bibliography

Bushnell, H. *Christian Nurture*. New York: Armstrong, 1876.

———. *Views on Christian Nurture and of Subjects Adjacent Thereto.* Boston: Massachusetts Sabbath School Society, 1847.

Cheney, M. A. *Life and Letters of Horace Bushnell.* New York: Harper, 1937.

Kirschenmann, F. "Horace Bushnell: Orthodox or Sabellian?" *Church History* 33:49-59.

Loewen, L. L. "An Evaluation of Horace Bushnell's Theory of Christian Nurture." M.A. thesis, Wheaton College, 1947.

Myers, A. J. W. *Horace Bushnell and Religious Education.* Boston: Manthorne and Burack, 1937.

Smith, H. S., ed. *Horace Bushnell.* New York: Oxford, 1965.

---

32. *The Religion of the Mature Mind*, p. 305.

24

John H. Kromminga

Abraham Kuyper
(1837-1920)

Abraham Kuyper was not primarily an educator or a writer on educational theory, but his contributions to the theory and practice of Christian education deserve consideration.

His profession was that of the gospel ministry. A gifted orator, he soon rose to national prominence in this calling, but his gifts of leadership and his popularity summoned him to other avenues of service. In succession or combination he filled the roles of leader of a Christian political party, member of Parliament, prime minister of the Netherlands, professor of theology, editor of widely-read periodicals, and prolific writer on a wide range of subjects.

What Kuyper had to say on educational theory was only a part of his total life's work, but it was an important part. Although the Antirevolutionary Party of which he was a principal leader was not a one-issue party, much of its attention was devoted to Christian education. The same cause made demands on Kuyper's energy as member of Parliament and prime minister, and as journalist he wrote thousands of pages in defense and propagation of this cause. Furthermore, the accomplishment most dear to his heart was the founding of the Free University of Amsterdam, which was intended to be the very embodiment of his principles.

Kuyper did not, in the main, originate the ideas he advanced. In working out his school program he built on foundations laid by G. Groen Van Prinsterer, and he shared honors with Lohman and other contemporaries.[1] But he wrote at great length in developing the theological background and support of these ideas, and he labored more effectively than any other person to put them into practice. These two activities are the focus of this chapter. The theological foundations will receive the principal attention; the practical implementation will be mentioned chiefly to illustrate and illuminate the theory itself.

The Theological Foundations

Born into a ministerial family, Abraham Kuyper was himself ordained to the ministry in 1863.[2] After serving a village church for four years and a church in Utrecht for three, he accepted a call to Amsterdam in 1870. During this time he had become active in Christian politics and in journalism. In Amsterdam he emerged as an outstanding critic and opponent of theological modernism. His term as pastor in Amsterdam ended in 1874 when he was elected to the Second Chamber of Parliament. He never returned to the ministry, but he remained an active churchman, serving as elder in the Amsterdam church.

Kuyper's political career continued. He served several terms in Parliament, and from 1901 to 1905 was prime minister of the Netherlands. He became head of the Antirevolutionary Party and in the meantime founded the Free University. His lectures in theology at this institution reflect his most profound theological thinking. The year 1905 marked the beginning of a gradual withdrawal from national politics.

Early in his ministerial career Kuyper had become an ardent devotee of Calvinism. Although it is widely recognized that Kuyper's Calvinism was an extension of original Calvinism, it is suggested that Kuyper followed Vinet rather than Calvin in allowing less authority to the government.[3] He considered Calvinism to be the source and guarantee of the constitutional freedoms of the Netherlands.

---

1. H. Colijn, *Levensbericht van Dr. A. Kuyper* (Kampen: Kok, 1923), p. 15.
2. Biographical items are drawn mainly from Frank Vanden Berg's *Abraham Kuyper*, the only complete biography in English.
3. F. W. Grosheide, *Kuypers Geloofsstuk* (Kampen: Kok, 1937), p. 10.

According to Kuyper, Calvinism has the deepest grasp of God's unity with His creatures:

> It does not seek God *in* the creature, as does Paganism; it does not isolate God *from* the creature, like Islam; it does not posit between God and the creature an intermediate fellowship, like Rome; but it proclaims the lofty thought that God, standing high in majesty above all creatures, still exercises unmediated fellowship with the creature through His Holy Spirit.[4]

Both predecessors and followers of Kuyper agreed with him in objecting to certain trends in the Netherlands. He could not accept the idea of a national church with all of its implications. This entered into his leadership of the *Doleantie,* a secession from the state church in 1886. One of his favorite aphorisms was that uniformity is the curse of modern life, pluriformity the gift of God. He regarded such uniformity as a real and present danger in the sphere of education.

The name of his political party—Antirevolutionary—renounced the secularizing spirit of the French Revolution, which made education an arm of the state. With reference to elementary education, the state attempted to suppress private schools and thus to rob Christians of their right to give their children a Christian education.[5] The all-powerful state also intruded into university education. Kuyper noted this tendency in the Netherlands, where the university as a free corporation had disappeared. The state determined whether and where universities should be founded; it appointed rectors, curators, and teachers; it regulated examinations and grades; and it provided funds.

Kuyper's reaction, and that of the movement with which he was associated, arose out of a religious-patriotic motif—the application of the (Calvinistic) Christian faith to all of life. He was convinced that these Christian principles were deeply integrated with the life and welfare of the Netherlands. It is obviously difficult to separate Kuyper's work as educator from his work as theologian, legislator, and journalist.

The slogan for *De Heraut,* a periodical which Kuyper edited, was "A free school and a free church in a free nation." He argued, according to Jan Van Lonkhuysen, "that since the children belong

---

4. *Calvinism: Six Stone Lectures,* p. 12; cf. *De Gemeene Gratie in Wetenschap en Kunst,* pp. 28ff.

5. J. Van Lonkhuysen, "Abraham Kuyper: A Modern Calvinist," *The Princeton Theological Review* 19 (1921): 139.

to the parents, and their education is the primary concern of the parents, therefore the school belongs to the parents...." Kuyper admitted that "state and church...may exercise supervision, to see whether the school is a free institution, the organ of a free society, or of parents united together in such a society."[6] This emphasis protects the rights of minority groups.

A motif that recurs consistently in Kuyper's writings is that of sphere sovereignty. Two outstanding instances are his inaugural address at the founding of the Free University[7] and his Stone Foundation lectures at Princeton Seminary in 1898. Each of the spheres—the state, the church, the family, science, art, and others— is sovereign in its own area. Each has its own place and its own role. They interact with each other, to be sure, but none can usurp the prerogatives of any other.

An even deeper motif is Christ's universal claim on all of life. The life principle instilled by Christ proceeds from the heart of the believer to every sphere: to the inner chamber, the church, life in society, the school, politics, statesmanship, the university, science, and finally to those deep principles of life which are the foundation of all national existence. It is the peculiar genius of Calvinism to recognize this sovereignty of God over all of life. If God has become man in Christ, there must always be a place for Christ in this world.[8]

In Kuyper's theology this was worked out in two related themes, common grace and its antithesis, special grace. These are two sides of the same coin and can be understood only in dialectical relation to each other. While God bestows His special grace only on those whom He has called to eternal life, He bestows His common grace on all men. The institutional church is unqualifiedly the terrain of particular or special grace.

> In the church only the life of special grace; *outside* of the church only the life of common grace.[9]

But in spite of this apparent disjunction, the two spheres are not unrelated to each other. The light of the gospel shines through the windows of the church and the church organism has certain effects on the national conscience, and this is a form of common grace.

---

6. Ibid.
7. *Souvereiniteit in Eigen Kring*, 3rd ed. (Kampen: Kok, 1930).
8. W. J. Aalders, "Dr. A. Kuyper," *Onze Eeuw* 4 (1921): 18.
9. *De Gemeene Gratie*, 2:273. Cf. A. A. Van Ruler, *Kuypers Idee Eener Christelijke Cultuur* (Nijkerk: Callenbach, n.d.), p. 18.

Kuyper left unanswered many questions as to how special grace influences the development of common grace. His broad vision was not always supplemented by attention to detail. His conception of common grace was historically conditioned by the nineteenth century; common grace manifested itself in some non-Christian cultures, but these were destined to disappear when Christian influence was brought to bear upon them. Europe and America were the particular spheres of common grace. History is Christian history.

A history of humanity in the rich, deep sense of the word becomes possible only by the action of a common grace ruled by Christ.[10]

The objects of God's choosing constitute the heart of the nation. Therefore the struggle for a Christian education is also a struggle for national development. Christian culture can be seen in narrower and broader focus. There is no essential difference between them, but the culture is better reflected in the narrower group, the confessing church. Election and special grace do not separate men from society, and common grace comes to completion only under the influence of special grace.

Christian is taken in two senses: that which is opposed to heathen, and the like; and that which is opposed to liberal, neutral, unbelieving. General-Christian culture fits the former; concentrated-Christian culture, the latter. In the former sense one can call all education in Europe and America Christian; in the latter sense there is a need for more Christian education. This distinction was clear and important for Kuyper, and it reflects something of the old problem of the requirements of the gospel versus the counsels of perfection.

The motif of the common grace doctrine lies not in cultural appreciation but in cultural activity. It gives the regenerated believer the possibility of existence, material to work with, and meaningful activity. Kuyper sometimes expressed himself in such a way that his common grace doctrine appeared to tend toward synthesis, but in fact it did not; the antithesis remained throughout.

This antithesis occurs between everything which proceeds from the life-principle instilled by Christ and everything which does not. This antithesis is all-pervasive, but apart from the church it is focused most sharply in the university. All science is based upon faith. Every person proceeds on his basic assumptions, which

10. *De Gemeene Gratie*, 2:184.

are either theocentric or homocentric. The national welfare is at stake here as elsewhere. If science is cultivated on a rationalistic rather than a Christian basis, the nation will inevitably be de-Christianized.

The antithesis as understood by Kuyper pervades the entire field of learning. It is perhaps less sharp in the material realm than in the spiritual, where the observer is more involved personally, but it is present everywhere. All aspects of life, properly seen, are ultimately unified in God. The recognition or nonrecognition of this constitutes a basic cleavage.

Common grace presupposes a certain amount of cooperation in education, but the antithesis also operates here. The Christian school is far more than a means of evangelism. It differs from a "neutral" school

> in the spirit which controls all of the education and in the influence and application which is brought to bear upon the child in every respect.... Christian education ... transmits Christian insights from generation to generation not only in respect to confession, but also in respect to everything that concerns the formation and upbringing of the child.[11]

This applies not only to propositions, but to sympathies, habits, viewpoints, and ideals.

If this is true of primary education, it is even more true at the university level. The neutral approach is invalid. Science is not neutral; an element of the spiritual is present in it, not only in the person making the inquiry but also in the subject which he is exploring. Kuyper sought to restore the subjective element of scientific inquiry to its rightful place. The distinction between regenerate and unregenerate men applies to all knowledge, not merely to spiritual sciences. Only he who is renewed by the Spirit is in a position to view all things in harmony with their essential nature.

It should be evident from the above that while Kuyper's ideas were profoundly theological, they had a direct bearing on educational theory. He sought to lay foundations for the position that all education ought to be Christian. He was concerned for far more than minority rights in so doing. As a practical politician he had to settle for some gains with respect to minority rights. As a party leader he urged the formation of separate organizations in

---

11. Ibid., 3:395.

the sphere of education (and in other spheres as well) for the effecting of ideas not held by all the people.

But his ideals were higher than that. It does not do full justice to him to say, as one commentator said, that Kuyper founded the Free University in order that "the Calvinistic people might not be destitute of leadership, but have their own ministers, lawyers, doctors, judges, statesmen, journalists, and professors in the various branches of science."[12] Worthy and ambitious as this objective is, Kuyper's vision went beyond it. He considered the Free University to be in the interests of the entire nation and beyond. Christian education is nothing less than a leaven for all of society.

The Practical Accomplishments

The tension between ideal and actual was especially evident in the practical accomplishments of Kuyper as statesman. To a great extent Kuyper, the man of broad vision, left to others the task of working out his ideas in practice. When all of his words had been spoken, the task of determining just how a school is fully Christian and how a subject is to be Christianly taught remained to be solved. With respect to establishing the legal right of existence for Christian schools of all descriptions, however, Kuyper was preeminent in his zeal, ability, and accomplishments.

It must not be supposed that Kuyper accomplished these things without a great deal of opposition. Long before he entered the political arena, he had become controversial because of the nature of his positions and his ardent espousal of them. He was vigorously opposed in the political sphere and bitterly lampooned in the public press. Some of his legislative efforts were failures, and in the end he had to settle for something less than he desired. Nevertheless the education law which he sponsored and the university which he founded were major achievements.

As early as 1869 he addressed the Calvinistic School Society. Under the title "The Appeal to the National Conscience," he discussed the national character, the national calling, freedom of religion, liberty of conscience, and parental autonomy in educational action. Kuyper believed that one sphere, that of the church, must be reserved wholly and directly for God. The rest—state, family, society, learning, and culture—can be only generally and

---

12. Van Lonkhuysen, "Abraham Kuyper," p. 140.

indirectly penetrated by religion. But even in these areas believers must organize themselves separately in order to apply their principles as intensively and extensively as they should. This approach is not ideal, but it must be applied when the entire populace can no longer be the organ of religious confession and life.

From his first entry into Parliament, Kuyper espoused the cause of the schools. He maintained that schools should have their autonomous organization, with local, provincial, and national boards. The state is to legislate standards, certify teachers, control and inspect, and require attendance. The state also has the obligation to make it financially possible for parents to send their children to the school of their choice. The state must respect the parents' freedom of conscience. It should reimburse nonstate schools for the money they are saving the state. Thus in defending the rights of the particular minority which he represented and which he considered to be the true representative of the national religious and cultural heritage, Kuyper fought also for the rights of all minorities.

The educational antithesis, as Kuyper understood it, can be posed as a question: Must youth be instructed neutrally, that is in fact atheistically, or must they be instructed Christianly, according to the demands of Scripture? In this context, the fight for the elementary school and the free university is one fight.[13]

Kuyper established the principle that free universities (free, that is, of both state and church) have full rights alongside state universities. He fought for the legal validation of the degrees awarded by such universities. Although he visualized the formation of many such universities, the only one to emerge was his own—and the Free University of Amsterdam may justly be called his own; his vision and energy were the greatest single factors in its establishment.

The Free University began with a theological faculty, of which Kuyper himself was the chief ornament. But he desired a genuine and complete university, not merely a divinity school. From the very beginning he worked for the ultimate accomplishment of this ideal. Some supporters of the Free University began to hesitate when studies progressed beyond theology, law, and letters to the natural sciences. But for Kuyper this was perfectly consistent, and he never wavered in his progress toward this goal, which has long since been achieved.

---

13. Aalders, "Dr. A. Kuyper," p. 18.

Although Kuyper's activities were carried on in many fields, there was a massive unity in his efforts, and although his work as educational theorist was not his chief professional role, very much of his activity was directly related to Christian education.

The distinctive theology which he worked out as professor at the Free University contained the principles of a science, law, letters, history, and theological encyclopedia. This was summarized in his *Encyclopaedie der Heilige Godgeleerdheid,* originally published in three volumes. A Condensation and English translation of this work is the one-volume *Principles of Sacred Theology.*[14]

The Christian education which Kuyper advocated was in no way intended to isolate the Christian community from the nation or from the world of learning. It involved separate Christian organization, to be sure, but such organizations are deeply immersed in national life. Because of his principles Kuyper could never rest satisfied with an ivory-tower existence. Christ has absolute claims on all of life, and His claims may not be ignored. Separate organizations exist not to isolate these claims, but to make them effective in society.

Thoroughly consistent with this was Kuyper's insistence that Christian education involves all of learning. A mere "school with the Bible" was poles apart from his intention. The antithesis carried the inescapable implication that no subject can be understood apart from Christian insight. Common grace, likewise, requires that these insights be applied to every activity.

Selected Bibliography

Kuyper, A. *Calvinism: Six Stone Lectures.* New York: Revell, 1899.

———. *De Gemeene Gratie.* 3 vols. Leiden: Donner, 1907.

———. *De Gemeene Gratie in Wetenschap en Kunst.* Amsterdam: Hoveker and Wormser, 1905.

———. *Principles of Sacred Theology.* Translated by J. H. De Vries. Grand Rapids: Eerdmans, 1954.

Vanden Berg, F. *Abraham Kuyper.* Grand Rapids: Eerdmans, 1960.

---

14. Trans. J. H. De Vries (Grand Rapids: Eerdmans, 1954).

25

James Merritt

William James
(1842-1910)

William James was probably the leading psychologist-philosopher in America during the late nineteenth and early twentieth centuries. He wrote much of value on religion, and his philosophy and psychology are relevant to the study of education.

His Life

James was the son of theologian Henry James, and in William's last letter to his father, he acknowledged his indebtedness to him as well as his differences:

> All my intellectual life I derive from you; and though we often seemed at odds ... I'm sure there's harmony somewhere, and that our strivings will combine. . . .[1]

Henry died before the letter arrived from England, and it was read at his grave by his eldest son and namesake, Henry James the novelist. William's father had enrolled in Princeton Theological Seminary in 1835, but in 1838 he left because of what was to him

---

1. H. James, ed., *The Letters of William James* (Boston: Little and Brown, 1920), 1:219.

its harsh Presbyterian theology. When in Windsor, England, in 1844 with his wife and two infant sons, Henry underwent a spiritual crisis which influenced him most markedly for the rest of his life. He emerged from it a Swedenborgian enthusiast if not disciple. Swedenborg's writings gave him the tangible hope of spiritual oneness and provided him with further justification for his break with Calvinism.

Although religion and philosophy were united in Henry's mind, his eldest son could not remember "an item of the detail of devotional practice" in the James home, or any "shade of an approach to 'keeping Sunday.' " Yet there was "a general liberty of living, of making ourselves as brightly as home might be, in that 'spiritual world' which we were in the habit of hearing as freely alluded to as we heard the prospect of dinner or the call of the postman...." There was much religion in the home but, the children later felt, "so little to show for it."[2]

The James family moved often, partly out of a desire to obtain for the children the best instruction available. William studied in schools in Boulogne-sur-mer (the College); Newport, Rhode Island; Geneva, Switzerland (the Academy); and Cambridge, Massachusetts (the Lawrence Scientific School). In 1865-66 he was part of Louis Agassiz's zoological expedition to Brazil. Between 1867 and 1874 he had several serious bouts with neuresthenia, a complex emotional impairment which remained with him for life. In 1869 he received an M.D. from Harvard University, but because of his health he never practiced medicine. In 1873 he began teaching at Harvard, and his career was, in the best sense, an extension of his education. He taught physiology first, then psychology, and finally philosophy.

Upon hearing of his father's death in 1882, William wrote to his wife of four years, Alice Gibbens James, that she must not leave him until he had come to understand "the value and meaning of religion" as his father had. He did not, however, consider religion the *one* thing needful in life, as his father had, but "needful with the rest." He wrote that

> my friends leave it out altogether, and I, as his son (if for no other reason) must help it to its rights in their eyes.

Ralph Barton Perry noted that James fulfilled this pledge twenty years later in writing *The Varieties of Religious Experience.* By

2. *Notes of a Son and Brother,* p. 157.

the very tone of his father's household, James had learned early that religion is essentially a matter of personal orientation. For James nothing was more important than to know how beliefs about ultimates do in fact operate in the daily context of personal experience.

His Philosophy of Religion

The task of reconstructing James's philosophy of religion is an overwhelming one due to the immense wealth of his prolific writings and the extensive exegesis which has accumulated since his death in 1910.

One theme we must pursue is his attack on the absolute. In his essays on pragmatism James was concerned to confront the erudite philosophers of the absolute with the more practical philosophy of observing beliefs in experience. He objected to the monism (or absolutism) which the American culture of the nineteenth century had thrust upon him in his youth. (His father's theology had been characteristically monistic, although he had replaced the older Calvinistic monism with one premised on God as love and on the "created creature" as independent.) James became pluralistic in that he gave up the notion of a single truth "out there," to be approximated by the best philosophical formulation. In pluralistic philosophy, contrasting theologies live side-by-side, as the printed and spoken versions of them exist side-by-side in the journals, the seminar rooms, and the popular lecture halls. But how is one to determine which theology is "more true" than another? In the pragmatism of James, that belief or system of beliefs which "works best" for the believer is true for him. The believer himself provides the validation for what "works best" for him. The term *working best* is not to be crassly applied; rather, it refers to the settling on genuine options through the choice of one belief over another which might have been chosen. If the belief chosen does illumine the very situation in which it is chosen and does not disagree with what one knows about the rest of the universe, then that belief for that person is true. There need be no reference to a "folio edition" of absolute truth.

We can approximate the "alpha and omega" of William James on religious education by noting two salient facts: (1) his parents did not indoctrinate him with any particular religious doctrines; and (2) in the last decade of his life he formulated his own metaphysics. The first fact suggests that if children are to grow up into genuine religious life, they should be reared in homes which provide the optimum encouragement for the free study of religion. The second fact suggests that every youth needs to learn as he matures what should be his relationship to the metaphysical study of religion.

What was the central thrust of James's philosophy? We have noted that James was pluralistic rather than monistic. Robert Ulich suggested that in time James also would be known as an "empirical idealist." John Wild redirected attention to the radical empiricism of James and showed its close relationship to the phenomenology of Edmund Husserl. Both James and Husserl looked for a system of inquiry into the givenness of immediate experience which is not dependent upon prior knowledge from the natural sciences.

James's radical empiricism does offer a profound challenge for religious education. The society of our "free world" is necessarily pluralistic, as the society of totalitarian communism is monistic. How shall the individual in a free society learn to use all of the freedom of religion which rationally he possesses? He must learn how to describe his immediate feelings in precise detail. Older systems of empiricism had described the primary units of perception in terms of sensations such as "white circles," "red spheres," and "green shapes." In the *Principles of Psychology,* James described feelings as they naturally occur in the stream of consciousness. In accounting for thoughts as they occur, there is no dualism of "mind stuff" and units of matter. His empiricism is "radical" in that it takes into account our very conceptions of ultimates as they become our knowledge through immediate acquaintance.

In concluding his Hibbert lectures on *A Pluralistic Universe* at Oxford in 1909, James affirmed the need for a new relationship of empiricism and religion:

> Let empiricism once become associated with religion, as hitherto, through some strange misunderstanding, it has been associated with irreligion, and I believe that a new era of religion as well as of philosophy will be ready to begin....[3]

The Hegelian notion of the transcendental ego was involved in this misunderstanding. Absolutists had taught that the ego is a precious receptacle for the revealed knowledge of God and an

---

3. P. 314.

agency through which God's will operates. Such conceptions have to be modified, and some even abandoned, if one wants a psychological account of the operations of the human mind. The prolific development of empirical science in the latter nineteenth century, spurred by Darwin's *Origin of the Species* (1859), forced many to reconsider their conceptions of God and man.

Theology relates mind and faith; some notions of mind became almost too sacred to analyze, let alone attack. But James did analyze them in his *Principles*. He had learned from his father that theology is something to reformulate, not merely cherish. He also learned that the dogmatism of science demands equal skepticism and reconstruction in the light of the best philosophical criticism available. In his Gifford lectures in 1901, he demonstrated how psychology can be employed to describe religion. While preparing the lectures, James wrote to a long-time friend, Frances R. Morse, revealing first that James was himself religious, and second that he was by no means the coldly objective scientist trying to explain away religion.

> The problem I have set myself is a hard one: *first,* to defend (against all the prejudices of my "class") "experience" against "philosophy" as being the real backbone of the world's religious life—I mean prayer, guidance, and all that sort of thing immediately and privately felt, as against high and noble views of our destiny and the world's meaning; and *second,* to make the hearer or reader believe, what I myself invincibly do believe, that, all the special manifestations of religion may have been absurd (I mean its creeds and theories), yet the life of it as a whole is mankind's most important function. A task well-nigh impossible, I fear, and in which I shall fail; but to attempt it is *my* religious act.

"Experience" is the backbone of the lectures, even if some in James's conservative audience were unconvinced that it constitutes the backbone of religious faith. James had intended to report man's experience with religion in the first ten lectures and to reserve the latter ten for philosophic justification. But the psychological matter became so extensive as he wrote that the philosophic justification, as he stated in his preface, had to be "postponed entirely."

The Varieties of Christian Experience (the published form of the Gifford lectures) should not be viewed primarily as an extension of James's expertise as a psychologist. In his teaching and writing as a scientist and scholar, his interest in relating to ultimate concerns was never absent. Alfred North Whitehead ranked James among the four best philosophers in the history of Western civilization who had worked on the prodigious data of the past.[4]

A full account of James's philosophy must include his having personally experienced the depths of existential anguish and despair and, on the constructive side, his having set for himself the lifelong task of working out a philosophical solution for his type of religious concern, the sort of solution which he could put before his philosophical colleagues but which the educated public also could comprehend. In *The Varieties* James provided a disguised account of his experience in lectures six and seven on "The Sick Soul." It is among the reports of "conversions" of persons who had lost all sense of their essential worth.

> Whilst in this state of philosophic pessimism and general depression of spirits . . . I went one evening into a dressing room in the twilight to procure some article that was there, when suddenly there fell upon me without warning . . . a horrible fear of my own existence. Simultaneously, there arose in my mind the image of an epileptic patient whom I had seen in the asylum. . . . *That shape am I,* I felt, potentially. . . . I became a mass of quivering fear. After this the universe was changed for me altogether. I awoke morning after morning with a horrible dread at the pit of my stomach, and with a sense of the insecurity of life that I never knew before and that I have never felt since. . . . The experience has made me sympathetic with the morbid feelings of others ever since. . . . I have always thought that this experience of melancholia of mine had a religious bearing. I mean that the fear was so invasive and powerful that if I had not clung to scripture texts like "The eternal God is my refuge," etc. . . . I think I should have grown really insane.[5]

Biographers have placed this event in January 1870. James strove to resolve his chronic distress, and on 29 April 1870 he came upon Renouvier's definition of free will—"the sustaining of a thought *because I choose to* when I might have other thoughts." James wrote in his diary:

> My first act of free will shall be to believe in free will. For the remainder of the year I will abstain from the mere speculation and contemplative *Grublei* [i.e., "grubbing among subtleties"] . . . and voluntarily cultivate the feeling of moral freedom (by both reading and acting). . . . I may perhaps return to metaphysical study and skepticism. . . . [but I shall] consequently *accumulate grain on grain of willful choice like a very miser;* never forgetting how one link dropped undoes an indefinite number. . . .[6]

---

4. *Modes of Thought* (New York: Free, 1938), pp. 2, 3.
5. Pp. 160, 161.
6. *Letters,* p. 147. Emphasis is mine.

This diary entry, in the view of James's son, Henry, not only reveals much of what went on in James's mind in 1870 but "suggests parts of the *Psychology* and of the philosophic essays that later gave comfort and courage to unnumbered readers."

Following the model of his own experience, James wrote about personal religion "pure and simple" in *The Varieties.* There is no abstract "religious emotion" which is a distinct, elementary mental affection by itself and which is present in every religious experience. But because religion is so difficult to separate from morality, many insist upon defining religion as a system of feelings and thought taught by the church, personal religion being only a fraction of this complex. James, however, defined religion as

> the feelings, acts, and experiences of individual men in their solitude, so far as they apprehend themselves to stand in relation to whatever they may consider the divine.

Used in this sense, religion describes much from which theologies, philosophies, and ecclesiastical organization may secondarily grow. The term *divine* should be interpreted very broadly to include any object which is godlike.

In determining which of the available accounts of religious activity to include in *The Varieties,* James employed the criterion of credibility: Does the report have the impact of a genuine effort to relate to the "divine" as the person conceives it? James included reports of nominally religious persons such as Augustine, Theresa, John Bunyan, and George Fox; of literary figures such as Walt Whitman, Leo Tolstoi, Thomas Carlyle, and Marcus Aurelius; and of lesser-known persons from pietistic literature and from James's personal acquaintances. A strong implication of this prodigious mass of testimony is that for many there is the need to relate more or less directly to the divine, in a manner which is independent of the teachings of religious institutions. There are, however, important substantive differences among the types of testimony. For example, Marcus Aurelius agreed with "the divine plan of the universe," while the Christian author of *Theologica Germanica* agreed with, and even ran to embrace, the divine decrees. The Stoic emperor's feeling was primarily one of morality, that is, relating oneself to duty and necessity.

> The moralist must hold his breath and his muscles tense; and so long as this athletic attitude is possible all goes well—religion suffices....[7]

---

7. *The Varieties of Religious Experience,* p. 47.

But if one is "sicklied over with the sense of irremediable impotence," religion can provide an added dimension of emotion. This comparison of an essentially moral attitude with an essentiall'' religious one becomes even more pertinent when we learn tha't James had considered himself a Stoic in his youth and had even considered suicide as a Stoic solution to other forms of chronic distress which preceded the traumatic events of 1870.

James sensed that the Edinburgh audience for his Gifford lectures was essentially absolutistic and Kantian (i.e., there is *one* account of God and Man and the moral law to be apprehended). He had in mind not only the dogmatists of theology but also the "dogmatists of science," those who had felt that if some events can be materially determined, so can all events—including the so-called "religious" emotions. The latter can be explained away, for example, by attributing them to a malfunctioning of the gastronomic juices. James wanted both of these groups to be aware that although empiricism had been employed in attacking religion, it could be and should be employed in developing it. In 1896 he had noted in his lecture "The Will to Believe" that one has a right to hold a belief about important matters even if the verifying evidence is insufficient; when one feels the need to believe about important matters including ultimate concerns, one should consider the true options and make the choice that shall "make a difference" for the good in experience. Thus the large number of extended accounts of religious feelings presented at Edinburgh indicate James's desire to make clear the wide variety of religious beliefs which have in various senses "worked." Religion is essentially an affair of the emotions, and in a pluralistic universe the choice of religious belief is inevitably paramount. In the realm of religion, articulate beliefs are cogent only after the inarticulate feelings have reached the same conclusions. James affirmed not that this is how it should be, but that the emotional does in fact exercise such a priority over the rational. "Instinct leads, intelligence does but follow," James asserted in "The Reality of the Unseen."

In each account of religious experience, there is at least some grain of truth, however quaint or bizarre the report. But how is a religious experience to be judged as significantly good and not merely as having some passing relevance? The answer of James was not in terms of the subject's mental health; this was the unwarranted approach of the medical materialists. In the realms of science and industrial arts, it is not required that those who offer truth have no record of physical or nervous malfunctioning. Spiritual judgments are to be tested not on the basis of their origin (e.g., an unstable, nervous person) but in terms of what it explains or what guide it provides for action.

> Immediate luminousness, in short, *philosophical reasonableness,* and *moral helpfulness* are the only available criteria. Saint Theresa might have had the nervous system of the placidest cow, and it would not save her theology, if the trial of her theology by these other tests were to show it contemptible. . . .[8]

It was James's intention to provide extensive data as a context for the study of religious experience. Accounts from authors whose lives bordered on the pathological should not be omitted, because some of the accounts may be valid.

Some states of mind have to be judged as superior to other states of mind, but none is judged superior on the basis of its antecedents. One of two entirely different criteria must be applied: (1) Which give us immediate delight? or (2) Which have the better consequences? What immediately feels best is not always most "true" when measured by the verdict of the rest of experience; if "feeling good" were all that counted, then drunkenness would be the supreme human experience.

James's willingness to study such a wide range of religious experiences does not mean that his was an unqualified relativism; he found so much "sad discordancy" in the realm of religious experience. How then can one spiritual opinion be tested against another? "Through logic and experiment" was James's general answer. But whose logic and whose experiment? The last resort has always been, in the long run, the common consent of mankind or the judgments of those who instruct and train. For example, one might find a philosopher's account with which he agrees. If that account also agrees with the general theological tone of the times, then it reinforces one's personal judgment. To ask what the "competent" should know about spiritual judgments is what theology and philosophy of religion are all about. It is in the latter area that James is so timelessly relevant.

According to a joke making the rounds of philosophy-of-education conventions, Deweyan philosophers behave as naturalistic atheists Monday through Friday but become dutiful theists on Sunday! But the pragmatism and the radical empiricism of James

---

8. Ibid., p. 18.

do not require such compartmentalization. James's belief in God was consistent with his pluralistic universe. The "man in the street" instinctively wants to believe in God, and this belief offends the educational researcher who has been brought up on the "puritanism of science."[9] The latter is James's description of the dogmatism which permits one to believe only that which is susceptible to verification.

The Varieties is potentially instructive for the person who looks upon the quest for a religion as a problem in self-education. James illumined the choice of a religion by referring to two types of temperaments: (1) the healthy-minded one and (2) that of the "sick soul." A healthy mind sees all things as good. One can be healthy-minded involuntarily, apparently inheriting it from one's environment. Or a person can become healthy-minded by voluntarily and systematically identifying himself with a positive doctrine which supports healthy-mindedness. All of us do this to some extent in that we frequently turn our attention away from disease, hunger, and corruption in government to more pleasant matters;

> ...the world we recognize officially in literature and in society is a poetic fiction far handsomer and cleaner and better than the world that really is.[10]

Religion for the healthy-minded temperament concentrates on good and avoids evil. One should get away from sin; when repentance is necessary, "the best repentance is to up and act for righteousness, and forget you ever had relations with sin."[11]

At the time of James's Gifford lectures, a popular movement known as "mind-cure" flourished; in brief, it was a doctrine of healthy-mindedness. James found the roots of the movement in such places as the four Gospels, Emersonianism, Berkleyan idealism, "spiritism," popular evolutionism, and Hinduism. Liberal Christianity of the day was in harmony with the mind-cure movement; it emphasized, instead of man's defects and hell, the basic goodness of man and the world, in accord with God as the all-in-all.

But James knew from his own crisis of 1870 that neither "mind-cure" philosophy nor liberal Christianity adequately explains the ultimate. In his Gifford lectures he spoke of a falseness in the healthy-minded philosophy; at best it offers a hollow security and

9. *Human Immortality*, p. 10.
10. *The Varieties*, p. 90.
11. Ibid., p. 127.

an irremediable sense of precariousness. We live on "the edge of sadness."

James was not saying that those with "healthy-minded" temperaments are ignoring evil; rather they want to avoid it or "play it down" both in their active concerns and in their conceptions of the universe. Spencerian evolutionism taught that evil is really good in disguise because it is a necessary means for progress in the social order. But the notion of "good in disguise" hardly explained for James why he suffered permanent heart damage shortly before writing the Gifford lectures.

But the religion of healthy-mindedness and the absolutistic philosophies which support it are not proved wrong or inadequate through rational argument, at least not in the Gifford lectures— their purpose was the psychological study of religious experience. In looking to James's evidence, we first ask what James knew about the temperament of people. To answer this, students of religion need to look long at the *Principles*. The caution which might be needed here is that in *The Varieties* James was not presenting a simplistic topology which categorizes human temperaments as "healthy," "sick," or "divided," although this is often how we find other people and ourselves at particular times and places. James had been a sick soul in 1870 and so had his father in 1844. His "conversion" was through the means of a conceptual choice which he believed would effectively reinforce his sense of genuine being. His own identity crisis led him to collect reports of others, and he found that much suffering and suicide can be traced to one's inadequate identity with the ultimates of the universe.

What makes a person conscious of his divided self? The question can be misleading because we do not have a "self" in the sense of a "pure substantive entity," that is, something which can be divided. What is felt as "a division in one's self" is two sets of apparently conflicting attitudes more-or-less related to the same object of attention. One's sense of identity (or his very identity) is his habitual feeling of being genuine. Without this his soul is sick. But this is not to accept the soul in an ontological sense. There is nothing which *has* the sickness. Rather the feelings which help one to feel generally that his being is genuine are not recurring with sufficient force and frequency.

One's habitual feeling of genuine being can be reinforced or threatened, depending on how he relates to the general conceptions which his society supports. When the philosophy of the establishment or of the enemy is out-and-out evil, to be genuine he has to be a rebel or soldier for the cause. In his essay "The Moral Equivalent of War" James discussed how a society can reinforce genuine being without recourse to war.

One's individual problem of self-education is: What can I do here and now to reconstruct my sense of personal identity? This is the moral problem of "What ought I to do?" applied to one's being. Society's problem is: What sorts of public knowledge should we agree on which are relevant to each individual's problem of wanting to feel genuine being?

James reported that in the hours of his acute distress, had he not "clung" to such texts as "The eternal God is my refuge" and "I am the resurrection and the life," he would have gone insane. Whether James continued to *cling* to such texts in later crises we do not know. We can be sure that he did not call on a God who as the Great Magician or the Supreme Miracle-maker needs to impress His subjects with His majesty. In James's hours of distress, God might have been in His heaven, but James knew that all was not right either with the world or in his own mind. Whatever God did, He did not create the *self;* that is a word we have invented to give coherence to our thoughts and actions. Descartes was wrong in concluding that the self is a pure essence, substantively existing a priori. James would correct Descartes's "I think, therefore I exist" to "I doubt, therefore something very important is going on." Thus, rationally, to account for our very self-identity we require the best of philosophy.

All who claim to be interested in education, either as professionals or as persons wanting to live genuinely, would do well to reconstruct James's experiences both with education and with religion.

Selected Bibliography

Allen, G. W. *William James: A Biography*. New York: Viking, 1967.

James, H., ed. *The Letters of William James*. 2 vols. Boston: Little and Brown, 1920.

James, H. *Notes of a Son and Brother*. London: Macmillan, 1914.

James, W. *Human Immortality: Two Supposed Objections to the Doctrine*. Boston: Houghton and Mifflin, 1899.

————, ed. *The Literary Remains of Henry James*. Upper Saddle River, N.J.: Gregg, 1870.

————. *A Pluralistic Universe*. New York: Longmans and Green, 1947.

————. *Talks to Teachers on Psychology and to Students on Some of Life's Ideals*. New York: Dover, 1962.

————. *The Varieties of Religious Experience: A Study in Human Nature*. Edited by J. Ratner. New Hyde Park, N.Y.: University, 1963.

Perry, R. B. *The Thought and Character of William James*. Boston: Little and Brown, 1935.

26

David H. Roper

John Dewey
(1859-1952)

John Dewey was born in 1859 in Vermont where his father owned a general store. As a boy he delivered papers after school and was an avid reader. He attended the White Street Congregational Church in Burlington, and later was a conscientious Sunday school teacher, holding an adolescent's uncomplicated view of New England theology.

Dewey graduated at the head of his class at the University of Vermont, majoring in philosophy. Later he studied at Johns Hopkins University under G. Stanley Hall, George S. Morris, and Charles S. Price. The philosophy department was influenced by German rationalism and especially by Hegel.

Dewey took a position at the University of Michigan as an instructor and married Alice Chipman, a coed. In 1894 he moved to the chair of philosophy and education at the University of Chicago. In January of his first year, under the auspices of the university, he opened the University Experimental School. The beginning was slow and tentative. Children came from the neighborhood, and the university supplied the teachers. Dewey had difficulty securing equipment, and the following incident was prophetic. He told a number of salesmen the type of student desk he desired, but none could supply it. Finally one salesman retorted, "You want something at which children may work; these are all for listening."[1] The children in Dewey's experimental school learned at phenomenal rates when compared to average children.

In 1904 Dewey moved to Columbia University, where he was when most of his 38 books and 815 articles were published.

Dewey's educational philosophy is consistently related to his overall philosophical system. In fact, agreement with Dewey's basic philosophy is the logical price of agreement with his educational theories since the two are so inexorably linked. An encounter with his dialectic is necessary to understand his educational philosophy. Therefore the first division of the chapter deals with his philosophy, and in particular with his epistemology (which provides the method for education), his metaphysics (which establishes a point of view toward life), and his ethics (which suggests the outcome of this point of view). The second section deals with his principles of education.

His Philosophy

Epistemology. Dewey's philosophy is usually called "instrumentalism." The implication is that knowledge is not simply a set of facts or a piece of descriptive information. Knowledge and thinking are instruments by which men manipulate the world about them. Others have called this "experimentalism" since the method employed is the scientific or experimental method.

Most systems of thought aim at finding out antecedent facts and passing them on to future generations. Dewey, however, insisted that antecedent reality does not exist as such in that it does not constitute a valid item of knowledge.

> ... tradition makes the test of ideas to be their agreement with some *antecedent* state of things. This change of outlook and standard from what precedes to what comes after, from the retrospective to the prospective, from antecedents to consequences, is extremely hard to accomplish. Hence when the physical sciences describe objects and the world as being such and such, it is thought that the description is of reality as it exists in itself. Since all value-traits are lacking in objects as science presents them to us, it is assumed that *Reality* has not such characteristics.[2]

---

1. J. Dewey, *The School and Society,* p. 32.
2. *The Quest for Certainty,* p. 136.

His point seems to be that historical entities do not exist as items of value in themselves, even though they may be verified by physical science. Science, to be truly scientific, must be completely dispassionate in its methods and therefore can attribute no value or reality to a thing which may be discovered. In the book *Experience and Nature,* Dewey offered a more lucid illustration of the problem of antecedent reality.

> The Norsemen are said to have discovered America. But in what sense? They landed on its shores after a stormy voyage; there was discovery in the sense of hitting upon a land hitherto untrod by Europeans. But unless the newly found and seen object was used to modify old beliefs, to change the sense of the old map of the world, there was no discovery in any pregnant intellectual sense, any more than stumbling over a chair in the dark is discovery till used as a basis of inference which connects the stumbling with a body of meanings.[3]

Knowledge, therefore, is not a grasp or contemplation of a known or given but rather a "way of operating upon and with the things of ordinary experience...." It is a "mode of practical action."

Dewey's instrumental use of knowledge is seen most vividly in a problem-solving context. He looked upon man as a biological problem-solving machine set in motion by the evolutionary process. As long as there are no obstacles, the machine tends to remain in motion. But in life there are basic indeterminates such as options or deficiencies in knowledge, skills, attitudes, or appreciations. These are units of experience that are problematic. When these problems are encountered, the machine grinds to a halt. There is a period of tension while a new direction is determined. The problem becomes the object of intense scrutiny until it becomes clear-cut in the mind. Then all the facts comprising this unit of experience are collected and observed. Ideas of possible solution may rise out of the situation itself, from research in adjacent areas, or the individual may cast about in his own mind for items of past experience which are relevant to the present indeterminacy. This is not an orgy of fact collecting, but rather a pulling together of pertinent elements related to the problem of the moment. Dewey rejected the indiscriminate collection of facts since facts are important only in that they provide hypotheses for action. In the final stages, observation and organization of this data tend toward the formation of a pattern. An analysis of the pattern becomes a

---

3. P. 156.

hypothesis upon which to act. Finally the hypothesis is tested. If the proposed solution is workable, motion continues as before until another indeterminacy arises.[4] Problems lead to experiences which call for reflective thinking, the result of which is items of knowledge which are used as tools to work upon later indeterminacies. Experience, then, is the source of all knowledge. Conversely, ideas and facts are the instruments for manipulating experience.

> Ideas are instruments used to alter present indeterminate situations so that an enjoyed future situation, itself noncognitive but worthwhile on its own account, will reliably ensue through the use of procedures which have proved their instrumental value in this capacity.[5]

Since any item of knowledge has validity only to the extent that it is wedded to ongoing experience, it follows logically that the value of any fact is not resident in the fact itself, but in its ability to work and alter existing situations.

> The test of ideas, of thinking generally, is found in the consequences of the acts to which ideas lead, that is, in the new arrangement of things which are brought into existence. Such is the unequivocal evidence as to the worth of ideas which is derived from observing their position and role in experimental knowing.[6]

Isolated facts, according to Dewey, do not have de facto qualities; "cold storage" facts that exist apart from experience do not constitute facts in themselves. For instance, the fact that two plus two equals four has no intrinsic reality. The value of this item of knowledge is the degree to which it is the result of, or means to, an experience. Nothing is valuable in itself. Facts are important only to the extent that they produce hypotheses for action. Therefore, knowledge is not the accumulation of isolated facts to be salted away in the mind for future reference but a method for integration and survival. Instrumentalism is not a philosophy of knowing, but of doing and living, hence the progressivist shibboleth, "We learn by doing."

Dewey felt that there is no finality to the problem-solving process. Objectives and values may be terminals within an experience, but fixed ends and means are equally fallacious. Life itself is a never-

---

4. D. Butler, *Four Philosophies and Their Practice in Education and Religion* (New York: Harper, 1951), pp. 428, 429.

5. "Experience, Knowledge and Value," in P. A. Schilpp, ed., *The Philosophy of John Dewey*, p. 557.

6. *The Quest for Certainty*, p. 136.

ending process of perfecting, refining, and maturing. This viewpoint is revealed in his recurrent predilection for using adjectives to describe the instrumental use of knowledge.

> It is a plausible prediction that if there were an interdict placed for a generation upon the use of mind, matter, consciousness as nouns, and we were obliged to employ adjectives and adverbs, consciously and unconsciously, mental and mentally, material and physically, we shall find many of our problems much simplified.[7]

Dewey insisted that nouns imply perfection and rigidity. Nouns are cold and hard and stand out in bold relief from the rest of experience. In contrast, adjectives are warm and fecund. A noun suggests the perfect, an adjective the imperfect. The imperfect, however, is not a falling away from perfection; rather, the imperfect adjective tends to become the perfect, sterile noun. A noun is the institutionalization of an adjective. Precisely for this reason a substantival form tends to become deadening because it insists upon conformity, compliance, acquiescence. When an adjective becomes hardened into a noun, that form is crystalized and tends to suppress new effort and expression. The status quo becomes the object of worship, and that which was expression becomes an idol blocking further expression. A good case in point is the matter of institutionalized religion. Dewey said that a religious quality should replace religion as such. Religion engenders the thought of cold, formal creeds without life and energy, but the religious quality of an experience suggests growth and vitality.

> To be somewhat more specific, a religion . . . always signifies a special body of beliefs and practices having some kind of institutional organization, loose or tight. In contrast, the adjective "religious" denotes nothing in the way of a specifiable entity, either institutional or as a system of beliefs. It does not denote anything to which one can specifically point as one can point to this and that historical religion or existing church. For it does not denote anything that can exist by itself or that can be organized into a particular and distinctive form of existence. It denotes attitudes that may be taken toward any object and every proposed end or ideal.[8]

Metaphysics. Naturalism is based on the principle of Lucretius, that "nothing has ever been created by divine power."[9] Bernard

---

7. *Experience and Nature,* p. 75.
8. *A Common Faith,* pp. 9, 10.
9. G. H. Clark, *A Christian Philosophy of Education* (Grand Rapids: Eerdmans, 1946), p. 31.

Ramm indicated five distinctives of naturalism: (1) reality is bound up in nature alone; (2) the universe is not interpreted by reference to higher levels but is self-existent, self-explanatory, self-operating, and self-directing; (3) the scientific method is the only reliable method of acquiring real knowledge (insight and intuition are uncertain until tested by the scientific method); (4) man is a product of nature rather than of divine creation; (5) there is a concerted effort to reach the minimum number of axioms from which the entire experience of man can be explained.[10] As George Santayana pointed out, "It would be hard to find a philosopher in whom naturalism, so conceived, was more inveterate than in Dewey."

Supernaturalism, according to Dewey, is the cause for the great preponderance of the world's troubles. He gave several reasons for his belief:

1. Supernaturalism is incompatible with our democratic system.

> I cannot understand how any realization of the democratic ideal as a vital and spiritual ideal in human affairs is possible without surrender of the basic division to which supernatural Christianity is committed.[11]

The division to which Dewey alluded is that of the sheep and the goats, the saved and the lost. This distinction, he claimed, creates a spiritual aristocracy which works against the democratic ideal.

2. Supernaturalism causes meditation on an ideal existence rather than releases intellectual energy upon more compensatory endeavors. Dewey wrote concerning speculative idealism that the ideal itself becomes the product of discontent with existing conditions.

> Instead however of serving to organize and direct effort, it operates as a compensatory dream. It becomes another ready-made world. Instead of promoting effort at concrete transformations of what exists, it constitutes another kind of existence already somewhere in being. It is a refuge, an asylum from effort. Thus the energy that might be spent in transforming present ills goes into oscillating flights into a far away perfect world and the tedium of enforced returns into the necessities of the present evil world.[12]

3. Supernaturalism leads to a false dualism of the sacred and the secular which precludes invasion of the scientific method into

---

10. *Problems in Christian Apologetics* (Portland: Western Baptist Theological Seminary, 1949), p. 55.

11. *A Common Faith*, p. 84.

12. *Human Nature and Conduct*, pp. 260, 261.

supramundane affairs. But the scientific method and its correlatives are relevant to every area of human inquiry.

> The argument that because some province or aspect of experience has not yet been "invaded" by scientific methods, it is not subject to them, is as old as it is dangerous. Time and time again, in some particular reserved field, it has been invalidated.[13]

Dewey felt that the religionist's claim to a "particular reserved field" is an a priori based upon supernaturalism, "which is the thing to be proved; it begs the question."

4. Supernaturalism is based on crass ignorance. The necessity of supernatural intervention is "just another instance of the old, old inference to the supernatural from the basis of ignorance." Dewey did qualify this pronouncement, however; this ignorance is based on a lack of scientific knowledge with reference to the nature of life.

5. Supernaturalism spoils religion in that it makes religion an absolute in which men find security in fixed doctrines and forms of worship rather than in the experimental method. Institutionalized forms of worship stand in the way of the fuller development of religious life. Individuals who seek this development must wipe the slate clean in their imaginations and free themselves from historical encumbrances before setting out to discover religious qualities in experience. There are no fixed creeds. New forms are always arising so religion must be kept flexible. Dogmatic definitions of religious experience are obstacles to religious living. Scripture itself constitutes a barrier to a religious life since any authoritative standard short-circuits the process of search and inquiry, and curtails the spirit of experimentation. Any formal statement of belief must be wiped out and replaced with experiences, outlooks, and functions which are religious. However, Dewey repudiated the idea that there is a "definite kind of experience which is itself religious." Even "poetry is called religion when it intervenes in life...." What Dewey sought were religious qualities which have the force of "bringing about a better, deeper and enduring adjustment to life." These religious qualities may pervade any experience.

Was Dewey a theist? *The Christian Century* in 1933-34 carried a series of articles discussing this question. Dewey himself entered the dispute but added little to the argument except a great cloud of semantic dust. In 1934 he published *A Common Faith,* and in

---

13. *A Common Faith,* p. 35.

it he dropped the usual inanities and ponderous jargon, and was very direct about his metaphysical leanings. In one sweep Dewey ruled out the God of the Bible, an absolute in ethics and moral accountability, immortality and the resurrection, and a supernatural Christ. Dewey used the word *God* in a far different way than Scripture does. Dewey conceived of God as the point at which the ideal becomes present, that is, an actual part of experience.

> It is this active relation between the ideal and the actual to which I would give the name God.[14]

In other words, as one progresses through life, ideals or values take shape in the mind. As events flow on, these ideals become actualities. God is found at the point of this union of the ideal and actual. Dewey wrote that the

> function of such a working union of the ideal and the actual seems to me to be identical with the force that has in fact been attached to the conception of God in all the religions that have a spiritual content.[15]

Dewey conceded that the use of the words *God* or *divine* may protect men from a sense of isolation and from consequent despair or defiance. He added,

> Whether one gives the name "God" to this union, operative in thought and action, is a matter for individual decision.[16]

The heart of this whole issue is the fact that Dewey did not allow for any supernatural being because it would inveigh against the principles of the scientific method. A transcendent God cannot be the object of any empirical verification. He cannot be omnipotent, omnipresent, omniscient because there are no absolutes. In short, God, as such, cannot exist.

Ethics. The most complete delineation of Dewey's ethical system is found in his *Human Nature and Conduct.* Dewey began with the premise that morals should be an intrinsic part of human conduct. His point was that morals can only be wedded to human experience if they are disentangled from supernatural rootings. Thus there are no transcendental moral principles and eternal verities. He pointed out that "those who wish to maintain the idea

---

14. Ibid., p. 51.
15. Ibid., p. 52.
16. Ibid.

[i.e., the objectivity of morals] unimpaired take the road which leads to transcendentalism." For centuries, Dewey believed, men had wasted their time in efforts to find a set of immutable moral truths to which human nature could be conformed. Their efforts were futile because all of life tends toward flux and change, and moral truth is constantly subject to adaptation and revision. Moral principles can be changed as their truth becomes obsolete. Since morals cannot be regarded as dogmatic, actions cannot be regarded as right or wrong in themselves; time and circumstances alter all.

Dewey admitted the difficulty of deriving authoritative moral standards from society, but he considered the question of authority "unanswerable whatever origin and sanction is ascribed to moral obligations and loyalties." A second difficulty concerns a criterion for change: Who is to say what changes in moral principles are valid, and whether or not those changes will accomplish social ends? Dewey could only suggest that habit and impulse furnish the method by which moral principles are changed and the aptitude for changing them. When Dewey stated that human nature is the workable source for moral principles, he did not view that nature with the suspicious eye of traditional Christianity. As for the depravity of man, "the conclusion does not follow from the data."[17]

Boyd H. Bode of Ohio State University, a disciple of Dewey, summarized well Dewey's view of ethics: "The moral factor of life, so it is assumed (by opponents of naturalism), must be derived from some theory of the universe, or of the cosmic order, or from eternal verities. It is hard to see how the American dream can come to fruition on the basis of the theory that moral values require cosmic endorsement to give them authority. This authority must come from their relevancy to the purpose of making men free through changes in social relationships. The solution of the moral problem lies in the future and not in the past."[18]

Dewey, however, never advocated moral license. He was a very austere man and expected a high standard of behavior from others. He scorned those who sought freedom from convention through license. Dewey wanted not to do away with morality and ethics but to emancipate valuable experience from the accretions of organized religion. In matters of social morality, this willingness to reexamine, and if necessary revise, current convictions is more

---

17. Ibid., p. 74.
18. Quoted in J. O. Buswell, "Public Education: A Propaganda for Atheism," *The Sunday School Times* 90 (1948): 135.

fundamental than any particular principle, but there is no place for license.

It is conceded on all sides that Dewey's influence on American education has been immense. His philosophy, however, has not been clearly understood. If it had been, enthusiasm for his teaching might have been tempered more extensively with fear, or at any rate with misgivings. Although many educators have been unclear about the metaphysical implications of Deweyism, he himself was singularly clear in his own mind. He was against the old institutions, including God, the soul, and all the props of traditional Christianity. He excluded the possibility of immutable law and fixed moral principles. He disregarded a divine purpose for mankind and made life an endless round of meaningless experience. Dewey's categorical imperative was, "So act as to increase the meaning of experience."[19]

His Educational Principles

Although progressive education is chiefly and properly associated with Dewey, it also had roots in the thought of Rousseau, Pestalozzi, Herbart, and Froebel; all sought to substitute natural methods for the traditional implements of learning. But it is Dewey who has dominated the educational scene for most of the last half-century. Robert L. Cooke wrote that "Dewey probably applied his philosophy directly to education in a greater degree and in broader ways than any other man." Cooke credited Dewey specifically for "the present emphasis on the educational value of experience, on scientific measurement and procedures in education and the project method in teaching."[20]

Dewey saw three educational worlds. The first is one of absolute order and uniformity, where change and growth are an illusion. In this world subject matter

> consists of bodies of information and of skills that have been worked out in the past; therefore, the chief business of the school is to transmit them to the new generation.[21]

Conformity to standards and rules of conduct formulated in the

19. *Human Nature and Conduct*, p. 283.

20. *Philosophy, Education and Certainty* (Grand Rapids: Zondervan, 1940), p. 167.

21. *Experience and Education*, p. 2.

past by adults is enforced. Since the subject matter, as well as standards of proper conduct, is handed down from the past, the pupils must be docile, receptive, and obedient.

The second world of education was that of the progressive schools.

> To imposition from above is opposed expression and cultivation of individuality; to external discipline is opposed free activity; to learning from texts and teachers, learning through experience; to acquisition of isolated skills and techniques by drill, is opposed acquisition of them as means of attaining ends which make direct vital appeal; to preparation for a more or less remote future is opposed making the most of the opportunities of present life; to static aims and materials is opposed acquaintance with a changing world.[22]

Dewey felt that this general philosophy may be sound, but it could develop negative principles of anarchy and disorder because of its rejection of the place and meaning of subject matter and of organization within experience.

The third world is one of growth which combines tradition and novelty, order and freedom, necessity and contingency. It is a much-needed middle ground between the two extremes. It combines freedom and order, mechanisms and values. Its principle is growth; its method is experimentalism. It offers partial freedom and partial control; some errors, some failures, but also cumulative and significant growth. This educational world commends itself in a democratic rather than an autocratic society.

Five basic tenets of Dewey's neopedagogy have been suggested: (1) child-centered education; (2) education through intrinsic motivation; (3) education through activity; (4) education as reconstruction of experience; and (5) social-centered education.

Child-centered education. Dewey wrote:

> It is a change, a revolution, not unlike that introduced by Copernicus when the astronomical center shifted from the earth to the sun. In this case the child becomes the sun about which the appliances of education revolve.[23]

Dewey had great respect for the individual child's personality. He felt that adults tame the "delightful originality of the child" by foisting adult customs and standards upon him. When the more

---

22. Ibid., pp. 5, 6.
23. *The School and Society,* p. 35.

mature members of society require the child to conform to such rules, they are both assuming a high order of intelligence in the child and distrusting this intelligence. Instead, "moral" habits should be instilled "which have a maximum of emotional empressement and adamantine hold with a minimum of understanding."

Basic to Dewey's system was the concept that children have one operating speed and their way is best. Thus the school is oriented around the child rather than around the thinking of adult administrators. The starting place of education is not a pre-perfected curriculum based on the judgment of adults but a psychological method of delivery based on the immediate needs and interests of the child.

> Subject matter must be derived from materials which at the outset fall within the scope of ordinary life experience.[24]

Training must be grounded in actual participation in practical situations with which the child is familiar.

Dewey stressed repeatedly that education should be directed not toward future adult needs but toward the immediate present, because the child must be trained to cope with his environment now. It is basic to his criterion of continuity of experience that the future be taken into account at every stage of the educational process. But the assumption is treacherous that

> by acquiring certain skills and by learning certain subjects which will be needed later . . . pupils are as a matter of course made ready for the needs and circumstances of the future.[25]

The ability of the child to cope with present needs is the guarantee of a similar success in the future. To the extent that the child is increasing his control of his own character and social relationships, he is being educated. Dewey stressed the concept of personality integration for the present. "The truly integrated child is the *summum bonum* of progressivism."

Education through intrinsic motivation. Dewey stressed the importance of interest to effort. The interested will is vital to the educative process. He decried rote and the

> emphasis upon drill exercises designed to produce skill in action, independent of any engagement of thought-exercises, having no purpose but the production of automatic skill.[26]

---

24. *Experience and Education*, p. 87.
25. Ibid., p. 47.
26. *Democracy and Education*, p. 209.

External coercive pressure and motivation extraneous to the thing to be done is likewise to be avoided. Incentive must come from within and grow out of the work. Dewey suggested that we

> do not have to draw out or educe positive activities from the child, as some educational doctrines have it. Where there is life there are already eager and impassioned activities.

The discipline of doing the disagreeable is outweighed by the value of working with a "full concern with subject matter for its own sake."

Discipline is rooted in the intrinsic method. Dewey felt that enforced control results in artificial uniformity and habits which account for the "mass of irrationalities that prevail among men of otherwise rational tastes." He pointed out that rigid rules and regimentation may control external activity but cannot control thoughts and desires. If the aim of discipline is not self-control, the student will act on whim and caprice when released from external control.

In this economy the teacher is a guide, not a dictator or a disciplinarian. Education is less what the teacher does and more what the students do.

> The teacher is a learner and the learner is, without knowing it, a teacher—and upon the whole, the less consciousness there is, on either side, of either giving or receiving instructions the better.[27]

Education through activity. Dewey insisted that true education begins with experiences which are going on. Because experience is not static in that it has variety and flow, learning takes place in a problem-solving context. Therefore, the school should provide opportunity for normal activity where the student can meet problems and solve them. The school should not be a collection of recitation rooms but a laboratory where

> opportunities exist for reproducing situations of life and for acquiring and applying information and ideas in carrying forward of progressive experiences.

The school which is a listening institution can have uniformity of material and method, but its curriculum can only be

> a certain amount—a fixed quantity—of ready-made results and accomplishments to be acquired by all children alike in a given time.

---

27. Ibid., p. 207.

Dewey's thinking with reference to the curriculum came from his criticism of educational methods. In his day the traditional curriculum was based on the concept that there is just so much desirable knowledge, and when the child has gone through twelve or sixteen years of school, he has mastered the whole, provided he has not forgotten what he learned first. But Dewey insisted that a content-centered curriculum isolates the child from concrete situations of experience.

> Abandon the notion of subject matter as something fixed and ready-made in itself, outside the child's experience; cease thinking of the child's experience as something hard and fast; see it as something fluent, embryonic, vital; and we realize that the child and the curriculum are simply two limits which define a single process. Just as two points define a straight line, so the present standpoint of the child and the facts and truth of studies define instruction. It is a continuous reconstruction of experience, moving from the child's present experience out into that represented by the organized body of truth we call studies.[28]

Dewey's whole educational philosophy hinged on the fact that experience, not subject matter, constitutes the curriculum of the school. Since experiences are going on all around the pupil, life itself makes up the curriculum. He saw two evils in a curriculum which is presented externally. (1) There is a lack of connection with what the child has already seen and felt and loved. It makes the material purely formal and symbolic. (2) There is a lack of motivation.

> There are not only no facts, or truths which have been previously felt as such with which to appropriate and assimilate the new, but there is no craving, no need, no demand.[29]

In line with his overall philosophy of education, John Dewey ruled out the departmentalization of courses into math, science, biology, etc. There could be no time-honored, sequential curriculum ("In the multitude of educations, education is forgotten") but a core curriculum in which there are no time schedules, no courses as such. The unit of study is not a given class period but an area marked out by a particular unit of experience. The insistence that the learning activities of children cease with the bell every forty-five minutes is aptly designated the "ridiculous imperative."

Dewey's philosophy of activity in education is the heart of the

---

28. *The Child and the Curriculum,* p. 16.
29. Ibid., p. 10.

progressive movement. It is most often expressed in terms of the familiar adage "Children learn to do by doing," which may be summed up in one concept—the project method. Education through this method begins with some indeterminate situation which creates tension and interest and a will to solve the problem. The problem begins to take shape as the student examines the situation. All data from former experiences are gathered and compared with those issuing from the present problem. These familiar factors are cast into a new pattern, and tentative solutions are worked out which relate to the new situation. Solutions are tested: those that are ineffective are discarded; those that are effective become the means for solving future indeterminate situations.

> In just the degree in which connections are established between what happens to a person and what he does in response, and what he does to his environment and what it does in response to him, his acts and things about him acquire meaning.... Purposive education or schooling should present such an environment that his interaction will effect acquisition of those meanings which are so important that they become, in turn, instruments of further learnings.[30]

In summary, Dewey felt that there is activity in acquiring the experience that will give meaning to learning; there is experience in trying to put it to use, both now and in subsequent experiences.

Education as reconstruction of experience. Dewey had little patience with educational systems that divorce subject matter from experience, but he would have been the first to admit that experience is the best teacher only to the extent that it is the right kind of experience. Some experiences may be miseducative in that they may: (1) arrest or distort the growth of further experience; (2) produce a lack of sensitivity or responsiveness to subsequent experiences; (3) increase automatic skill but in the process cause the individual to fall into a rut; or (4) fail, because they are too disconnected, ever to be linked together in a meaningful fashion.[31] To solve the problem of miseducative experience, Dewey suggested the principle of continuity, or the experiential continuum, or as it relates to education, the continuous reconstruction of experience.[32] This experience draws upon experiences that have gone before and modifies to some extent those that come after. Every experience

---

30. *Democracy and Education,* pp. 13, 14.
31. *Experience and Education,* pp. 13, 14.
32. Ibid., p. 24.

draws upon data from past experiences in solving problems. In turn, these data become the instruments for working upon subsequent experience. By this continuum Dewey exploded the pedagogical myth of purely theoretical knowledge. He pointed out that knowledge is what the student has found out by personal acquaintance and by study of what others have ascertained and recorded. But this is only knowledge to him because it supplies the resources for interpreting the unknown things which confront him, filling out the partial facts, foreseeing their probable future, and planning accordingly.

An ounce of experience is better than a ton of theory because it is only in experience that any theory has vital and verifiable significance.[33]

Social-centered education. Dewey stated categorically that

the measure of the worth of the administration, curriculum, and methods of instruction of the school is the extent to which they are animated by a social spirit.[34]

Two conditions make possible this "permeating social spirit": (1) The school itself must be a community of effort. Dewey described the progressive school as one of cooperative effort rather than passive receptivity. Nevertheless, Dewey felt that the truly educative processes go on in a context of group activities and experiences. Mere facts can be acquired in isolation, but the meaning of those facts "involves a context of work and play with others." (2) The school must not maintain the traditional separation of "town and gown" or cultivate "academic seclusion." Learning in school should be continuous with that outside school. The concept that education only takes place contiguous to the little red schoolhouse contributes to a monastic type of education where an

idealized past becomes the refuge and solace of the spirit; present-day concerns are found sordid, and unworthy of attention.

Dewey's answer was an

educational scheme where learning is the accompaniment of continuous activities or occupations which have a social aim and utilize the materials of typical social situations.[35]

33. *Democracy and Education,* p. 169.
34. Ibid., p. 415.
35. Ibid., p. 418.

The American education scene was changing. A free-to-all but compulsory-universal system was introduced, forcing the teacher to deal with large numbers of students from different backgrounds. Dewey introduced a system of education that took into account the complex needs of the general public more than the intellectual appetites of the intelligentsia.

During Dewey's lifetime there was a rapid growth of modern vocations; work was becoming specialized; new technical occupations were arising. This demanded scientific investigation of problems and data, and a careful evaluation of the future. Creative ways to teach had to be invented, and technical content had to be dealt with in new ways rather than by old classifications and curricula; Dewey did both. The scientific world was calling for a new psychological way to deal with children and learning, one that was more consistent with their nature, and Dewey's *Experience and Nature* supplied this.

Dewey has been called the first original American philosopher, a pragmatist and instrumentalist who so reflected the new, growing American spirit that contemporary observers had difficulty determining if he shaped American education more than America shaped him.

Selected Bibliography

Dewey, J. *The Child and the Curriculum.* Chicago: University of Chicago, 1902.

———. *A Common Faith.* New Haven: Yale University, 1960.

———. *Democracy and Education.* New York: Macmillan, 1943.

———. *Experience and Education.* New York: Macmillan, 1958.

———. *Experience and Nature.* New York: Dover, 1958.

———. *Human Nature and Conduct.* New York: Holt, 1922.

———. *The Quest for Certainty.* New York: Capricorn, 1960.

———. *The School and Society.* Chicago: University of Chicago, 1915.

Schilpp, P. A., ed. *The Philosophy of John Dewey.* 2nd ed. New York: Tudor, 1951.

Index of Persons

Adam, Melchior, 101
Adamnan, 64, 66, 68, 69
Adler, Mortimer J., 183
Adrian VI, 85
Aeschylus, 267
Aesop, 148
Agassiz, Louis, 298
Agricola (Martin Sohr), 85, 87, 155
Albert (Albertus Magnus), 71, 78
Alsted, John Henry, 177
Ambrose, 54, 58
Ammann, Johann Jakob, 134
Aquinas, Thomas, 61-62, 71-81
Aristotle, 74, 79, 92, 95, 99, 100, 148, 153, 155, 171
Arnold, Thomas, 208, 210, 264-69
Augustine, 14, 54-59, 95, 99, 114, 119, 303
Averroës (ibn-Rushd), 78, 79
Avicenna (ibn-Sina), 78

Bacon, Francis, 180, 186
Badius Ascensius, 83 (n. 3)
Barclay, William, 49

Bark, William Carroll, 63
Beardslee, William A., 45
Beck, Paul, 195, 196
Bede, 64, 65, 67, 69
Bell, Andrew, 240
Bell, Hannah, 227
Bellamy, Joseph, 227
Beraud, Francois, 169
Beza, Theodorus, 169, 171
Black, Matthew, 22 (n. 8)
Blair, E. P., 34 (n. 37)
Bode, Boyd H., 318
Body, Alfred H., 213
Boethius, 79
Bonnard, P., 33 (n. 34)
Bourgeaud, Charles, 170
Brandon, S. G. F., 15 (n. 2), 34 (n. 38)
Brick, William, 231
Brubacher, John S., 45, 182
Bucer, Martin, 85
Bugenhagen, Joseph, 120 (n. 36), 150, 157
Bultmann, Rudolf, 31 (n. 31)

Bunyan, John, 303
Burleigh, John H. S., 55
Bushnell, Horace, 211, 278-87
Butts, R. Freeman, 157

Caesar, Gaius Julius, 170
Calvin, John, 62, 85, 90-91, 162, 167-
    75, 289
Camerarius, Joachim, 146, 154
Carlstadt (Andreas Rudolf
    Bodenstein), 158
Carlyle, Thomas, 303
Cato, Publius Valerius, 113
Cele, John, 85
Ceporinus (Jakob Wiesendanger),
    133, 134
Chadwick, W. Edward, 40
Chevalier, Antoine, 169
Chrysostom, John, 119
Cicero, Marcus Tullius, 54, 92, 95,
    113, 148, 155, 170, 171, 267
Clarke, William Newton, 27 (n. 22)
Clement of Alexandria, 96
Coe, George Albert, 278, 285, 287
Coleridge, Samuel Taylor, 279
Colet, John, 100, 265
Collin, Rudolf, 134
Columba, 61, 63-70
Comenius, John Amos, 11, 89-90,
    176-89, 215-16, 240
Cooke, Robert L., 319
Copernicus, Nicolaus, 320
Crum, J. M. C., 22 (n. 9)
Cyril of Jerusalem, 55 (n. 2)

Darwin, Charles, 301
Demosthenes, 148, 171
Descartes, René, 308
Dewey, John, 11, 211, 310-26
Dilthey, Wilhelm, 151
Donatus, Aelius, 113
Dringenberg, Louis, 85
Duke, John A., 68
Dunkel, Harold B., 259

Easton, B. S., 31 (n. 32)
Eavey, C. B., 197
Eby, Frederick, 174, 187, 192
Eck, John, 158

Eckhart, Johannes, 84
Ellis, E. E., 29 (n. 28)
Erasmus, Desiderius, 85, 89, 92-102,
    113, 115, 124, 146, 155, 214
Euripides, 147

Faber, John, 125
Farel, Guillaume, 168
Farner, Oskar, 131
Fenton, J. C., 34 (n. 37)
Fichte, Johann Gottlieb, 240, 250
Fleming, Sanford, 279
Fox, George, 303
Francke, August Hermann, 89, 90,
    190-99, 200, 201, 204, 205
Froebel, Friedrich, 240, 319

Galen, 129
Galilei, Galileo, 100
Gamaliel I, 43
Gamaliel II, 42, 43
Gansfort, Wessel, 85
Geldenhuys, J. Norval, 32 (n. 33)
Gerhard, Johann, 119
Ginneken, Jacob van, 83
Grant, F. C., 34 (n. 37)
Grebel, Conrad, 133
Greeming, James, 227
Groen van Prinsterer, Guillaume,
    289
Groote, Geert, 61, 62, 82-88
Groser, W. H., 231
Gross, John O., 219
Gut, Walter, 125

Hall, G. Stanley, 310
Hartfelder, K., 144 (n. 2)
Hauser, Joel, 227
Hegel, Georg W. F., 252, 310
Herbart, Johann Friedrich, 90, 101,
    210, 240, 249-63, 319
Herodian, 171
Herodotus, 261
Hilary, 114
Hodge, Charles, 284-85
Homer, 146, 147, 171, 261
Hughes, Thomas, 264, 269
Hus, John, 177
Husserl, Edmund, 300

Isocrates, 170

Jacob, E. F., 83
Jacobus de Voragine, 137
James, Henry (brother of William James), 297, 298
James, Henry (father of William James), 297-98, 301, 307
James, Henry (son of William James), 303
James, William, 211, 297-309
Jerome, 114
Jesus, 13, 14, 15-38, 39, 44, 46, 51, 52, 69, 75, 93, 95, 96, 101, 117, 120, 121, 129, 130, 131, 137, 138, 145, 146, 147, 149, 151, 157, 163, 194, 196, 202, 203, 204-5, 206-7, 245, 285, 286, 291, 292
John of Saxony, 110, 111
Josephus, Flavius, 40
Jud, Leo (Meister Leu), 133

Kant, Immanuel, 250, 251
Keatinge, Matthew, 179, 180, 186
Kessler, Johann, 134
Kingsley, Charles, 272
Knox, John, 90, 91, 161-66
Kuist, Howard T., 40
Kunze, J. C., 198
Kuyper, Abraham, 210-11, 288-96

Laurie, S. S., 179
Lefèvre d'Etaples, 95
Locke, John, 216
Lodolph of Saxony, 137
Lohman, A. F. de Savornin, 289
Loyola, Ignatius of, 91, 136-43
Lucretius, 314
Luther, Martin, 11, 62, 90, 93, 94, 95, 96, 101, 103-23, 146, 147, 156, 157, 158, 177, 207

McClintock, John, 229
McGeary, Thomas, 222
McGiffert, Arthur Cushman, 279
Machiavelli, Niccolò, 96, 97
Maclure, William, 240

Maimonides (Moses ben Maimon), 78
Majors, John, 162
Manz, Felix, 133
Marcus Aurelius, 303
Marty, Martin, 193
Maurer, Wilhelm, 150
Mayer, Milton, 183
Melanchthon, Philip, 90, 105, 113, 144-60
Merrill, George L., 229, 230, 231, 234
Meyer, Adolph E., 185
More, Thomas, 97
Morris, George S., 310
Mosselanus, Peter, 113
Mühlenberg, H. M., 198
Murmellius, John, 86
Myconius, Oswald, 127, 134

Neander, Johann, 64
Neef, Joseph, 239
Newman, Albert Henry, 191, 192
Newman, John Henry, 210, 271-77
Nicholas of Cusa, 85
Niebuhr, Reinhold, 47

Origen, 15 (n. 1), 24 (n. 14), 96, 119
Ovid, 113, 170
Owen, Robert, 240

Paul, 12, 39-53, 119, 145, 146, 152-53
Pellikan, Konrad, 134
Perry, Ralph Barton, 298
Pestalozzi, Johann H., 90, 210, 236-48, 251, 319
Philo Judaeus, 41
Pico della Mirandola, 95, 151
Pirckheimer, Willibald, 97
Plato, 78, 92, 95, 140, 148, 171, 261
Plautus, Titus Maccius, 113
Plotinus, 54
Plummer, Alfred, 20 (n. 7), 32 (n. 33)
Plutarch, 99, 148, 171
Polanyi, Michael, 276-77
Polybius, 171
Porphyry, 54

Potter, G. R., 125
Price, Charles S., 310
Prince, J. W., 218

Qualben, Lars, 192, 195
Quintilian, 92, 99

Radewijns, Florentius, 84
Raikes, Robert, 210, 226-35
Ramm, Bernard, 314-15
Ratke, Wolfgang, 177
Reid, W. Stanford, 169, 172
Renouvier, Charles Bernard, 302
Renwick, A. M., 165
Reuchlin, Johann, 133, 146, 158
Rhenanus, Beatus, 85
Rice, Edwin, 227, 230, 231, 232, 233, 235
Rousseau, Jean Jacques, 90, 186, 208, 236, 238, 240, 246, 319
Rubin, Jerry, 276
Rückert, Oskar, 126
Rüsch, E. G., 131
Ruysbroeck, Jan, 84

Santayana, George, 315
Schelling, Friedrich Wilhelm Joseph von, 250
Scott, C. A. Anderson, 43
Seneca, Marcus Annaeus, 171
Smiles, Samuel, 269
Smith, H. Shelton, 280 (n. 8)
Sophocles, 267
Spener, Philip, 190-91, 192
Spinka, Matthew, 178
Stanley, David M., 48
Stork, Thomas, 230
Sturm, John, 62, 85, 136
Sullivan, Richard, 63 (n. 2)

Tagant, Jean, 169
Tasker, R. V. G., 23 (n. 10), 25 (n. 16)

Terence, 113, 145
Theresa of Lisieux, 303, 305
Thomas à Kempis, 62, 85
Thorndike, E. L., 188
Thorndike, Lynn, 83
Thucydides, 265
Tolstoi, Leo, 303
Torrey, C. C., 22 (n. 8)
Tyler, Bennett, 282 (n. 14)

Uelzen, Hermann, 250
Ulich, Robert, 192, 300

Van Lonkhuysen, Jan, 290
Vergil, 113, 170, 267
Vieth, Paul H., 278
Vinet, Alexandre, 289
Vives, Louis, 96

Walker, Williston, 193
Watts, Isaac, 224
Wesley, Charles, 224
Wesley, John, 90, 198, 209-10, 212-25, 226-27, 228, 234, 265
Wesley, Susanna, 214-15, 216
Whitefield, George, 224, 228
Whitehead, Alfred North, 301
Whitman, Walt, 303
Whitridge, Arnold, 266
Wild, John, 300
Wimpheling, Jakob, 85
Winthrop, John, Jr., 178
Wolff, Christian von, 250
Wycliffe, John, 119

Xenophon, 171

Young, G. M., 266, 267

Zeller, Tuiskon, 262
Zinzendorf, Nikolaus Ludwig, 89, 90, 198, 200-208
Zwingli, Huldreich, 90, 124-35